SURVIVING THE BOSNIAN GENOCIDE

SURVIVING THE BOSNIAN GENOCIDE

The Women of Srebrenica Speak

SELMA LEYDESDORFF

TRANSLATED BY KAY RICHARDSON

Indiana University Press
Bloomington and Indianapolis

Publication of this work has been made possible with the financial support of the Dutch Foundation for Literature.

This book is a publication of
Indiana University Press
601 North Morton Street
Bloomington, Indiana 47404-3797 USA

iupress.indiana.edu

Telephone orders	800-842-6796
Fax orders	812-855-7931
Orders by e-mail	iuporder@indiana.edu

Originally published as Selma Leydesdorff, *De leegte achter ons laten: Een geschiedenis van de vrouwen van Srebrenica* (Amsterdam: Bert Bakker, 2008).
© 2011 by Selma Leydesdorff

English translation © 2011 by Indiana University Press

Manufactured in the United States of America

Library of Congress Cataloging-in-Publication Data

Leydesdorff, Selma.
    [Leegte achter ons laten. English]
    Surviving the Bosnian genocide : the women of Srebrenica speak / Selma Leydesdorff ; translated by Kay Richardson.
        p.   cm.
    "Originally published as Selma Leydesdorff, De leegte achter ons laten : Een geschiedenis van de vrouwen van Srebrenica (Amsterdam: Bert Bakker, 2008)"—T.p. verso.
    Includes bibliographical references and index.
    ISBN 978-0-253-35669-7 (cloth : alk. paper) — ISBN 978-0-253-00529-8 (pbk. : alk. paper) 1. Yugoslav War, 1991–1995—Atrocities—Bosnia and Hercegovina—Srebrenica—Personal narratives. 2. War widows—Bosnia and Hercegovina—Srebrenica. I. Title.
    DR1313.32.S68L4913   2011
    949.703—dc22
                        2011011589

1 2 3 4 5   16 15 14 13 12 11

All people are born free
All people are equal before God
All people are innocent until proven guilty
All people are good until some do evil
All people are righteous until some do the unrighteous
All men of Srebrenica were alive until some were murdered
All people are innocent until those who committed crimes are judged
Evil is forever, but not absolute
Good is absolute, but sometimes absent.

We have come here to listen
To those who cried for help
To the Heaven and the Earth
To the Day and to the Night
To the Word and to the Omnipotent.
In order that the sword be taken away
From those who have murdered during the day and the night.
We have come here
To see the truth with our own eyes, about ourselves and about them.

Teach us that tolerance is the highest form of power
And the desire to wreak vengeance
The first sign of weakness.

If we sin against people
Give us the strength to ask forgiveness
If people sin against us
Give us the strength to forgive!

May grief become hope!
May revenge become righteousness!
May the tears of the mothers become prayers
That Srebrenica never happens again.

—IMAM CEKIĆ, reis-ul-ulema of Bosnia-Herzegovina,
at the memorial for Srebrenica, July 11, 2005

Contents

Translator's Note

I would like to thank Ian Priestnall, an old colleague and dear friend, for his superb professional advice on the finer points of translation and his personal encouragement and support during the process.

Preface: What Happened Before

When war erupted in Bosnia in 1992, it was not a huge surprise. What used to be Yugoslavia—the multiethnic communist state held together for decades by Marshal Josip Tito—was crumbling. New nations based on old ethnicities began to declare their independence; Bosnia did so in 1991. What did surprise everyone, including the participants, about the war was how deliberately vicious it was. Thousands of people, in particular the Muslims, were forced to flee what would later be called "ethnic cleansing." In eastern Bosnia, Muslims were the victims of a brutal and bloodthirsty purge that involved murder, rape on a massive scale, plundering, and forced relocation. Images of the violence there stunned the world. (In this book, Bosnian Muslims are referred to as Bosniaks, a term used in the region. Bosnian Serbs are usually referred to as Serbs, while the Serbs who live in Serbia are referred to as Serbians; these distinctions are also common in the region. In the interviews, the aggressors are sometimes referred to by the derogatory term Chetniks.)

The situation was so out of control in 1993 that the United Nations designated "safe areas" or "safe enclaves" in the region and sent troops to protect the Muslims. Srebrenica, a small town sequestered in a fertile valley in eastern Bosnia and known since ancient times for its silver mines and mineral springs, was one of them. Before the war began, the town's population was approximately 9,000 [1] After it was declared a UN Safe Area, thousands of Muslims from surrounding villages fled to it in search of safety.

The troops sent by the UN had a limited mandate and were insufficiently armed to keep peace in an area where a violent war was raging. Beginning in January 1994, the Canadian troops in Srebrenica were replaced by various units of Dutch soldiers. Despite the UN's guarantee of protection, Srebrenica was under constant shelling from the surrounding hills. The peacekeepers could not prevent a humanitarian disaster. There were no medical supplies, water and electricity had been shut off, food convoys were denied access, and the population was starving.

In July 1995, the enclave was taken by Bosnian Serb troops led by General Ratko Mladić. The more able-bodied men and some women tried to flee to safety through the woods on the surrounding hills. The remaining women, children, and elderly men sought shelter under the protection of the Dutch Blue Helmets within the enclave known as the Dutch Compound in Potočari, an industrial area where the Dutch soldiers had their camp. Potočari is located halfway between Srebrenica and Bratunac, a town on the Drina River (see the map on p. xii). Some men accompanied their wives to Potočari, but most of them were murdered, although some of the elderly were spared. All of the older boys (12 years and up) were also murdered.

According to the 2009 estimates of the International Commission on Missing Persons, there were 8,100 Srebrenican genocide victims, although that number is debated. Of those, 6,186 had been identified through DNA analysis as of 2009.[2] Men were not the only victims; information on the number of women and children killed is still coming to light.[3] In 1995, there were 731 missing children, mainly adolescents between 16 and 18 years of age, although that number also includes babies. More than 5 percent of the victims were younger than 15.[4] From the beginning of the war, children's deaths were often collateral damage; in Potočari, however, children were deliberately targeted.

The largest genocide in Europe since the Second World War took place under the eyes of Dutch soldiers. I am one of those in the Netherlands who believes that examining the role of the inadequately armed and unprepared soldiers, as well as the failed leadership of the military and the Dutch government, should teach us a lesson.[5] Instead, from the beginning there have been attempts to cover up what happened, and that has not changed over the years. Soldiers were ordered not to speak, rolls of film vanished, and contact with the victims was discouraged. The first few days after the fall of Srebrenica, the press was informed that the mission to protect its population had been successful. The Dutch crown prince (who probably had not yet been briefed) celebrated the completion of the Dutch soldiers' mission by drinking beer with them in Zagreb. News of the mass murder broke several days later. It was reported that the Dutch soldiers had watched while the Serbs separated the men from the women—a clear and ominous sign of what was to happen.

This standing by and watching events unfold was criticized by many. One of the most vocal was Fred Grünfeld of the University of Utrecht,[6] who compared the role of DutchBat in Srebrenica to that of the United Nations in the Rwandan genocide. In both instances, Grünfeld noted, the genocide was predictable and the United Nations had the opportunity to prevent the massacres. He also noted a lack of solidarity with those who later became the victims, given that no attempt was made to stop the slaughter. Grünfeld regards those bystanders as morally and legally abetting the genocide, because they did not give help to the people in need. This is confirmed by the testimonies of a number of survivors in a complaint against the Dutch state and the United Nations.[7]

International debate over who is responsible has continued since the fall of the enclave. This debate is no longer focused on the role of the Netherlands, although the failure of the Dutch military is generally acknowledged. In her book *A Problem from Hell*,[8] Samantha Power regards Srebrenica as yet another failure of American foreign policy, which repeatedly looks the other way when there is mass murder. The political analyst David Rieff places what happened there within the framework of an ineffectual United Nations that does not keep its promises.[9] The body of work about Srebrenica continues to grow, with contributions by scholars, journalists, and filmmakers, as well as literary accounts.[10] There are a number of explanations as to why Srebrenica happened, and the research continues.

Within Bosnia's public arena, there are two ways of talking about Srebrenica. The first accuses the Bosnian Serbs and the Serbians of cruelty. Everything possible was done to get an acknowledgment of guilt from the Serbian state.[11] Both the Serbs and the Republika Srpska, or Serb Republic (the region within Bosnia-Herzegovina now controlled by Bosnian Serbs as a result of the Dayton Accords),[12] were tried by the International Court of Justice in The Hague. The judgment was that the Bosnian Serbs were guilty of genocide, but the army of the Serb Republic was not. This is why Serbia continues to deny any responsibility. In the regional literature, which is part of the growing cultural memory of Bosnia, Srebrenica has become a painful reminder of Bosnian suffering during the war and a metaphor for ultimate betrayal and suffering, much like Auschwitz in many respects. Yet even in this context, the voices of the survivors are not heard.[13] Political and military facts—not emotionally charged testimonies—are given importance and accorded a place in history.

In 1996 the Netherlands decided to commission an investigation into the role of the Dutch soldiers and to determine who was responsible for what happened. The Netherlands Institute for War Documentation (NIOD; Nederlands Instituut voor Oorlogsdocumentatie) carried out the research, which was finally published in 2002.[14] The report was enormous (3,760 pages) and scrupulously avoided the judgment many officials had feared—that things could have gone differently. It found the role of the Dutch military to have been ambiguous, which was interpreted to mean that DutchBat and its commanders were not to blame. After publication of the report, the sitting Dutch government took responsibility for the events and resigned.

The French government also commissioned an investigation, but again there were no clear conclusions. What happened at Srebrenica remains incomprehensible. The two men most responsible, Radovan Karadžić and Ratko Mladić, had absconded years earlier; some believe that they may have been protected and sheltered by those who benefit from their silence. Karadžić was caught in 2008, and presumably Mladić will be in the future.

In the debate surrounding the report, some historians objected that government-commissioned reports are often the result of endless negotiations.[15] My greatest complaint is that there is still little or no interest in the experience of the victims; this is also apparent from my correspondence with the compilers of the Dutch NIOD Report. When that report appeared in 2002, the Dutch parliament decided that an official inquiry was necessary. That inquiry[16] also failed to answer the question of whether there could have been a different outcome, which the survivors assume was possible. During the formal presentation of the NIOD Report, a group of women survivors walked out in anger. This was later dismissed as hysteria or (some suggested) because the women were being politically manipulated. I doubt that. The women felt abandoned and unsupported because no one was willing to listen to them. They stood face to face with Dutch officials and military personnel, expecting answers. But the state refused repeatedly to answer the most important questions of all—why and how this had happened—because of "document confidentiality."

The focus of this book is on the survivors. I have distanced myself from the Dutch obsession with unresolved guilt and self-chastisement, which ignores the survivors;[17] even the parliamentary inquiry left the survivors' experience out of the event's history. Their voices have not been heard. The opportunity to speak with them and to listen was lost; instead, all attention was focused on the question of governmental responsibility and the role of DutchBat.[18] It almost seems as though the real victims no longer exist. The Dutch government's position—that responsibility should be placed elsewhere—is strained, uncaring, and characterized by fear of legal liability. Clearly, the responsibility for the actual murders lies elsewhere, but that does not erase the need for a thoroughgoing discussion of the Dutch responsibility for what happened.

The soldiers of DutchBat and their psychological problems have received much attention in the Netherlands. They suffer from feelings of guilt and fear, they were treated badly when they returned, and they were placed under a gag order regarding what they had seen. Although well aware that something was amiss, they assured that they had performed well. In 2006 some of them were even given medals for their service. I was among those who protested this in public debate. Approximately one-fourth of the soldiers did not attend the presentation ceremony. Having compassion for those who served there and now have problems is not the same as feeling solidarity with the real victims. I argue for more openness and for giving the victims access to accurate information about what happened. It is unfortunate that the Dutch government never apologized for the impotent performance of its army, and still refuses to do so. As a result, the affair escalated into legal proceedings, in which the Dutch deny any responsibility. In this case of genocide, it is unforgivable that the victims must resort to such measures to get justice.

In this book, the Muslims who can do so recount their memories. They are mainly women; the men are dead. The complaints and sorrows of the survivors are great, and their lives are often scarred by unresolved grief, dislocation, and poverty. They have not been listened to, and little has been written about them. In 1999, *Srebrenica, het verhaal van de overlevenden* (*Srebrenica: The Survivors' Story*) was published, which included 104 testimonies about the role of the United Nations in the genocide against the population of the UN "safe haven." (An English edition, *Pillar of Shame,* was published in Tuzla in 2007.)[19] Eyewitnesses tell their stories, but the testimonies are fragments.

The victims want to know what happened. They want to know where the men in their families are. They have run out of patience with the soldiers, who decry the inadequate military command structure and use their inability to refuse orders as an explanation for what happened. For the victims, it is as clear as day that the outcome could have been different and that anyone who does not question what happened is complicit in keeping a horrible secret. That secret was known to the Clinton administration and leaders of other governments, who collaborated on a policy of non-intervention while the population of Srebrenica died, first through hunger and shelling, and finally by mass slaughter. Because of that, the Bosnian Muslims—the Bosniaks—lost faith in the United Nations, as represented by DutchBat.

The victims have told their stories and have made accusations. Their stories may contradict one another, and no narrative is complete; there are only shreds of memory and lots of grief. To understand, one must listen carefully and accept the confusion. These broken stories compel us to consider what it is like to be forsaken and to have no one left. Only then can we begin to realize how difficult it is to remember after such trauma. Although their memories are fragmented and in tatters, this is how memory presents itself in such cases.

There is another reason for the fragmentation and confusion. The survivors grew up in Tito's unified, communist Yugoslavia and then later lived through its disintegration. They had been told that all the "nations" of Yugoslavia were equal and yet they knew that was not true, especially for Muslims. They had also been told to live together peacefully, which they did, despite their differences.

Within a decade, those differences became important again, and the redistancing led to a war in which old friends and neighbors morphed into enemies and murderers. Men with whom one used to socialize were suddenly in military uniforms, forcing one to flee hearth and home. Under such circumstances, remembering how things used to be becomes almost impossible. What should be remembered—the friendship or the rancor and aggression?

During 1992–1995, thousands lived in the enclave of Srebrenica; despite the poverty and the misery, they did their best to survive with decency and integrity. They had not yet been abandoned—they felt protected by the United Nations—and there was hope that things would return to normal. Of course, it would not be the same as before, but it would be a world in which one could exist peacefully. Now, in the twenty-first century, the survivors can barely remember their hopes during those years, let alone their emotions and how life really was. The horrors of 1995 were so violent and traumatizing that it seems better to forget the peaceful times, or at least to repress them. What remains in their memory is a hole that matches the desolation in their current lives, lives bereft of a hopeful future. Can they ever live in peace? They escaped, but to where, to what? The world of the past no longer exists, but no one knows quite how to restore things as they should be.

The mood in the Netherlands is changing, but it is a slow process. I would like to see more official recognition that something went horribly wrong in Srebrenica. I would also like to see no further attempts to conceal what happened, but this is not yet the case. There have been no attempts at reconciliation with the women. Apparently, that will take a few more years, yet I have an abundance of hope and also patience.

Acknowledgments

These are the names of the women and two men who told their stories to me in Bosnia and gave me permission to record them. I thank them, and also those who did not wish to be mentioned: Vahida Ahmetović, Sabra Alemić, Fadila Alić, Šuhra Alić, Šefika Begić, Ajša Begtić, Nura Duraković, Fazila Efendić, Nura Efendić, Sabaheta Fejić, Hatidža Habibović, Behara Hasanović, Sevda Hasanović, Rukija Hasić, Mejra Hodžić, Kada Hotić, Hadžira Ibrahimović, Safija Kabilović, Edina Karić, Ajkuna Kremić, Sabra Kulenović, Jasmina Ljeljić, Hidajet Malagić, Hafiza Malagić, Hatidža Mehmedović, Hanifa Muhinović, Timka Mujić, Suada Mujić, Šuhreta Mujić, Ćamila Omanović, Devleta Omerović, Šida Omerović, Magbula Pašalić, Abdulah Purković, Kadira Rizanović, Refija Salihović, Binasa Sarajlić, Haša Selimović, Zumra Šehomerović, Šuhra Sinanović, Bida Smajlović, Haša Smajlović, Nermina Smajlović, Razija Smajlović, Munira Subašić, Nezira Sulejmanović, Hazreta Tabaković, Zehta Ustić, Ramiza Zukanović. I also thank Fadila Memišević.

Vahida Buljabašić was interviewed about 1995 on the other side of the Drina, in Mali Zvornik, Serbia. Mirsada Bakalović in Australia gave Ger Duijzings permission to use a transcript of an interview he had with her.

Students interviewed the following survivors in the Netherlands: Said Atić, Ajka Buhić, Fadil Hotić, Fikreta Hotić, Zejna Jasarević-Fejić, Muška Omerović-Begović, Ramo Ramić, Ševala Salkić, and Beriz Šehomerović. The students were Anna Albers, Jan Bernhardt, Lara Broekman, Arieke Duijzer, Femke van Leeuwen, Ragna Louman, Eilen Ros, Mark de Vries, and Esther van Zeiden.

All the interviews were transcribed by Sanela Zahirović, who also acted as interpreter on many occasions. The translation of the transcripts into English was done by Gordana Kisić. Sanela and Gordana were my key team; they never gave up, even when I was exhausted.

In Bosnia, I thank Branka Antić of Tuzla, a physician at Snaga Zene, for years of friendship and the manner in which she always helped me in my endeavors. We understood each other from the beginning. The same applies to Asta Zinbo of ICMP in Sarajevo. She helped me to remain objective and to ask questions. She took responsibility for maintaining contact between the women and NIOD, and comforted me when it all became too much. I also thank her team members Alma Mašic (who no longer works there), Violeta Burić Milosević, and Lidija Skaro for their patience and their translating; I will never forget. Dragana Jovanović of the research team The Netherlands–Srebrenica was always there for me in Srebrenica. As part of that team, Abel Hertzberger, who introduced me to Dragana, always gave me sage advice. Over the years, Jacob Finci of Sarajevo, now an ambassador in Switzerland, was a good counselor and wise friend. Most of all, I thank Bertie Stauber for his friendship and all those days together in the car.

Meldijana Arnaut and Velma Sarić contributed to this book by researching the organizations of women survivors; this took place under the supervision of Professor Smail Čekić at the University of Sarajevo. I also thank the Institute for the Research of Crimes against Humanity and International Law.

I collaborated with Selma Kapidzić and Jagoda Gregulska under the supervision of Mirsad Tokaca of the Research and Documentation Center (RDC) in Sarajevo. In October 2006, Selma and I organized a course on oral history in Sarajevo.

Professor Rusmir Mahmutcehajić gave me the opportunity to present my material to the International Forum, Bosnia.

Suada Pasić helped me to find survivors in the Netherlands; she has become a friend. Margriet Prins, the good-willed staff member of the Office of the High Representative, is someone I wish I had met much earlier. It was a joy to travel with someone who could interpret; she made the interviews in Bosnia much easier. I also thank Zlatko Hurtić for his friendship and never-ending belief in this project.

I thank Dr. Ger Duijzings, reader in the anthropology of Eastern Europe at the School of Slavonic and East European Studies (SSEES), University College, London, for giving me access to the materials prepared by Kirsti Thorsen, and for permission to use some of his interviews in this project. I also thank Kirsti Thorsen for her cooperation and Professor Fred Grünfeld for allowing me to use his unpublished material. If only all researchers were so generous!

In addition to the collaborators named above, I also thank the interpreters Suada Salihbegović, Sonja Akašamija, and Zlata Gatić, with whom I worked many times, and Selma Gasi, with whom I worked during my first very difficult trip to Bosnia. Hasan Nuhanović gave me permission to use material from his book. Puco Danilović assisted me with materials a number of times and also translated this book into Bosnian.

The following women from Bosnia gave me permission to read the material regarding them in the NIOD archives: Munira Beba Hadzić, Hajra Catić, Sabaheta Fejić, Fatima Husejnović, Hatidža Hren, Edina Karić, Fadila Memišević, Sabra (Šuhreta) Mujić, Ćamila Omanović, and Zumra Šehomerović.

The following persons helped me at various times in Sarajevo, Tuzla, and Srebrenica: Zehira Imanović (hospitality), Hajra Salimović (hospitality), Amra Delić (finding an article), Edina Suljić (transcription), and Ismir Korjenić (transcription).

I thank the management team at Hotel Tuzla in Tuzla and Adis and Nermin of Hotel Bosnia in Sarajevo for their help and the manner in which they provided me with security. Professor Mient Jan Faber (IKV) and Dr. Karel Vosskühler (former Dutch ambassador in Bosnia) gave me their cooperation. I thank Professor Onno van der Hart for our written discussion regarding trauma. Jehanne van Woerkom of the political committee Stari Most helped me with data regarding the "general pardon." Dr. Guido Snel shared his opinions with me. Professor Christien Brinkgreve has been my sounding board for years and is an integral part of my life. Kanita Kaunić assisted me with the diacritical marks. Professor Philomena Essed and Professor David Goldberg read an early research outline and encouraged me. Dr. Jet Bussemaker, a member of the lower house of the Dutch parliament at that time, aided me in approaching the lower house.

I am grateful to Dr. Elly Touwen-Bouwsma (NIOD) and Professor Hans Blom (NIOD) for their cooperation.

At the University of Amsterdam, I received support initially from Astrit Blommestijn; we share history. Selma Hinderdael of the university's liaison office helped me with the formal proposal for the Dutch Ministry of Foreign Affairs and with much more. I received a great deal of support from Hotze Mulder when I found myself in a new unit of a new faculty, and from Kees Ostendorf, who never seemed perturbed by my rather strange expenses. I also thank Professor Jan Willem van Henten and Professor Athalya Brenner for the peaceful atmosphere that characterizes my current workplace in the Department of Religious Studies, and Professor Aafke Hulk, the dean during this research, for arranging a place for me to work. Sanja Zivojnović knows the language and did more than just secretarial work.

For many years I worked with Professor Mary Chamberlain and Dr. Nanci Adler on the book series Memory and Narrative. Dr. Andrea Peto of Budapest also participated and was a discussion partner. Professor Richard Candida Smith organized a seminar in Berkeley and Professor Albert Lichtblau did the same in Salzburg. I presented papers in Istanbul when I was a guest lecturer at Sabanci University; in Xiamen, where I taught in 2006; and in Tbilisi, where I gave a seminar and helped to organize the Women's Fund and Memory Research Center. I thank Professor Leyla Neyzi, Professor Li Minghuan, and Dr. Marina Takubashvili.

Professors Margaret Jacob, Lynn Hunt, and Ellen Dubois organized a seminar at the Center for Eurasian and European Studies, UCLA.

Marieke van Oostrom of Bert Bakker Publishing was an editor whose precision I could not match during the completion of the Dutch edition. Ansfried Scheifes continued his good work as the copyeditor of a number of my books. Marjan Lucas and Marion de Zanger also read the text. Marjan helped me to break into the field; Marion read and read. I could not have finished without them. The same applies to the anonymous reviewers.

This book was made possible by financial aid from the following organizations: Stichting Democratie en Media (Foundation for Democracy and Media); Fonds Bijzondere Journalistieke Projekten (Fund for Special Journalistic Projects); and Hivos-Cultuurfonds (Hivos Humanist Institute for Development Cooperation). Their generosity preserved this research and contributed to giving the survivors of Srebrenica a voice.

Siep Stuurman has been listening to my doubts for years. Were all those conflicts worth it? Wasn't I getting too exhausted? In addition, he always read along with me. Best of all, he was just a phone call away when I was alone in Bosnia and an interview had left me perplexed and sad. He was my anchor and made it all worthwhile.

OCTOBER–NOVEMBER 2007

ON THE PUBLICATION OF THE ENGLISH EDITION

After the publication of this book in Dutch, I reworked and shortened it. I have tried to make it more understandable for the American reader.

I am grateful to the late Tony Judt, former director of the Remarque Institute at New York University, and his staff for the generous offer to work there. I was warmly received at NYU and supported by Professors Linda Gordon and Marion Kaplan. Rachel Bernstein taught me what students know about oral history.

Dori Laub of Yale University has been an unwavering partner in the discussion about trauma. He and Ben Kiernan organized a guest lecture in the Modern Genocide and Contemporary Challenges series at Yale.

I also spoke about trauma at the Trauma and Violence Interdisciplinary Studies program at NYU and at the East-West Gender in Transition: Women in Europe workshop. I thank Nanette Funk.

The invitation to the Freeman Spogli Institute for International Studies at Stanford was quite special. I thank Katherine Jolluck, who supported my work, and also her husband, Norman Naimark, for the discussion on ethnic cleansing.

My work received an award from Bosnjaco.net in New York. I thank Esad Krcic for his support. In 2009 I was chosen by the Bosnian community in the Netherlands, with support from several organizations in Bosnia, to be the "person of the year" for writing this book. I was honored during a ceremony at the Bosnian embassy in The Hague.

The reception of the Bosnian translation of this book, *Prazninu ostaviti iza nas: Istorija žena Srebrenice* (Sarajevo: Rabic, 2009), has been remarkable. The first presentation was to the American Bosnian Association in New York; for a moment, it felt like we were in Sarajevo. In particular, I thank the women's organizations for their love and tribute. They arranged for the Bosnian president, Dr. Haris Silajdžić, to receive a copy during a ceremony just before the commemoration in 2005.

Finally, I thank Kay Richardson, my translator, and Janet Rabinowitch, my editor.

Abbreviations

ICMP	International Commission on Missing Persons
ICTY	International Criminal Tribunal for the Former Yugoslavia
IKV	Netherlands Inter-Church Council (a Dutch NGO)
MSF	Médecins sans Frontières (Doctors without Borders)
NGO	nongovernmental organization
NIOD	Netherlands Institute for War Documentation
OHR	Office of the High Representative (Bosnia-Herzegovina)
RDC	Research and Documentation Center, Sarajevo
UNHCR	United Nations High Commissioner for Refugees
UNPROFOR	United Nations Protection Force

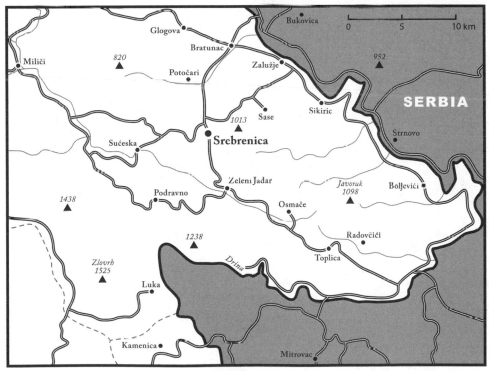

SURVIVING THE BOSNIAN GENOCIDE

SABAHETA'S STORY

*It is easier to bear the pain of loss than the pain of a guilty
conscience.*

—MUNIRA SUBAŠIĆ, president,
Mothers of the Enclaves of Srebrenica and Žepa

When I first interviewed Sabaheta, we were sitting in a small, bare room next to the office of Mothers of the Enclaves of Srebrenica and Žepa in a suburb of Sarajevo. The room belonged to no one; because there was no money, there were only three chairs. The organization housed next door had an overly full space; its walls were covered with photos of the giants of the earth who had visited to show their solidarity with the women survivors of Srebrenica and then left. In the room where we sat, birds had visited recently. It was cold and damp, as Sarajevo often is in the autumn. Sabaheta's face was pale; she was tense. She began to talk, and so began our friendship.

> My name is Sabaheta. When Srebrenica fell in July 1995, my son, my only child, was taken prisoner by the Chetniks right in front of the Dutch soldiers. And my husband, who went through the woods, did not reach the safe area. . . . My whole life up till then, my life since I was born, is ruined. Everything good is gone. All the happiness and joy were replaced with pain and grief for my son and my husband.

The couple had lived in Srebrenica since 1975. Their son, Rijad, was born in 1977. In 1992, when the war in Bosnia-Herzegovina began and the town was no longer safe, their peaceful life was disturbed. The family fled into the woods and lived there for 12 days in the open air. She described how Srebrenica was flooded with refugees from the surrounding villages after the war began, and how it all ended in 1995:

> When the Chetnik offensive against Srebrenica began on the 11th of July in 1995, I went with my son and many other people to the compound in Potočari. I thought we would be better protected

there than if we went with my husband and the other men through the woods. But the protection didn't happen. On the 13th of July, 1995, the Chetniks took my child from me, right in front of the eyes of the Dutch soldiers.

When asked why she had trusted the Dutch, she said: "Because I thought that we would be protected in the compound." But after the fall of the town, the Serbian soldiers made their way among the people and began to take men and girls with them. "And the Dutch soldiers just watched and did nothing." According to Sabaheta, they actually helped the Serbs because they kept things orderly.

I arrived on July 11 [in Potočari], and was alone on July 13. They took my son, although I tried to fight with the Chetniks, but I couldn't. They pushed me into a truck that was going to Kladanj, where a couple of acquaintances picked me up. Then I tried to commit suicide, and I thank God that I did not succeed. Because if I had succeeded, who would look for my son and husband now?

It's true that for a while I was not a stable person, but I came to my senses among the other mothers and wives, who had begun immediately to find out what had happened to our families and where they were. We organized meetings and protests . . . to find out what had happened to them and where they were. We asked the International Red Cross, our government, the Dutch government, and the Bosnian minister of foreign affairs. But there was no information, nobody wanted to answer us. If one day thousands of children are taken from their mothers, and so many women and men, more than 10,000, disappear in the forests and nobody knows where they are—I can't understand that. I understand that everybody wants to forget about the genocide of Srebrenica. Fighting against that amnesia gave me the strength to search for what happened there. I can't forget my son and my husband and I want to know what happened to them. . . . I still don't know anything about my husband and my son, but I do believe that the veil over Srebrenica will be lifted and we will find out who was responsible for Srebrenica and the crimes committed there.

She admitted that it was difficult for her to talk about the events in Potočari and she always tries to avoid it. However, she told me anyway.

On July 11 at around five in the afternoon, my son and I arrived in Potočari. There were already a lot of people there. The night of

July 11–12 my son and I slept in the open air, although I tried to get into the covered part of the compound. There was a hole in the fence to let people in. But they wouldn't let us in. I was concerned about my child's future. On July 12 at 10 [o'clock] we were turned over to the Chetniks. The Chetniks immediately began walking around, pointing to the men: "You, you, you." And they took them with them, supposedly to question them, and said they would be brought back after that. But they never did. . . . I was really afraid, but I managed to hide that from my child. My mother was with me; she is still alive and lives with me. We were together in Potočari. I sat down and thought about what I should do with my child. I had the feeling that I would not be able to get him through this.

When the deportations began, we heard a rumor that they were going to separate the men and the children [Sabaheta means the boys] without regard to age. It was a large site—a factory complex, an industrial zone—and it was now full of women, children, and men who had been driven out of Srebrenica and were waiting to be deported. Among the Serbs, I saw [two people I knew]. The first was my next-door neighbor. He was with his son. His son and mine were the same age and went to school together. I decided to ask him for protection. I tried to push my way through the crowd to reach him. While I did that, I had a strong intuition to return to my mother and my son. It was so strong that I turned back. I went back to where I had left them; my mother was in tears. But my Riki wasn't there. "Mother, where is Riki?" Crying, she told me, "There, they have taken him." I looked around; about 100 meters farther up I saw a group of our men standing in front of armed Chetniks. My Riki was among our men. I ran there, stood in front of my son, and told a Chetnik, "Why have you taken my child? This is my child. Give him back!" They began to curse me out and yelled, "No, we won't give him back, all we want to do is question him. Then we will give him back." "You give him back now, give him to me now. If you want to question somebody, then question me. Leave this child alone; he hasn't done anything." One of the Chetniks said, "Take him." So I took him and went back to the place where my mother was.

Sabaheta had counted on the Serbs being reasonable, and it worked. Probably, some of the men knew her. She and her son sat there, barely talking and afraid. She did not know what to do.

We stayed there that night, afraid to go to the buses that would deport us, so I stayed another night. It was a dreadful, terrible night full of screams and fear. You heard someone screaming, and then we all stood up, maybe 15,000 people, and we screamed in unison. Can you imagine 15,000–16,000 people screaming at the same time? I think that half of Serbia could hear us. And the world didn't know what was happening? Everybody saw what was happening. But they didn't want to help.

The next day, Sabaheta decided to talk openly with her son about their circumstances. She felt that things might go wrong for him. "He understood the situation. I saw it on his face and in his eyes. I saw from his behavior that he was aware of the situation. I said to him, 'Son, your mother needs to talk with you.'" She proposed suicide, which he refused. Then she said: "Good. If you don't do it, then your mother won't either." They decided to go to the buses.

I took his arm and we began to walk. We passed the line of Dutch soldiers and immediately I saw that the Chetniks were standing in a row along the street. A hundred or 200 meters farther up, the buses and trucks stood ready for the deportation. My son and I went slowly, arm in arm; 50 meters behind us were other people and in front of us were also people, two by two in a row. When we came to the Chetniks, they said immediately that my son had to go to the right and I had to go straight on. We didn't listen, we kept walking straight ahead together. But that wasn't good; they followed us immediately and said that he had to go right and I had to go straight on. I didn't want that [but] they grabbed him. I pulled him to me, and they pulled him away. . . . I begged them to let him go: "Please don't do this, he is my only child, he hasn't hurt anybody; if anybody is guilty, it's me—take me." They cursed and pushed me, . . . they hit me, I couldn't do anything. They were stronger and armed, and so they took my child. The only thing Riki could do when he realized what was happening was to look at me, and I looked at him—it was a brief moment. Huge tears rolled down his cheeks. He hugged me, kissed me, and said, "Go, Mother, please." They grabbed him. I couldn't walk any farther. I knelt down and begged them, "Please, kill me, kill me, you've taken my only child. I don't want to go farther. Kill me and end this." They began to yell, scream, curse me, curse my Muslim mother, Alija Izetbegović [the Bosnian leader]. . . . They told me to go away and that they would bring my child back, that they only wanted to question him. I said to them, "If you are going to give him back, then give him back now. I won't leave; if you won't give him back, then kill me." One of them took a gun and pointed it at me, but another one told him not to kill me.

Sabaheta was thrown into one of the waiting trucks and lost consciousness. Looking back, she said: "My life stopped in 1995 when I realized that my son and husband were not coming back. Since then, I am a robot that gives itself orders."[1]

Sabaheta still cannot forget that those who committed the murders were not strangers, but people she knew and trusted. Not surprisingly, she is now one of the survivors' representatives who relentlessly seek out the truth. What happened? Where are the missing? For her, the world is one enormous lie and a conspiracy against her desire for the truth. She cannot understand how she lost her stability and how her life fell to pieces as a result of deeds that once seemed unimaginable. How could her friends, her acquaintances, turn into murderers? How could they have been so well prepared to murder? And how could the world turn a blind eye to what happened?

CHAPTER ONE

FAREWELL

The Desolation, the Women

There is always a story about saying goodbye—to a husband, a son, a sweetheart, a father, or another family member. A man and a woman embrace each other for the last time, their faces strained and wet with tears. A father hugs his daughter hastily, both knowing they will never see each other again. A child cries and calls to her father who is being taken away, "Come back, come back!" A mother grips her young son tightly and begs the soldiers to leave him with her. "Don't take him, he hasn't done anything, he's so young!" She pulls, trying to free him from the soldiers' grasp, but without success.

Perhaps the farewell took place on the streets of Srebrenica, when many men and a few strong women left, hoping to escape through the woods to safety behind the lines of "their" Bosnian army. Or maybe it was nothing more than a last glimpse—just after the men had been separated from the women—as the buses at the Dutch compound in Potočari were being loaded. Although they hoped to see each other again, they knew in their hearts that this farewell was final. Yet the women have waited, at first for their husbands to return, then for news that their bodies had been found. Many are still waiting.

One might ask if this approach is a proper way to write history, if including such images will give us a historical narrative. I argue that history is the totality of such small, sad moments; although seemingly insignificant, they are of great importance to the people who lived them. How can I bring order to the myriad "facts," the little incidents that were told to me by the survivors of Srebrenica? For years I listened, and discovered that their totality does create a history of how people survived the fall of Srebrenica and then continued on with their lives. Time seems to have passed but, sadly, for many of the survivors, time has stopped. Some stories shocked me deeply, moved me to compassion, and filled me with admiration for the teller's courage in talking to me, a Dutch citizen. I come from a nation the survivors consider complicit in the fall of the town where they thought they were safe; some even consider the Dutch guilty of murder.

It took a great deal of time before I could allow myself to feel the enormity of their grief. It took even longer before all those tatters of grief could be woven into a larger tapestry of what it was like to live there before the 1995 genocide, and then to survive. Some images continue to haunt me—hands reaching for each other one last time, a husband and wife turning to look at each other before disappearing into the crowd, a heart that seemed to stop or just became empty. There was often a moment when the women couldn't breathe, because everything ached. Then the waiting for news began, despite knowing there was little hope of survivors. Gradually, news of a body being found became good news, because it made a decent burial possible. These are the things that define their memories; this is their history.

Safíja Kabilović, an older woman in a refugee camp, was still waiting for her son in 2004

> I waited for so long, until I got a death certificate [in 2004] for the son who was found and dug up. I waited for the younger son until last year, hoping that one way or another I would learn that he was still alive. We felt like he might have been taken to another country and hadn't been able to contact us. There are cases of people who were taken elsewhere, and then after a certain time they send a message. But when my oldest son was found, I lost my hope. I knew. I went to the funeral, and I know where his body rests. I still pray to God that I will hear that my other son is somewhere. There is a saying that you can't give up hope until you've seen it with your own eyes. May God hear my wish that he is alive somewhere, that he is somewhere.[1]

After the massacre in 1995, the grieving women who had lost their husbands, sons, fathers, and brothers appeared on television. From that moment, I wanted to hear their stories. Their men were dead, but they had survived. These women had watched their men being taken away, knowing what was happening in their immediate surroundings and fearing the worst. Of course, they did not know everything; there were so many people and the slaughter took place at a number of sites. I wanted to listen to them because I am convinced that the survivors' stories are a necessary part of the mass murder's historiography.

The survivors have had to fight to talk about their experiences. The fall of Srebrenica is an enigma that has developed into a struggle in the media; the eyewitnesses are considered annoying because they refuse to be silent and continue to ask why this happened. The survivors tell their stories to show that what they saw does not agree with what they have been told. Some historians feel that such eyewitness accounts are untrustworthy and biased. I disagree, although I do agree with the American historian Hayden White, who noted in 1978 that both eyewitness accounts and historiography are never neutral. He called the denial of the value of such personally colored documentation "the fictions of factual representation."[2] The representation of extreme situations poses myriad problems for the historian, because the survivor's response is inevitably interwoven with emotional impressions and grief that are difficult to comprehend.[3] In order to understand traumatized memories, it is necessary to listen to the traumatized story. Recovering and recounting such difficult memories also are crucial for a healthy relationship with the past; they contribute to a more critical and accurate way of remembering, which in turn leads to a more mindful, ethical, and charitable attitude in the public sphere. I am in favor of an approach in which every answer to questions about Srebrenica brings about new explorations for truth.

Most historians do not see value in interviewing the survivors. Their reluctance seems to stem from the discomfort of facing the overwhelming grief that remains. The survivors do not tell us hard facts.[4] Instead, they provide impressions, traumatized pieces of the past, and stories of grief that come together in a historical picture that accords suffering a place. This is a picture that the survivors can relate to.

According to the American cultural historian Dominique LaCapra, valuing the memories of others is important for developing a discerning memory. By accepting others' memories, even if we find them strange and unpleasant, we are laying the foundation for a legitimate and democratic approach in the future.[5] Listening was not easy during my research. It is always difficult to listen to stories of trauma; we have a natural resistance to them. Even though I had no problem in feeling empathy for the women during the interviews, I did feel resistance to listening to yet another horror story. I became aware that survivors who do not talk about what happened have increasing difficulty over time in doing so. And when the obstacles cannot be overcome, it is emotionally so difficult that it seems better to forget or repress the memories. As a result, some women have become passive and others depressed. Severe physical and psychological distress have major consequences for the functioning of the body and for the ability to think about who we are and about our physical well-being.[6]

We know from other atrocities that the survivors' testimony adds an essential dimension to the history of a war and its genocide.[7] Of course such testimony must be critically studied, and there has been important research in this area. Survivors' stories are open to multiple interpretations, they are not stable, they are dominated by a grief that has taken on a life of its own, and some moments of blind panic are nearly impossible to describe.[8] Despite these difficulties, it is now accepted that writing the history of such events requires listening to the survivors.[9]

In *Vectors of Memory*,[10] Nancy Wood examines the culture of memory in Europe after 1945. She discusses how the philosopher and Holocaust survivor Jean Améry admits that his memories are embedded in what Nietzsche called "resentment." Resentment is not a desire for revenge, it acts as a stimulus for critical and moral reflection; this is also evident in the work of Primo Levi. According to Wood, this feeling of resentment is a "trenchant rebuke" against the moral decay within a society whose victims trusted it. Even stronger, "these reflections on memory-as-resentment still speak to us today, not because the genocides to which we are witness are analogous to the Holocaust, but because, like Améry, victims have experienced their fate as one of abandonment by the outside world."[11] This means that in writing about genocide—including what occurred in Srebrenica—emotion and ostensibly objective research are inextricably interwoven. This is inescapable. It is the task of the historian both to decode and to deconstruct the accounts of the eyewitnesses. This requires deciphering the emotionally laden language of survivors' accounts as well as using the more traditional methods of historiography.

Is it indeed possible for the survivors to talk about what happened? That was my first concern. Time and again, I was warned that I was beginning an impossible task, yet the survivors trusted in me, and the interviews were successful. "Trust" is of critical importance for those who have lost their understanding of it. They trusted their neighbors, who then became rapists and murderers. Then they trusted the soldiers of DutchBat, who were supposed to protect them. Why should they tell me what happened? Some interviews turned into a collaborative search for the past, admittedly hampered because I had to work through interpreters, even though the interpreters did their best to help me communicate directly with the women. I was taken into their confidence and they told me their stories, although on occasion it was just too much for an interviewee to talk about what happened and the resulting confusion. In 2002, someone threw a clump of dirt at my interpreter and me in Srebrenica; now, that is unthinkable. Today, I am fully accepted, and there is mutual respect and warmth.

The interviews had various patterns, yet there was always the unexpected. There was never a set template of testimony, as there was at the International Criminal Tribunal for the Former Yugoslavia (ICTY) in The Hague, where the goal was evidence. Witnesses there were asked to describe precisely what happened in a manner suitable for an indictment. Those statements do not tell about how life was in the enclave before and after 1995, and what the fall of the enclave meant to their lives. How did the women say goodbye to their husbands before the men attempted to escape through the woods to the safety of Bosnian-held territory? When was the last time the women saw their men before they were separated? Did they expect the slaughter, or did they believe in the protection that had been promised to them? Did they expect the United Nations or NATO to intervene? And how do they feel about the foreign soldiers who did nothing? Did they feel betrayed when it happened, or did the feelings of betrayal only develop later?

These women have taught me yet again that one's current situation affects how one views the past. For many of them there is no future, hence their stories are of total loss. Since being driven out of Srebrenica in 1995—and before as well, when they were driven from their villages in the preceding three years—life has lost its meaning. They survived, but most of them have not found a new reason to live. The trauma of their family members being murdered is too great to integrate emotionally. Because they live in poverty, making plans for the future is impossible. They simply exist. If there is the possibility of a new house, perhaps in the region around Srebrenica, then at least some peace might be found.

In Dutch, this book was entitled *Leaving Desolation Behind,* but it could also have been titled simply *Desolation.* It is about the lives of those who have been rent from the social fabric. The loss of their families and networks has torn a hole in their psyches. Their world is gone, and with it a part of themselves. As we will see, the grieving (and often poverty-stricken) widows are considered disruptive, and their continual complaints about what happened too confrontational.

In 2003 the historian Omer Bartov proposed a microlevel historical approach to studying the escalation of hate in such situations.[12] He suggested examining limited areas and territories where the origins of hatred can be observed, as well as its growth into violence and, ultimately, genocide. He feels that the devil is to be found "in the local."[13] The research should look at how the social equilibrium—the mortar that holds a society together both materially and spiritually—becomes disturbed. How does this happen, and why does a person kill another with whom he has lived in peace for decades? It is almost impossible to understand, and yet there must be an explanation.

I left my books and the library to search for answers. I met approximately 100 women and recorded the life histories of about half of them. In 2006 a group of students interviewed survivors in the Netherlands. During the years of this research, much changed, even as the world of the women of Srebrenica has changed. In the beginning, I learned about the problematic thought processes of the women who could not return to their old locations, but were convinced that anything was better than living in the camps. Later, I heard the stories of the difficulties of returning to Srebrenica from those who had moved back.

As I write this in 2009, it appears that the number of returnees will increase. Life in the camps and in temporary housing is unbearable for many survivors. However, there are women who cannot return; they do not dare, they don't have the necessary papers, or they are not capable of rebuilding their lives in the villages around Srebrenica or in the town itself. There are thousands of such women. It is their loss of context, of meaningfulness, that shocked me the most during the years of interviews. It was not only the loss of their men that had devastated their lives, but also being alone, exiled from their former home, having too much responsibility and no one to share it with. The family network and its daily support are gone; even in families where some of the men survived, the structure is damaged and the normal relationships no longer apply.

Whoever studies genocide at length asks why it happens. How can there be so much cruelty? How can one person do such things to another? Testimony (not only from my interviews) has taught me that nothing is unthinkable and that cruelty can have infinite variations in a setting in which fear of reprisal or punishment is absent.[14] And still, it seems incomprehensible how commonplace torture, rape, and murder become. Potočari was a pandemonium that stank of death and gore, where people walked around smeared with the blood of the butchered. The banality of evil was not, as Hannah Arendt wrote, the clerk at the desk, but the routine gesture by which a throat was slit, a woman raped, a husband separated from his wife, and a little boy yanked from his mother's arms. Evil became so commonplace that the perpetrator thought nothing of it. The lust for murder was so strong that resistance seemed futile, yet a few did resist. There is the story of the man who let an old acquaintance escape, thus putting himself in danger.[15] At the beginning of the war, there were many stories of Serb neighbors who shared food supplies, helped with an escape, or even hid friends, despite the danger. It was only later, and especially in Potočari, that the social fabric was radically and perhaps irreparably torn; every feeling of common humanity was replaced with hatred and apathy.

Hatred is the result of years of provocation and bullying. But the Serbs did not simply hate: they no longer regarded the Muslims as fellow human beings. For those who do not know what happened, the photos of General Ratko Mladić handing out candies seem to show a somewhat inebriated but average man; for those who know, the photos show a mass executioner.

Ramiza, surviving in a void

In 2006 I asked Ramiza, who lives in the provincial town of Tuzla, specifically about the desolation and loss of context. She was grieving for her family: spouse, father, brother, and especially her mother, who was murdered in the winter of 1992–1993. She missed her mother the most. We were in a neighborhood of Tuzla composed of houses built by the Dutch government for the survivors of Srebrenica. Ramiza was satisfied with her house and hoped that she could stay there. Because so many refugees are forced to move, she was uncertain about that. Indeed, insecurity was now a part of her existence. She spoke little about the murders of the men in her family; she felt that she would never know what really happened, although she would like to know the truth. "What am I supposed to do? I don't have any hope left. . . . I feel hollow in my soul. In every respect, I have no one . . . , no future, no prospects, nothing. I only have my child, she is my only hope and comfort. I fight for her . . . , [but] I have no plans, no ideas." When asked if she was interested in taking an educational course, she answered: "Nothing in particular, I don't want anything. There is a garden behind the house. If I'm not in the garden, then I'm doing handwork. I make lunch for my girl, I wait until she comes home. . . . I dream of my mother a great deal, and of Hamed [her husband]. I dream of them both."[16]

The void for Ramiza is not only personal and psychological, but an objective fact if we look at her life now. The social fabric and the interconnections of her existence are lost. Her life is missing the same thing that is missing from the lives of other survivors in the camps and shelters—context. Their existence lacks cohesion, and they seem to operate in a social vacuum. This is most palpable among those who returned to Srebrenica; they try stubbornly to reweave the social fabric, but cannot. They live in poverty and insecurity in a town that offers them no safety.[17]

Timka, a story of trauma

Survivors' stories are sometimes too shattered and they are too traumatized to be understood immediately. Timka taught me to listen well in such instances, because the loss of context is also a context, and sometimes its resonance is overwhelming.[18]

Timka explained to me how normal life used to be. As a child in school, she socialized with all her classmates. She knew they weren't Muslim, but that didn't matter.[19] The children played together and sat together in school. One of her friends was a Serb, but that only became important much later; Timka lost that friendship because of the war. The two women belonged to different parties, parties that, after having lived together, began to murder each other, and then could not forgive each other. That is how Timka perceives it. Before the war, she had a full life; she loved her husband and children and the home they shared together. The only void in her life before the war was caused by the death of her father, but that was different. She was 14 when he died; in that era, it was uncommon to lose one's father as a young adolescent. His death changed her life dramatically; there was suddenly a great deal more work to do on the farm and she had to quit school. She only completed four years of school, although she was a good student.

Bosnian Serb and Bosnian Muslim children went to school together and played together in Srebrenica. As they got older, they danced and flirted with each other; in Timka's generation occasionally they married each other. Her entire account of the war is influenced by the fact that this situation no longer exists and never will again. She lives near her sister-in-law Šuhreta in an area occupied by Serbs; her former classmates are now her enemies, and she is afraid of them. Her life there is more difficult than that of survivors who returned to Srebrenica.

When I interviewed her in 2004, she had been living in her old house for a while. I met Timka through her sister-in-law, who lives next to her in a small village in a valley about a half hour's drive from Srebrenica. It is an area where ethnic cleansing was successful. The two houses of the Muslim women who returned stand next to each other; for the rest, there are only "the others." The women have no one to protect them. If shooting breaks out tomorrow, anything is possible. They are aware of that and are afraid.

It had been safe there before. When I asked her about that era, when Tito was still alive, she told me: "Yes. But now, for example, now that I've returned, I'm alone. Serbs live across the street. . . . I'm not comfortable when I lock up the house at night before going to bed. I'm nervous. There are nights when I can't sleep at all. I'm always afraid. You don't just get over that. When Tito was alive, you could go out in the street and leave your house open. You could do that if you wanted to."

Her world has changed since then. She lost her husband and her son; she last saw them in Srebrenica, before they fled through the woods. They decided it was better to go their separate ways. The men were wary about leaving their families, but they were also afraid that the women and children would not survive the long trek through the forest. Timka, her daughters, and her daughter-in-law went one way, and the men went another, toward the hills and the forest, toward the vast expanse of Bosnia. Everything seemed to be in slow motion; she can still recall how it felt to say goodbye, although she prefers not to. It was one of the most painful moments; the grief she felt then took her breath away. Here again was that inevitable farewell, where one must pause. Timka regained her composure and continued: "I can't describe saying goodbye. My son's last words were, 'Mother, we are going now. Take care of the children.' Then they left and I haven't heard from them since." She learned later that her husband, son, and son-in-law were all captured.

After the farewell, there was nothing else for the women and children to do but to join the enormous crowd that was making its way to the UN base in Potočari. They were swept along in the sea of people and ultimately arrived at the base, which already contained thousands of refugees. Timka spent three traumatic days herded together with thousands of others, days of fear during which she tried to be a support for her family. There was nothing to eat and they were under constant threat, treated like cattle in a holding pen. It is still difficult for Timka to talk about the events of those three days. Timka survived; like the others I interviewed, she tried to pick up the thread of her life. She would prefer not to remember, because the images are of all she has lost. Timka was apologetic, "but please don't ask too much about that."

When I interviewed Šuhreta, Timka was in distress. She was gasping for air, as though to let us know that she, too, had suffered. The contrast between Timka and her sister-in-law, who was adamant about telling everything regarding the brutal murder of her husband, was striking. I could barely listen to the details; he was slowly tortured to death in a manner guaranteed to cause the most pain. Later, I became used to hearing such accounts, because the Serb strategy was to torture first and then murder, or sometimes to rape first and then kill. But at that time, Šuhreta's interview was difficult for me. I was still learning how to witness by "crying silently," as I later named it. This is weeping without uttering a sound. Occasionally, I entered a hall in Bosnia where 10 women would be crying silently; it was always a disconcerting experience.

As the interview with Šuhreta progressed, Timka became less agitated. Clearly, she is high-strung. Her hands are those of a woman who works the land. She is an endearing and charming woman, as is her sister-in-law. The house has neither running water nor electricity, yet it is clean. The interview dragged on and the situation was tiresome. The story itself is not long, and yet it took the whole day. We tried to put her at ease; we drank coffee. She complained:

> I am dying of loneliness. I sit within these four walls, day and night, I have no one to take care of—no brother, no sister, no father, no mother, no spouse, nothing, nothing. But the heaven is high and the earth is low, and I have to live. Wherever I am, here or somewhere else, my soul aches and I am alone. I have no one who can fetch something for me [her sister-in-law is too weak]. If I can't cook, then no one does it for me. I returned here. I can't work. I own a good bit of land farther up in the village, but I have no one to work it for me.

It is characteristic of interviews with traumatized persons that everything seems both distant and incredibly close, in the past and happening now. Time melts and yesterday's events are mingled with those of long ago.[20] The stories are told within a no man's land that has no time or lies just beyond its boundaries.

Events are not discussed chronologically. The interviewee (in this case, Timka) searches for the right words, but the images before her eyes are blurred and in disarray. With the aid of my interpreter, I kept trying to help her clarify her story. I wanted to know more than just her complaints. I wanted to know how she lived before, and how the misery she had experienced fit within a longer life story. We drank coffee, we sat silently; we drank juice and ate her fruit preserves. These are calming rituals, and I have learned that a calm atmosphere is needed to make room for the telling. I know that the past is painful, that all three of us will be on edge at a given moment in the story, and that we will all become exhausted. It has also become clear to me that, although all the women talk of Srebrenica unceasingly, it is seldom about the trauma, and no one has really listened to their stories. I am there to listen. I know that later, when my interpreter and I are gone, she—like all the women—will be grateful for the undivided attention, grateful and somewhat confused.

Nermina: Nothing is left

Nermina, whom I interviewed in 2005 in Mihatovići, also talked about the desolation. Mihatovići is considered a "model camp," but I found nothing good about it. At best, it is a model of gloom and depression. In 2005 it was estimated that about 2,500 people who were originally from Srebrenica lived there. In 2006 more families returned to Srebrenica. From a distance, it seems a nice place, but as one comes closer the chronic lack of maintenance, the filth, and especially the stench become obvious. Even on a cold, snow-covered day in winter, the camp stinks. Its permeating reek surprised me when I visited for the first time. Our car was stuck in the snow, so we had to walk to the camp. We walked past groups of loitering boys. It did not feel safe. There is nothing to do in the camps, and many residents talk about the high levels of crime,[21] which is the easiest way to acquire money. "They should put a fence around it," sighed one of the residents, "the world here is too dangerous." The biggest problem is the distance to the world where work is available and the lack of transportation. How is it possible to get to a paying job on time? There are always a few who manage, but logistics are not the only problems. People who have been in the camps for 10 years cannot simply begin working again. They have lost the daily routine of holding a job, and their sense of time has been damaged.

The poverty-stricken and miserable existence of the residents is obvious. The "richest" are the widows of soldiers, who receive about 350 KM (*konvertibilna marka,* or convertible marks, the currency of Bosnia-Herzegovina; 2 marks are equal to €1). All the women I talked to told me that life in the camp was unbearable. They wanted to return to their old homes, but that required that there still be something standing. Many houses were damaged or in ruins, the deeds had been lost, and there was no work to generate money for repairs and maintenance. Most important, the houses needed to be safe and must feel safe. That last demand is the most difficult. How can you feel safe in Srebrenica, when those in power since the war and the Dayton Accords are the same ones who tried to murder you? Nermina has returned to Srebrenica since we met, but at the time of the interview she doubted that she could ever do so. She was desperate.

We sat together and talked in a bare room. Our discussion was interrupted frequently. Her three boys were supposed to be playing outside so that we could talk in peace, but they kept coming inside. Although there was snow and it was cold, it was a lovely day. The boys wanted to warm themselves and to get a snack. Nermina is a small, nervous woman. She speaks rapidly and wants to tell everything all at once; she stumbles over her words, and yet her story comes out.

After a while, I said, "I want to ask you something, but you don't have to answer. It may be too painful. You hoped that you would see your husband again. Can you tell me more about that hope?"

> I have always hoped. I could swear on my life that he would appear from somewhere. I know that he never hurt anybody; he wouldn't harm a fly. That's why I find it so difficult when I think about it. Sometimes I cry day and night. And now . . . no organization gives me money. I pray to God that I may leave here. There are drugs here, and roaming children. I wish that I was in my own home, whatever God may have in mind for me. You don't get money to repair houses so that you can finally find some peace. I mean, if you have a little house with a bit of ground around it, then your child can play there and not in this uncivilized world. . . . No one takes care of us here, no one asks if we need anything. And now, the medical service that used to come here all the time has stopped. I have three children who go to school, I have no money to buy a piece of land or an apartment. Mainly, I don't have enough money.
>
> When I heard that we were going to get compensation for war damages, I was happy. Believe me. But there is no money that can make up for losing my husband. It hurts every time one of my children says "Papa." I took my children to the doctor, and the youngest began to cry, as he usually does there. He asked, "Mama, when is Papa going to come and hold me?" My soul aches, my heart is heavy. If I could buy something [a house] for the children. . . . Not so much because they need it, but because they miss their father so much. But I should take them away [from the camp]. I don't have money to buy anything for my children. I don't see a chance to renovate the house and return, although I fret about it.[22]

This was how Nermina expressed her ambivalence about returning to her old home. Since the interview, she has received money to repair her house and has returned. But she lost 10 years waiting for that to happen. We met again in the summer of 2009.

Interviewing the Women

A person who manages to tell about her suffering and explain how it has affected her life might also succeed in rediscovering her place in the world. Even if one's web of relationships has been severely damaged, giving an account of what happened puts things in order and is a step toward the world of "normal" relations. After interviewing survivors of World War II, the historian James B. Young argued that, when people tell their stories, they recreate a place for themselves in the world.[23] This was also observed by Dori Laub, the psychiatrist and gifted listener; war survivors who initially could not speak about their trauma discovered that, if someone listened to them, they could speak about it. In the process of doing so, survivors also discovered that the unspeakable was replaced with the ability to give their traumas both meaning and context.[24]

This was well expressed by Zumra Šehomerović in the 2006 film *Srebrenica,* as she walked through her old house. Zumra had been one of the key interviewees in the 1999 film *Srebrenica: A Cry from the Grave,* in which she told how her husband was separated from her.[25] I often encountered Zumra in Sarajevo, but was not aware that she was considering returning to Srebrenica. In the spring of 2007, that was still not possible because she had no funds for house repairs. In the film, she had said that the possibility of returning to her old home made her happy. "It connects me with life" and also with memory. As she walked through the house, she talked about how her children had been born there. Although it will never be the way that it was, it is still a space that gives her life both context and meaning.

During my research, some of the interviewees were also witnesses at the ICTY in The Hague. They chose to do that without "protection," hence their testimony is available. Everyone I interviewed knew what being a witness meant: hostile interrogations, barrages of confrontational questions, having the accuracy of one's memory questioned. Often, the boundaries of common decency were crossed. Because their testimony was legal evidence against the aggressors, perhaps that was necessary. However, a major consequence is that the accusatory has become the main form of discourse when talking about the war. Legal witnesses give a different kind of account than what I am interested in.[26] The indictments were not my focus, yet they colored everything. The interviewees were always surprised when I asked about the time "before," that I found such "silly" things important and wanted to hear about pleasant memories. Often, I entered a house and was greeted with the words, "When the Dutch soldiers betrayed us . . ."

What is always remembered in the region is a political debate rife with controversy. During the period of my interviews, there was no generally accepted history of the war that could serve as a reference point. Various factions have different interpretations of what happened in the war. Within this cacophony of conflicting collective memories and historiography, the survivors' voices have been barely audible. The survivors organizations joined that debate and demanded a voice as victims and accusers. The Mothers of Srebrenica and Žepa, the best known of the groups, collaborated with the filmmakers of the documentary *Srebrenica: A Cry from the Grave;* others have contributed to similar documentaries.[27] As a result, these films have influenced the stories of a number of interviewees. Every July, journalists arrive in Bosnia looking for instant interviews; many survivors have learned how to give the desired sound bites. This made it difficult for me to explain why they should speak differently to me. I also spoke with many women who had never been interviewed and were thus uninfluenced.

Religion is another powerful way to give structure to what happened. From the beginning, the Islamic authority in Bosnia accorded the women a public place for mourning. The *reis-ul-ulema* gives an open prayer every year on July 11 in Potočari, in which he prays that the tears of the mothers will prevent similar murders in the future. Religion can act as a backdrop that helps to mend the social fabric, thus giving the women a sense of belonging. Nevertheless, the survivors' stories often unfold in a void in which the women ask themselves where they fit in this new and incomprehensible world that has rejected them. I do not know the answer. The survivors are here, they defend their rights, they protest, they make a nuisance of themselves. During the years in which I worked on this book, their voices became louder. They organized and merged with other groups; they debated with others and made deals. But their experiences were not taken seriously, and on occasion they were accused of exaggerating.

Haša remembers well a discussion she had with a Dutch researcher for the NIOD Report, which was published in several volumes; she was in the Netherlands protesting the neglect of the survivors. The discussion was about the slaughter of the children at Potočari. She told me about it when I interviewed her in Lukavać, not far from Tuzla, in 2006. Although Bosnian publications had already reported that the children were massacred, the Dutch researcher was apparently not aware of this. Haša tried to tell him that the children had been murdered. His attitude toward her is indicative of the way that many academics regard the stories of "uneducated" women. She was still furious when she told me:

[He] said that there were no children. "There were no children at Potočari," he said. "What do you mean, there were no children?" "There were none," he replied. I took my papers, which I had brought with me to Holland, out of my purse. [The papers confirmed her son had been killed during the fall of Srebrenica.] I asked him, "Did I kill my child? Did I undress him?" He repeated, "There were no children, no one knows where you women hid them."[28]

The researcher finally backed down after looking at Haša's papers.

Although the women wanted to talk, grief hindered them and made it difficult for them to speak about what happened. Bida, whom I interviewed in her restored house in Potočari, discussed this when I asked about her grief.

I don't know, I can't talk about it, it is so difficult. If I start talking, believe me, then I can't go on. I lose my voice. . . . You don't know how difficult it is for me. After this, . . . I know I will have a headache. Believe me, I'll be sick. But sometimes when we get together [she still has female family members], we talk about the war, how we survived, and our fear. Occasionally, someone says, "Why do you talk about it?" I don't know. I would like to avoid it. . . . And yet we sit with each other and we cry. We can't help it. But the worst is when I lose my voice, something happens. . . . Most of us have a problem with it, and we can't help it.[29]

Ajkuna was slowly losing her memory and rather happy that she no longer remembered everything.[30] I had interviewed her daughter a year earlier. They were living in a deserted school; each classroom housed a family. Ajkuna's daughter-in-law Mejra was the head of the family; Ajkuna also had several beautiful granddaughters. When I interviewed Ajkuna, her family was moving into a house; the interpreter, Ajkuna, and I sat in an empty room in the school. She was anxious and was worried about Mejra, who had to do everything herself: "There is no man who can come and help you, who can cut down a tree for you, or saw off a limb. There is no pension . . . , there is no money, we have been brought back to nothing. . . . There is no one, and no one comes."

Before the war, Ajkuna had an extensive social network; since 1995, no one has visited her. I was her first visitor in 10 years. She had lost "all the men," including a number of nephews. "I have no one any more," referring to her large family. No matter how kind her daughter-in-law is, she remains an in-law and not a blood relative.

I am so happy that you have come. You are the only one who came looking for me. Nobody has ever sought me out. Bajram [Turkish for "festival," it refers to the two major holidays of Islam] comes, Bajram goes, New Year's comes. . . . I shut myself up in my room and cry all day. No one knocks on my door, no one asks, "Where are you, Granny? Where are you, Mother?" No one. . . . we had a large family; my mother had six children.

All of Ajkuna's brothers and sisters are dead; six of her children are dead, and she knows how two of them died. Four of them did not make it through the woods in 1995. We were only 10 minutes into the interview when the separation of the men and the women at Potočari came up, and it was impossible to talk about anything else thereafter. Her husband was loaded into a bus to be murdered. After a great deal of questioning, I learned that she and her family had fled their home for the first time in 1992. They hid in the woods for a couple of days. They had no food and they slept in the snow, but at least they were together.

Fear, Grief, Hatred

Many of those I met live among the shards of a world that was shattered. They drift through the hours of the day with neither direction nor purpose. Often the loneliness is unbearable, as it is for Timka. Because Timka lives among her former enemies and is afraid of them, all her feelings are amplified. That is understandable, given her past, her present situation, and how the events of 1995 affected her personality.

Remarkably, in many of the interviews I found little hatred. To the contrary, these women realize better than most that the world goes on, and that anything is better than war. Some were able to talk about the feelings of friendship they had for the "others," albeit after much hesitation and difficulty. Occasionally, one of them referred to "our Serbs," meaning those who lived in their village and were part of their society, as opposed to "Serbians," the enemy in national politics sent or indoctrinated by a strange power. They also refused to call it a "civil war," as is common in the West when talking about the former Yugoslavia; rather, they call it a "war." The aggressors came from outside, from the nationalistic greater Serbian polity as represented by Milosević, which had gradually laid the basis for what happened. The aggression was in sharp contrast to the years of peaceful coexistence that preceded it. That past is why they could remember with affection a time when the world was whole, the family had its usual daily ups and downs, and there were still men around. That is the past they continue to construct and interpret.

Much has been written about the falling apart of the former Yugoslavia, the rise of Serbian nationalism, and the resulting aggression, and many explanations have been given.[31] This book will not address those questions. Srebrenica was at the end of a violent chain of war and murder, of attack and counterattack. "Ethnic cleansing" became the term used during the wars in the region to denote the eradication of all but the dominant nationality by both deportation and murder. All sides involved were guilty of murder, but in East Bosnia ethnic cleansing was the hallmark of the Serbs. Mark Danner became famous for his coverage of the misery in Bosnia and Kosovo in the *New York Times Review of Books,* in which he described the phases in the process that led to murder.[32]

All stages of the isolation and murder of the victims involved the rape of women of all ages.[33] Excluding murder, rape is the most extreme form of ethnic cleansing, because the resulting children are considered to belong to the ethnicity of the rapist. Women lived in fear of being raped, while men felt humiliated and enraged by the rape of their women. We are also beginning to learn that men were also sexually assaulted.

The situation of the thousands of women who were rape victims is still unresolved. Žena-žrtva rata, the organization of rape victims, and its impressive president, Bakira Hasečić, have not yet succeeded in lessening the enormous taboo surrounding the crimes. Women do not talk about it; often, the victims are scorned by their families. The Islamic religious authority became aware of the problem early in the war, as rape swept across East Bosnia. In 1993 Derviš Ahmed Nuruddin wrote an open letter to the people of the region. He urged men and families not to reject women who had been raped. Clearly, the future psychological consequences threatened to be enormous. Both the women who were raped and the children who resulted from those rapes deserve respect, according to Nuruddin.[34] He was also concerned about the many infanticides of children born of rape, and tried to explain that this was murder. These children are the victims of an injustice that ultimately will be punished.

Since that early plea in 1993, the Islamic religious authority has continued to support the rape victims. The aftereffects of the epidemic of rapes are ongoing. Organizations that deal with these problems (e.g., Snaga Zene and Viva Zene in Tuzla, Medica Zenica in Zenica) are overwhelmed. No one really knows what to do with the children, although some mothers have accepted them, love them, and are rearing them. These children are a by-product of war, as is the question of their place in society.[35] In 2009 Amnesty International published a report that shows how inadequate the national judicial system is in cases of rape. According to the report, there is no public support for rape victims, and no desire to provide such help. The women are left out in the cold, with only sporadic help, mainly from NGOs.

Of all the painful and destructive aspects of war, rape is second only to mass murder in its devastation of a society and of the women who are scarred by it. Yet I believe that the murder of one's child is the most horrible of all. Sabaheta's story, which began this book, tells of such a loss. Sabaheta and I stood arm in arm in Potočari on July 11, 2007. It was raining and more than 460 men were being buried. She was upset; she told me once again that her life had lost its meaning since the death of her beloved son. Sabaheta was one of my first interviewees; I regard her story of loss as a gift to this project. It is a penetrating description of how one woman's world was shattered. How tragically fitting that her story ended in her temporary unconsciousness.

Searching for Truth

Central to all these women's lives at present is the search for answers; the women want to know what happened and where their husbands, brothers, fathers, uncles, and sons are. That is the truth that surfaces most often in the survivors' stories, but truth in this book has more than one meaning. The women told me how they remember the events and how they interpret the history, yet their truths are in conflict with the generally accepted version of what happened. The survivors told me what they think should be remembered, and I have tried to record what happened from their perspective, thus giving their vision a place in the history of the Srebrenican genocide. I can do this because I am not one of them—I am a foreigner, a Dutchwoman, and an academic. But our differences do not preclude friendship; without reciprocal affection, they would have told me nothing. My compassion for them was and is genuine. As a descendant of a Holocaust survivor and of a former prisoner under Japanese occupation in Indonesia, I understand how deeply their lives have been disrupted. I also understand how important it is to listen patiently. Grief and rage are not foreign to me, and neither is hypocrisy. My family was deported while too many Dutch citizens looked on and did nothing, "because there was nothing we could do." I am familiar with firsthand accounts of those who looked away and pretended not to hear.

The women resist what they rightly suspect is a tendency (albeit sometimes unconscious) to forget their suffering. Without a deliberate effort to record their stories, their history will disappear. Some of the interviewees did not have such long-term goals; they simply found it important to tell their stories to someone who was willing to listen. They also talked about the future and how they would like their lives to be; their stories convey a longing for an innocent world in which nations and cultures live together in peace. Rediscovering the peace and quiet of that world is important to them. Peace and a future are more important than hate, yet finding peace and one's place in the world as it is now is difficult. Living in peace is the only possible model; otherwise, life is not worth much.

The first phase in writing the history of a great trauma consists of nothing more than breaking the silence and giving voice. Telling the story to an outsider has a certain dynamic. The outsider is not supposed to repeat what is private and personal to other survivors; neither should the outsider judge. In the history of the disaster that overcame them, every interviewee—even if only for a minute—was at the center of what happened, thus giving her story context. They also told me how they had been left out of the recorded history of the events, how their own histories had disappeared. Their marginal position in society also has influenced their perception that history has forgotten them.

Identification and distance, the closeness of the outsider from another world, belong to the moment when the women speak. All who have spoken with survivors and are shocked by the grimness of what happened also know how much these stories add to what is already known from the official reports. It is not about the outsider's feelings of accountability or helplessness, but about the helplessness of someone who lost all that was precious to her in that violence, and who is in danger of losing her human dignity. It is also about how it is possible to survive, to go on, and yet to be forced to look back. Zumra described it well:

> His hand was on my shoulder, trembling, . . . somewhere deep inside me it still trembles. . . . It seems to me that every moment I feel it here on my left shoulder and that hot whisper of his that was reaching my ear as he told me not to worry, that everything would be all right. [He told me] when I come to Tuzla, to tell my son that he sends his warmest regards and to tell him to listen to me. And when I talk to my daughter, who is in Slovenia, by phone [he said] to tell her that her daddy has been missing her very much and that he cannot wait until the moment he will see her. . . . But he never lived to see that moment. These were his last words. They separated him [from me] and I stayed mute, I could not talk. . . . I passed and he stayed with his black jacket, which he held in his hand. . . . I never saw him again and don't know what happened to him. I regret so much that I did not say, "Don't take him"—that I didn't scream or shout for help. Maybe it would be easier to live now. I just left silently and could not speak, although my tears were flowing like a river and still do today, believe me.[36]

CHAPTER TWO

AN ORPHANED WORLD
Life before the War

T he war reached East Bosnia in the spring of 1992, although it had been raging in other areas of what used to be Yugoslavia for a whole year. People from different ethnic and cultural backgrounds who had lived together in peace were now at war with each other. The threat was palpable before the war's outbreak, but no one expected it to be so violent; in East Bosnia, no one expected neighbor to attack neighbor. But the prewar world vanished. They had grown up with each other, Serb and Muslim, and the younger generation felt even less alienation from the others than their parents had. There were mixed marriages, albeit fewer than in the big city of Sarajevo. But East Bosnia had been modernized, as had the former Yugoslavia, despite rural areas where residents were slow to change. Parts of the country had prospered, houses had running water and electricity, and the shops were reasonably well stocked for a province. Given the prosperity, the destruction of that world and a war did not seem possible.

Yet that world has been destroyed, and Srebrenica has been a ghost town since then. War damage is visible everywhere, especially in the villages around the town; buildings are riddled with bullet holes. The current residents have no work. Despite gradual improvement over the years in the town's center, the situation remains dismal. What happened in 1995, when its residents either fled or were murdered, haunts today's residents. Sitting on a café terrace, it was difficult for me to imagine that once people strolled along the main street, that women and men danced with each other, and that the town residents enjoyed an everyday happiness. Even when the current residents celebrate with feasting and dancing, the pall of war is still evident. Early in 2007, those who had returned to Srebrenica threatened to leave again; living conditions were deteriorating, and threats and insecurity were unacceptably high.[1] After months of negotiations, there were promises of improvement.

The fall of Srebrenica was a massive dislocation in the lives of my interviewees. After the fall, everything had to be rebuilt. In that sense, a historiography based on life stories differs from one about the town's capitulation and the mass murder in the following days. People also told of their youth and the society that has since vanished. Through these stories, I learned what the town's destruction meant. I began to understand how radically their world had changed and what it meant to lose one's web of social connections.

An important part of that residual misery is no longer in Srebrenica, but in the "temporary housing," miserable shelters where the survivors who cannot (or will not) return live. They are overcrowded in the camps, and live on the edge of an abyss that many Bosnians refuse to acknowledge or that they deny. Hanifa, who wanted to tell me about her life, lives in such a place. When I entered her shabby cottage in the refugee camp, I was shocked. Where did the millions given by the Dutch government for Srebrenica go?[2] Of course, as is true of all public works contracts, part of the funds were for infrastructure and projects yet to be decided by people other than the survivors. But after reviewing government budgets, I found no funds apportioned for the survivors, to whom the Netherlands should owe a debt of honor. Ježevac, a refugee camp in the canton of Tuzla, is an unsuitable place to live (as are all the camps), although the residents try to make it habitable.

Hanifa has lived in Ježevac since surviving Potočari in 1995. In 2004, little cottages were built by a Norwegian NGO. There is a bus twice daily to Banovići, the most important town in the valley, but, just as everywhere else, there is no work there. Finding regular work for those who live in the camps is unthinkable because of transportation problems. No one can afford a car, and public transportation is expensive. Ježevac's little cottages seem pleasant enough on a sunny day; with several necessary changes (the main one being to alleviate the overcrowding), they might be made habitable.

Born in 1949, Hanifa is an example of what happens to a person accustomed to physical labor who is now inactive. She arrived with other women who survived Srebrenica. Her appearance and clothing are poor but neat, and her cottage is clean, which is remarkable, given the circumstances. She wants to tell me about Potočari; she felt so alone there, so terribly alone. But she has been alone her whole life, and that is what she really wants to tell me: "I had no father." A detail from her youth indicates the rather primitive conditions in which she grew up:

> I was two and my brother was a baby in diapers when my father died. I never knew him, I was two. My mother took care of us, she worked on the land for money. She had no education. Working the land was how she managed to feed us. Two years later she fell ill. I never asked what she had. I never even asked my uncles. My uncles got her to the hospital; they had to carry her on their backs. There were no cars, so they carried her.

I tried to imagine her uncles with a very ill, dying woman on their backs. There were no cars, no roads that reached her village in the early 1950s. Carrying her to the hospital did not help; she died five years after Hanifa's father. Hanifa wound up with her uncles and aunts. Being an orphan in the homes of others was the beginning of her trajectory of loneliness; it is a recurring theme in her story.

> Our uncles and aunts loved us like their own children, but the aunts yelled at us and sometimes hit us. Their own children were small. At one point, I was big and their children were still little. They worked the land, but we didn't have to work. But you know, people love their own children more than someone else's. When my mother became aware that she would die soon, she made the aunt who was going to take care of us swear that she wouldn't send me to school.

Hanifa stayed at home and learned more about housekeeping than farming; more wasn't necessary. "My father and my uncles were rich. Not that they had a lot of money, but they did have land and livestock. They worked, we had barns full of grain, corn, oats. See, we were rich." In her world, being rich was still about land and cattle. She never owned anything else, except some clothing. In our world, her lifestyle would not be considered privileged:

> We all slept together, my uncles, my aunts, their children, and the two of us, my brother and me. When we were older, they built another house and there were separate rooms. But we still slept with one of the uncles, his wife, and their four children. We didn't have a room of our own. No one denied us food; we ate what they ate. For example, we had breakfast, but if we kids got hungry, they gave us something to eat before lunch. But you know, I would have been happier if I still had my parents, even if I didn't have enough to eat. I've been through a lot; I've suffered so much. When they hugged their children, I was so sad—I would have given all my meals for that. They told their children, "Come here, Papa/Mama loves you." I can't remember if I ever said "mother" or "father." It's different now. My child has no father, but there are children all over the place without fathers, here, there, everywhere. But back in the day, it didn't happen too often that someone died young. Our parents died. I was young, healthy, I was happy with a piece of bread, but if someone called "mother" or "father," . . .

Hanifa lost her husband at Potočari. He was not in danger at first because he was older, but he was finally separated from her.

My child cried, "Papa, where are you going? Papa, come back!"
And the policeman or soldier asked, "Whose child is this?" He
was suspicious, because we were somewhat older but were carrying a child. The soldier tried to console the child by saying his
father would come back. We went to the bus, there were still seats.
I looked behind us and didn't see any buses or trucks. Those in
front of us were full. I couldn't see anything. I saw them [soldiers]
walking back and forth. I thought that my husband would come
later. The bus was filling up, but there was no driver. When he
came, he started the bus. After 2 or 3 meters I looked to the left.
. . . There was a meadow in front of a storehouse that was strewn
for about 10 meters with backpacks, and caps and berets hung in
the tall grass. There were blankets that people had brought with
them to lie on. There was a lot there. Then I realized that my husband hadn't come. I haven't seen him since. We cried in the bus,
everybody cried.

She didn't know where he had been taken, and the child also began to cry. The
bus driver asked the women why they hadn't fled sooner and cursed them for
being so stupid. However, he did bring them to a safe area. After she arrived,
Hanifa's misery was still not over.

Life had been difficult for Hanifa before 1995. When she was a refugee in
Srebrenica, she was pregnant and had no place to stay when the town was being
cut off by Serb army units. Over the years, Hanifa kept losing her belongings
and—even worse—the people she loved. The fall of Srebrenica was not her only
trauma, but it was the worst. She lost her husband, whom she loved, after 16
years of marriage. He was the first person to give her the love she needed. He
took care of her when she gave birth to their child amid the wounded in the
overcrowded hospital in Srebrenica, and he was there for her during the days
in Potočari. Their separation, which had no farewell, was the worst moment.
It came at the end of living in a blockaded town for three years as food became
increasingly scarce. Despite her advanced pregnancy, she could not get enough
salt and real medical help was not available. The trauma of Srebrenica is not
only about the fall of the town, but also the history of the siege that preceded
it and of the people there who tried to survive. She was only one of many from
the surrounding villages who landed there.

It was important for Hanifa to tell of her loneliness—she always survived,
but she was always left alone. She could not talk about the past without referring to her current situation and the consequences of what happened in 1995. As
a small child, she had cried for her father; in 1995 her child begged his father to
stay; and all the children playing outside her cottage now have no fathers. That

seems to be the new normal. Are the children today better off than she was? Of course not, but they do not miss the love of both parents, as she did; they have at least one parent. We sat quietly in her cottage, listening. My interpreter, Suada, was weeping, and not just because of the story of Potočari. The juxtaposition of lifelong abandonment reflected in the crying child who does not understand what is happening, with the half-orphans playing in the camp who have the love of at least one parent, had moved her to tears. Hanifa's unselfish and gentle spirit is obvious. History dealt her a heavy blow, but the orphaned woman in this new world of orphans has dealt with it and survived. She bears no one ill will for what happened, not even history. I will see her again, and she knows that I will return.

After several months, I returned, as I try to do with many of my inter-viewees, even if they are not on my route or live in an area that is difficult for me to reach. I feel welcome. They all tell me in their own way about how their world used to be, a world in which children could not sleep if a parent was gone; and now also children cannot sleep. Hanifa's story shows that I could not have understood her if I had only asked about those horrible days in June and July 1995. Like all the others, she grew up in a world that has been destroyed and is no longer imaginable. So much has happened. The great divide is the siege of Srebrenica. In Hanifa's case, there was grief before as well.

Ethnic Separation and the Birth of the Bosniak

After World War II the various pieces of Yugoslavia were brought together in a communist federation, and all population groups were formally regarded as equal. That is not to say that there was no informal inequality and discrimi-nation; however, towns such as Sarajevo and Tuzla already had multiethnic societies, and this influenced the general image. Other places were less tolerant and people were in need of education. The communist worldview was con-stantly propagated through a network of organizations and institutions that managed people's lives. In addition to school, there were countless youth orga-nizations and folk-dance groups; there were labor organizations at the worksites and in the neighborhoods and villages. Every life was lived within this social framework.

With the death of Tito, communism in Yugoslavia collapsed and the soci-ety began to change rapidly. The country moved toward capitalism and the multiethnic society faded. It was turning into a world in which money was more important and people networked and bonded through their ethnicity rather than through their enthusiasm for communism. Being a Bosniak became important; it no longer meant just discrimination, but rather new possibilities.

The interviews are saturated with confusion because of these rapid changes in the society.

Economic changes came first. Yugoslavia's large debts from the 1970s were due. This led to a national economic crisis that was made worse by the world-wide oil crisis in 1979 and the recession that followed. Money lost its value due to inflation, and many people sought work abroad.[3] This was especially true for the poorer Muslim population of East Bosnia, where money earned abroad led to a shift in relations. In the region of Bratunac-Srebrenica, Muslim residents used that money to acquire a large percentage of the land.[4] In the years before the war, there was a sense of malaise. Many people, both Muslim and non-Muslim, were uncertain about their future economic and social security. This anxiety created a layer of fear in the society that became a breeding ground for negative emotions and hatred.

The nation's political and administrative structures were also changing rapidly. After Tito's death and the federation's collapse,[5] the idea of everyone living together—with their different beliefs, cultures, and ethnicities—lost political legitimacy.[6] Integration began to fall apart at the microlevel; they had been old friends, but the new voice of nationalism declared that the "other" was inferior.[7] Multiethnicity and multiculturalism were illusions of the past. Nationalist sentiments were encouraged, especially in Serbia, which in turn provoked reactions from others. There had always been differences; the harmony under Tito was only a brief but lovely intermezzo. Tolerance used to be a sign of refinement; in some parts of Bosnia, this is still true. But the multicultural idea of living together lost ground against increasingly strong feelings of nationalism.

The past became a major actor amid all these nationalistic emotions. Historical events were cited as evidence that living together was an unrealistic communist ideal. The myths surrounding those events fueled resentment against the "others," who had been the enemy in past centuries. The massacres in Muslim villages by the Serbs in World War II contrasted with Serb memories of Croatian concentration camps, in which Muslims were sometimes used as guards. Who stood where—and who was "good"—is one of the most difficult questions in Bosnia. The Second World War, in which the citizens fought against each other and were anything but brothers, had been whitewashed with communist rhetoric.[8] The official version of that history ignored other perspectives and denied the hostility.

The Serb leader Slobodan Milosević stepped into this historical vacuum with a message of "revitalizing our national legacy." He preached repeatedly that the Serbs were the root stock of Yugoslavia, and that ruling over other peoples could come easily to them. His most famous speech was at the 1989 commemoration of the 1389 Battle of Kosovo, known as the Battle on the Field of

Crows. The Serbs had repelled a Muslim onslaught; their leader, the Christian prince Lazar, died in the fighting. Milosević elevated the battle to the realm of national myth and positioned himself as the new prince who would defeat Serbia's enemies.

As wonderful as the multiethnic society sounded, it was not realistic. Even during Tito's lifetime, the ideal did not match the reality; adjustments were required.[9] No one was simply Yugoslav,[10] and perhaps only a few had ever really been just that. The plan was impossible to implement. As early as the 1960s, different ethnicities were demanding a share in political power. In 1961, the Bosnian Muslims were given the right to register as Muslims (as a strictly ethnic identification, of course). In 1971 they received the status of *narod,* a word that is difficult to translate; literally, it means "nation" but usually it is rendered as "people."[11] As a political designation, *narod* meant that every government institution, council, and village committee (as well as any public-sector administrative unit) required a proportionate number of Muslims, along with Bosnian Serbs and Croatian Bosnians. *Narod* and ethnicity did not coincide with religious experience. In a number of interviews, I was told about a world in which the differences between religions were becoming less important. People were becoming less religious and more Bosnian. Nonreligious Bosnian Muslims could be Bosniaks.

There are no reliable statistics on the degree of secularization, only an impression that the society at that time was tending toward the secular. Group differences did hinder intermarriage, although in Sarajevo things were different; mixed marriages were more common there.[12] In her study of a mixed Muslim-Croatian village, Bringa noted that there were few marriages between Muslims and other groups.[13] Other sources confirm that such marriages were rare,[14] but there are no hard data for East Bosnia. There is no reason to assume, however, that the pattern Bringa observed in a region that was three hours by car west of Srebrenica should be different. The populations of both the valley Bringa studied and the valley of Srebrenica-Bratunac were mixed, and they both have long histories of tension between ethnicities. In his epic novel *Blood and Vengeance,* Chuck Sudetić also noted that interethnic marriages were rare and described them as Romeo-and-Juliet marriages. Sudetić studied the region long enough, in preparation for writing the story of the Celik family, to be a reliable observer.[15]

The religious identity of the Muslims gradually flowed into a more worldly Bosnian identity, and Bosnian Muslims began to be called "Bosniaks." In the 1980s this led to a fierce debate over the meaning of Bosnian Muslim identity and a search for the historical continuity of the Muslim nation. The 1991 Census listed 43.6 percent of Bosnia-Herzegovina's population as Muslim (or Bosniak),

31.3 percent as Serb, and 17.3 percent as Croatian.[16] Exact data are also available for certain regions of East Bosnia. In the region of Srebrenica (including the surrounding villages), 72.9 percent of the population was Muslim and 25.2 percent Serbian, and in Bratunac it was 64.2 and 34.2 percent, respectively.[17] Being Bosniak did not mean having a specific political orientation. For the first time, there were large numbers of Bosniaks in positions of leadership. The number of Muslim representatives in councils and other administrative bodies grew, and the problem of political representation played out at even the lowest levels. Many of the interviewed women had a relative or acquaintance who was politically active in one of the many representative bodies in the region. When new groups enter a political arena, it creates a new situation that differs from when the previous elites were in power. The possibility of becoming part of the elite class through political participation made it attractive to join with others in the struggle for leadership. Muslims had just as many different political attitudes and opinions as did the other nationalities.[18]

A former teacher told the Dutch anthropologist Ger Duijzings[19] how the different groups lived separately. About 10 years before the war, a school was to be built in Brezani; the question was where. The village was half Serb and half Muslim, and the two parts of the village were six kilometers apart. The school was built in the middle, in the forest, because placing it in one part or the other was unthinkable.

Modernization and Secularization

The residents of East Bosnia had lived with each other for many years and were accustomed to each other.[20] They knew no other way, especially in areas with mixed populations; no one thought that things had ever been different. Daily life in Bratunac and Srebrenica are good examples. Increasingly, there were places where one could have a good time, regardless of one's identity. In the summer, the Drina River was a lovely place to visit; no one asked your religion or ethnicity when you rented a summer cottage. Some villages were exclusively Muslim, and the schools and daily life were not mixed. In general, such villages were considered backward; there, it took time before it was considered normal there for girls to attend school. Ger Duijzings was told that many Muslims hesitated to send their daughters to school. So, they did not register their daughters with the local authorities, which made monitoring their school attendance impossible. The interviewee estimated that this was the case for between 10 and 20 percent of the girls in remote villages.

Literacy, with an emphasis on primary education, was a cornerstone of Tito's policy. In 1958 schooling for children between the ages of 8 and 15 became mandatory. In 1979 the policy was modernized, and in the 1980s almost all children received formal education, and 70 percent of those received secondary education.[21] This remained true through the late 1980s, although the required school attendance for girls was often ignored. What was taught in school was not considered important for girls, although in most areas people were aware that a girl was better off with at least a basic education. Today, women who attended little or no school often regret their lack of education and regard it as a deficit. For those who did attend school, their world consisted of school and home; there was little else. Staying at home meant different things; for some, it meant helping with the housework, but in many villages, for economic reasons, staying at home meant heavy farm chores. Behara, whom I interviewed in Sarajevo, told me:

> I had to work hard. And remember that my father was an influential member of the village council, *muhtari* it was called. He was powerful in the region, but even he wouldn't let a girl go to school. In his opinion, the morals of a girl who attends school are lowered. I really regret that, as a result of that prejudice, I couldn't finish school. My oldest brother loved me, and because my parents wouldn't let me buy a notebook, he gave me paper and I did the homework he got; I was good at it. My teachers tried to convince my parents that it was a pity not to let me finish the remaining two classes. I was one of the best students. I shouldn't talk about it, but it is true.[22]

I asked her what she did all day; my question must have struck her as rather stupid. "My dear, it was life on a farm, and there was always a lot to do. You tend the cows and the sheep, you plow, you pick fruit. You do everything that farmers do. In the winter we knitted, spun wool, and weaved. I knew how to do all those things. We embroidered as well. . . . We had two houses; one was the old one and the other was for guests. That was how things were."

Where the population was mixed, children went to school together. Ramiza was born in a mixed village (Zaluže, near Bratunac) in 1966. The school she attended had both Muslim and Serb children.[23] A person's origin does not matter to Ramiza, even though now the differences and the hatred are so great. Ramiza assumed I knew how integrated the two groups used to be, and thought it was not even worth mentioning.

Different Histories

Ramiza's observation about the close contact between and apparently successful integration of the population groups was confirmed again and again.

Ćamila's story was similar. I interviewed her at length; she was a well-educated woman who represented the people of Srebrenica during negotiations with Mladić.[24] Ćamila's sophistication was apparent during her interview; she told me about her childhood, her marriage, and all the things that were so important to her, but she did not talk about the political history of the "events." She had testified at the tribunal in The Hague against Radislav Kristić regarding his part in the Srebrenica genocide. Her testimony and that of other women showed that many of the Serbs at Potočari were not strangers to the victims, and there had been no problems with them previously. She had known Serbs as neighbors and friends, and could not understand what drove them to act as they did. Ćamila, like many others, appealed to their friendship and good will after years of living together. She told about her meeting with Mladić:

> I entered the room and saw my schoolmate Miroslav Deronjić. I was really scared. At one point I turned to him and said, "Miroslav, my old friend, what are you going to do with all these people? Help us. They don't have weapons, they are hungry, they are barefooted, and they were driven like cattle into a pen and left to the whims of those men. They shoot at them, they aim at them." Then Mladić ordered me to sit down, because we knew each other.

The judge asked her what was the result of her request to Miroslav. "He tried to explain that he was also moved by the victims of the war, but Mladić interrupted him." Throughout her story, there are incidents of encountering familiar people from the other side who had done no evil up until then. Because this was a criminal case in a court of law, that kind of testimony was not of interest to the judges. They wanted to know if certain crimes had been committed; whether the perpetrators were known to the witness was not relevant. Yet such stories give us insight into how the two sides previously interacted with each other and how unthinkable wanting to kill each other was in the past.

It is important for our historical understanding of that time and place to realize how closely knit these groups were. Looking back during our interview, Ćamila was still surprised by this. "I never knew a person's religion, it wasn't important to me. We were just together, we walked, we sat together, we went out together. If I liked a boy, then I would look at him and giggle. Perhaps he made a remark or two, and that was that. That's how we got to know each other. . . . We never made any distinction. We never thought about who was what. . . . I didn't think it was important."[25]

Bida, whom I interviewed in Potočari, also could not remember a difference between the children of different groups. She has since returned to her old house, which was renovated. Born in 1952, Bida is a true child of Tito's era, when it was decreed from above that there were no differences, and in any event they didn't matter.[26] "There was no separation, we were together—the Serb Bosnians and us. There were a couple of Croatians, but most were Muslim or Serb." A number of small schools in the villages had only five grades; for the sixth grade the children attended a school in Bratunac. If the children had not come in contact with "others" in the villages, that changed in the sixth grade. "We knew each other, we were integrated. . . . The teachers were Muslim and Serb, no separation, no difference or anything." She had Serb girlfriends: "One day we agreed to do our homework at my place, the next day at Ratna's. . . . Five or six of us were always together. That way, we learned more and we helped each other. Thus, no distinction." One didn't even think about it.

In all the interview materials, it was not possible to find any details about the equal treatment of different population groups among adults and how they shared the same public space. The women assumed that I knew this, even though I asked them about it. It was all so normal. Yet it is also obvious that the memory of this togetherness has become problematic, like all memories, and remembering the war in this region exacerbates this. Muslim memories and Serb memories diverge not only between the two groups, but also among those who now live in Bratunac and Srebrenica.[27] There is confusion; one's former classmates and fellow residents had turned into murderers, or didn't protest or even supported the murderers. Nobody really knows how and why that happened. It is less confusing if one forgets the positive feelings, but that isn't really possible. Those friendships were once a part of their lives, so they are left feeling ambivalent. It seems—and is—so very difficult to make sense of it all.

Those friendships come up whenever one expresses surprise at what happened and every time one searches for an explanation of why things went wrong. The majority of the women feel that the hatred did not come from religion. As Hatidža put it:

> I think religion teaches us in particular not to hate. I think we are all religious to some degree, but I have no desire to be—and refuse to be—fanatic about it. No religion, no holy book, teaches you to hate, to hurt others, to murder them. If such a book exists, show it to me. But such a book doesn't exist. A neighbor was more important than your own brother. You had to respect your neighbor, because you got as much respect from others as you gave. And that is the truth.[28]

Religion is not an explanation, although many feel it is used as an excuse for not having to explain what happened. No one understands what happened; it remains inexplicable.

Most people knew the Serbs well and were comfortable with them. Fikreta, who now lives in the Netherlands, told Camilia Bruil that she knew the Serbs because they were her instructors and teachers. "You didn't talk about that back then. It was communism and nobody was supposed to say 'you're Serb' or 'you're Muslim.' That just wasn't done. You knew from the names; if you said a name, then you knew if they were Serb or Bosniak. Usually you knew, but nobody cared. It was just—warm and sociable."[29]

Longing for What No Longer Is

The world of then, that innocent world, will never return. Because I showed interest in the interviewees' entire lives, including periods no one had asked about for a long time, remembering was quite a task. Asking concrete questions (e.g., about their school relations) helped the process along. The difficulty in remembering is intensified by the trauma in 1995; in a sense, the time before 1995 has been sealed off. Bida told me about her school experiences while describing the school and the educational tracking system. Talking about the school in general gave her a break from her own story, but that ended when she told how she had to leave school prematurely. At last, she talked about herself.

> I finished the sixth grade and in the seventh I left school. It was an impulse; I didn't want to go to school any more. That was stupid of me, and now I regret it. For years I dreamed of going back to school, and [I feared] that all the children knew I had left school and was ashamed. I was bigger than that generation of students, but in my dream that didn't matter to me. I went to school. I don't know what came over me, why I didn't want to go to school. I left after the first semester of the seventh grade. . . . I left school without reason, and it would have been better if I had stayed. But I stayed home with my mother to work on the land.

Remembering the good times with her mother in their old home is overshadowed by grief for her brother, who died in 1995, and for her husband, who did not survive Potočari. This was clear from the beginning of the interview. Directly after the above statement, Bida said:

> There were five children, four girls and a boy. There are now four of us; our brother is no longer here. He meant the world to us—our very precious brother. I can talk about the past, but when I talk about this, I can't go on. I lose my voice. We never called him by his name, Meho. We always called him *Brad* [Brother]. . . . I can't explain to anyone how much he meant to us. We are all healthy,

but I would rather that none of us had survived. It's useless. He isn't here. We never heard anything about him. I can't continue to talk, my voice quivers when I try and it gets weaker. It's been that way since the war started. No matter what is said, I can't talk about it. I just can't. I cry and I lose my voice.

Escaping Overwhelming Emotions

It is not unusual for people in emotionally laden situations to lose their voices. I have seen how intense grief can lead to physical consequences. Many women who were abused at Potočari have psychological trauma as well as physical complaints: residual pain from bones broken by being kicked and stomped on, stomach and back problems from sexual violence, and neck problems from being dragged. These physical ailments spill over into the psychological.[30] A number of survivors also suffer from weight problems. Previously, they did heavy physical labor, but now they are sedentary. They continue to consume the same amount of food, but it is usually cheaper and therefore inferior to their former diets. The food of the poor often leads to obesity, and this is certainly the case in Bosnia. According to physicians, obesity is the result of refined carbohydrates (white flour and sugar) combined with fat. An obese woman may be unhealthy, but she is not necessarily unattractive. However, if there is no longer a loved one to notice how she looks, she may lose interest in her appearance. This, combined with a lack of money to buy anything more than utilitarian (and usually second-hand) clothing, can lead to a variety of psychological complaints.

At an emotional moment, the trauma can begin to dominate an interview; the story becomes fragmented and consists only of snippets. Talking about childhood was a way around the grief and helped to establish a soft contact that made the conversation seem pleasant. The interview never just shifted suddenly to being lost in her own grief; rather, it usually started with who the others were, why the interviewees loved them so much, and why it was all so sad. The French sociologist Pierre Bourdieu calls this technique "nonviolent communication" in his writings on interviewing in difficult circumstances.[31] Allowing the traumatized to speak demands space. Talking about how things used to be is a way around talking only about grief. The interviews were a wobbly balance between openheartedness, simple conversation, sharing what happened and is happening, and bogging down in grief. In most interviews, there was a moment when the process threatened to break down. Talking about how it was to live on the land was a way to continue, as was the term *ašikovanje*, which I will discuss later.

Nostalgic memories of a happy childhood were—and almost always are—pleasant, or perhaps "sweet" is the best word. Bida, who still mourns her brother, told me:

> Our house . . . was perhaps the largest house at that time between
> Srebrenica and Bratunac. It was built over cellars, and there was an
> upstairs and a downstairs. It was big, big enough for two families,
> ours and my uncle's. They also had children and we were like one
> big family. We loved each other so much, as though we had the
> same mother and father. In truth, our mothers were sisters and our
> fathers were brothers. Two sisters married two brothers. We were
> so close and we loved each other. It really was one big family. The
> house had two entrances, one on either side. We played outside,
> running around the house, sledding, that kind of thing. As far as
> work goes, there is always something that needs to be done on a
> farm, pitching hay and mowing. Mowing was done with a scythe.
> Later, when combines were used, it was easier. But even then a
> scythe was used. Grain was threshed with an automated thresher.
> There was a lot of work. Stalks of wheat that were left behind were
> cut. But we couldn't do it all ourselves. Whatever we couldn't finish,
> Mother paid day laborers to do. We were always farming; we never
> neglected our 25 *dunams* [a little over 6 acres] of land.[32] My uncle
> also cultivated his land. When we returned here, everything was so
> overgrown with weeds that we didn't know where to begin.

She sighed, and we waited. Obviously, she was reliving her return to the house,
a return without the brother she loved so much and without her husband, who
lost his life in Potočari. These are the unpredictable moments in an interview
when one doesn't know quite how to continue. Her face was so sad, and the
sister who sat next to her also looked sad. Most of the chores she mentioned
involved heavy labor and were usually done by men; now, women do them,
because there are no men left in the family. I realized this was a story about the
family, and not about Bida's work. I knew she had probably done traditional
women's work in the past, but perhaps by repeating, "They are gone, I miss
them, and so I talk about them," she was avoiding talking about herself, which
Bida finds extremely difficult.

Bida baked bread and pies,[33] as did all the women, because those goods
were not available in stores.

> We grew wheat, and when the mill was grinding white wheat, my
> mother took [our] wheat there [to be ground]. . . . Then we baked
> bread and other things. We made our own food. We made sure
> that the grass grew; we had wheat, beans, potatoes, vegetables,
> everything. We only bought what we didn't produce ourselves, but
> we produced most of what we needed. We had everything. We had

meat, chickens, sheep, milk, we had everything in our home. . . . I
helped my mother with the cooking. I knitted and crocheted, that
kind of thing. I did many things. I'm still good at using my hands.
I know how to do things and I love doing them. I can't sit still and
do nothing; I love to be busy.

All the women said they loved to be busy. This is in sharp contrast to the
vacant lives many have now, in which time weighs heavily on their hands. Anyone
who has visited a refugee camp knows there is not much to do. Against this drab
background, the happy life before the war seems even more desirable. Those
women who do not live in refugee camps do tasks now that were unthinkable
before (e.g., chopping wood).[34] Women are heads of families in communities
that consist mainly of women. Some young men who survived are just over the
age of 20 and physically mature enough to take over the heavy labor. These men
grew up without a father and in a culturally abnormal family structure that has
not changed over the years. Many women now act as the heads of families, and
are also responsible for administrative matters, such as housing and pensions.
Often, it is too much and they complain bitterly. Sometimes this is expressed
not as a complaint, but as a comparison with how things used to be and how
difficult life is now.

Hatidža Habibović told a different story; she was already accustomed to
taking care of herself. In the 1980s, she dealt with the untimely death of her
husband, and succeeded in setting up a boardinghouse. The rest of her family
lived in Tuzla. She was not as traumatized by the events of 1995 as some of the
other women. She only stayed one night in Potočari, and admitted that she went
through less hardship than many others. But when she returned to Srebrenica in
2002, she faced many problems; her story is an example of how difficult conditions were then. Like all women who were children in the 1950s, school was not
a given, and she regretted that.

I went less than a year. My father took me out of school. He didn't
want me to go, but he did want my brother, who was born after
me, to go. That was how it was then. So I couldn't attend school. I
had to do other things. I cried because I wanted to go. But I know
many things and no one can make a fool of me. When I did go
to school, we learned to print the alphabet and some arithmetic,
all sorts of things. I bawled my eyes out; I wanted to go to school.
But my father said it was better for my brother to go instead of me,
because there were things I had to do. Later, my father regretted it,
he thought it was a shame, but there was nothing to do about it.
I wasn't the only one, you know, many of us didn't go to school.

> . . . I had to work in the house. My father didn't have any help in
> the house, it was just my mother and him, and there was a lot to
> do. In general, he earned a good living, he had a good job, and we
> lived well. . . . He paid people to work the land, but there were also
> cows and sheep that had to be looked after, and other things that
> needed doing in the house. . . . If someone works for you, you have
> to make coffee for them and offer something to eat.

She pays people to work for her now as well, but for a different reason; there
are no men in the house and she has to pay for everything. "We women have
to pay, we have to make coffee, and also do other things." By that, she means
tasks that she did not do in the past. She prefers a more traditional woman's
role, and finds this difficult.

Hatidža Habibović started the boardinghouse after her husband died;
her clientele were mainly women who came to "take the waters" at the spa
above Srebrenica. "Because I was single, all the women wanted to stay with me.
Everybody wanted to stay in a nice, honest house. They came to *my* house, you
see, not to a house where there were men. It was a good period. One woman
lived in my house for eight years. She liked me because I was honest, and she
liked being there. I let her have the ground floor. I was good to everyone." Her
father had a larger house and rented rooms to Serbs as well as Muslims. She is
not bitter; she wants to use the opportunities she now has to make Srebrenica
a peaceful town.

She makes a distinction between good and bad Serbs. I asked her about
the Serbs in Potočari: were they all bad? She answered that she was not afraid of
them. "Some of them even spoke to us. My father got along with everybody; he
never argued with anyone. We were used to chatting. People complained about
everything, but we didn't look for trouble; we just got in the bus. Nobody did
anything to us, . . . nobody did anything to us. But the others whined about
everything. I can't say it any other way, because God watches me and I must be
honest."[35] I asked her if she still has contact with the Serbs she recognizes from
the war. "I run into them and that's okay. Nobody ever harmed me. But we
are sad and grieving—you know how it is. I never harmed anyone and nobody
ever harmed me. . . . You can't just walk past someone without speaking. What
could I do differently? Those who greet me and were good to my brothers and
my father think what happened to my family was dreadful."

Hatidža Mehmedović, one of the best known and most active women in
Srebrenica, is bitter about the differences between then and now:

> We had a healthy environment, very healthy. But it couldn't stay
> that way, someone had to destroy Yugoslavia and bring us this
> poverty, make us poor, so that now we get crumbs and wait for

packages. We had factories. . . . Now we have nothing and some want us to be part of Europe. We've become poor, with nothing but the clothes on our backs, as the saying goes. Until we become part of Europe, we'll probably lose our clothes as well. Then we won't even have clothes. In the past, we knew who was a beggar. Now we're all beggars. We could all beg if someone was handing out alms. We could all stick out our hands and ask for alms. Let's stick out our hands in the streets of Srebrenica. I'll go first. Let's see how much we get. I say we won't get anything, because there are no salaries, no jobs, nothing. There is no one who can give you something. In the past, beggars who sat on the street with their hands out received money. They could get more than a month's salary. Now, everybody can beg, but it's useless. How many families can live well on 150 KM [€75] [per month]? An entire family has to get by on 150 KM. And there are people with no income at all. If they can garden, that's all they have. But how can they buy oil, or coffee if they want it, or sugar? How can they pay the electricity? And so it goes. There are families like that, I know them, because I visit villages in the surrounding areas.[36]

For most of the women, talking about the past brings up tremendous grief. Sometimes, talking about it stirs up unresolved issues, which is not necessarily a bad thing, although it can be exhausting. Nezira Sulejmanović was among the last women to leave Potočari, at the end of the third day. She had her four-year-old with her. Her two sons had been murdered; before that, she had already lost a daughter. She is depressed from so much loss. Her husband was in Libya at the time of the fall. Nezira is one of the few women soldiers I interviewed; she is proud of her participation in the war. "I am a demobilized soldier, and my two sons are dead. I was on the front, at headquarters; there was a radio transmitter in my house. If they had caught me, they would have burned me alive. And now, no one understands me. The earth is too hard and the heavens too high. I must fight, but I can't. My body can't do it anymore, it just can't."

I knew from experience that sometimes when an interview becomes too depressing, it needs a cheerful twist. Sonja Akašamija, one of my interpreters, suggested asking when the women began ašikovanje, a combination of hesitant and not-so-hesitant ogling at boys. It was a flirting ritual at the dances and feasts that were part of marriage festivities. This old-fashioned custom, which has almost died out, embodies the innocence of the first meetings with the opposite sex. Ašikovanje also happens when groups of lanky teenage boys and girls stroll along the main street, eyeing one another, and perhaps secretly getting a bit closer. Asking when the women began ašikovanje always brought a smile.

Talking about Marriage to a Spouse Who No Longer Is

Nezira's husband was not at Potočari and had not been killed in the woods. I dared to ask her about their relationship and how they had gotten to know each other. I had tried in other interviews, but my questions usually resulted in tears and silence. The resulting stories were too fragmentary and not suitable for retelling. In general, Yugoslav marriage customs in the 1970s and '80s were surprising to me. Some girls ran away from home and considered the first night with their boyfriends as the beginning of their marriages. Other girls respectfully asked parental permission; after the union was blessed by a cleric (or not, and sometimes weeks later), the couples registered themselves as married. Occasionally, there was a large celebration that could last for days. Parents watched their daughters anxiously and wanted sexual relations to end in marriage. Tone Bringa wrote that there were three options. Besides a real wedding, eloping without parental consent was also a possibility, with the parents pretending to be unaware of the situation. The third option was a combination of these two possibilities.[37]

Nezira portrayed her family as very strict. "I didn't dare tell them that I was seeing a boy. I don't know how I managed to find one. Unlike girls today, I didn't dare say anything." I asked her how things had developed.

> I had other friends, neighbors. We went to the movies or there was a film at school, and we went to meetings at the school. But when the boy who became my husband came along, I forgot all my friends. I was tending sheep with other kids. It was all part of what we called *ašikovanje*. . . . Every Friday, there was a dance in front of the school. Then my husband, who is now dead, appeared. I saw him. He was tall, a nice fellow. . . . They came to ask me if I would marry him. At first I thought I'd say "yes," and later "no." You know how it goes. But I was in love. I was in love and I didn't know how. I had no idea. We went out together two or three times, and then he said he wanted to marry me. He had finished his military service and I was 15. He didn't have a mother and he lived with his father. So I said I would marry him, but that I couldn't cook.[38]

Her father was asked for permission, but he strongly opposed the marriage and locked Nezira in her room for seven days. Then he let her out and she ran away with the boy. Even though she had to work hard in her new home, she was content. Her new family was more religious, which she liked, and they seemed to understand her better than her parents did. A child was born exactly nine months later. Like all of the women I interviewed, she had known nothing about birth control, or even what sex was; it was all so overwhelming.

A woman who chose to remain anonymous confirmed this general ignorance: "Of course I didn't know about sex. I'm somewhat embarrassed to say that; I don't really want to talk about it. It was a disaster. Everything went so fast and then you can't enjoy it. No tenderness. You need some tenderness at first, before you have sex. Well, everything was over so quickly; I felt nothing. Believe me, those kinds of things can't be rushed."

Sevda had learned a great deal by listening to the conversations of older women, so she knew what was happening when her first period began. Her rearing was modern and she went to school, despite criticism from her mother's friends and acquaintances. Sevda also told about dances, meetings, and *ašikovanje*. Premarital sex was, of course, forbidden—she learned about sex only after her marriage—and even kissing was not allowed. By her own account, she married in order to be loved. He was a distant relative. Even though she had a secondary education, she wound up being a traditional housewife. I asked if she had expected that. "I thought I would work. I loved to work. When I left school, I registered for a job at the labor office. I wanted to work, but my mother didn't approve. When I began to go out with that boy, my future husband, I wanted to take a temporary job in Bratunac, but he told me, 'If you want to be with me, I don't want you to work. Never try to find a job.' What could I do? I was young."[39] She decided to earn money by doing needlework.

Her parents were against the marriage, so she ran away. That was normal, and seemed to be the only solution. She climbed out the bathroom window. But Sevda's parents were right; the young man drank heavily, and she was treated badly by her new family. She was disappointed when she realized her mistake. Her husband had seemed a good choice—he had a good job and she thought they would have their own house fairly soon. She found his family's custom of eating from a communal pan instead of individual plates uncivilized, which conveys a sense of the cultural differences between them. Sevda knew that she could not return to her parents' home. After one month, her husband began to beat her, just as he did his sisters. The beatings did not stop during her pregnancy, but Sevda did not dare to tell her religious parents. Instead, she worked at the many tasks in her new home. She was eight months pregnant when her labor began; she was chopping wood at the time and knew there would be no help with the delivery. Her daughter grew up without a father; despite everything, Sevda tried to give her daughter a positive impression of the father she had barely known. He did not survive the trek through the woods, and neither did her father and one of her brothers.

Ambivalence, Trauma, Impotence

Sevda has recovered from her miserable marriage, and her story resembles that of a number of women in this book. In the Bosnia of that era, women were beaten, as in other traditional societies; they talked about it as a normal part of their past. If he was murdered, then talking about his abuse came more easily. He was a brute, nothing more, but he didn't deserve to be murdered. The murder of the father of your children is a blow and raises the question of what to tell his offspring. At the same time, mourning one's husband blends into mourning one's father, uncles, and brothers; so many are missing, which creates confusion, and this is also part of the unresolved horror of Potočari. Some men did become more reliable and kinder to their wives during the difficult times in Srebrenica. They were more aware of their responsibilities and supported their wives. That was also the case with Sevda's husband; toward the end, he behaved better. Despite all the grief he had caused her, she waited years for him to return. Sevda was sad as she told about hearing that he was not in a Serb camp, which had been her last hope. Witnesses saw him surrender during the flight through the woods; her waiting was in vain.

> One of his nephews made it through the woods. I heard that he had seen my husband in Kravica [a Serb village near Srebrenica][40] and that he had surrendered. I asked him why. He said that he couldn't go on. He had changed his clothes [probably to shed anything that might be construed as military]. I hoped that his clothes would be found in the woods where he had changed. Then, someone came to inform me. . . . He had surrendered on the third day. He surrendered after he changed clothes. Then I heard about my father and one of my husband's brothers. One was murdered when he crossed the road near Kamenića. I know they are still looking for where they are buried. But I know about no one; no one has informed me of anything. All I know is what I heard from his nephew who saw him, who was with them, on the third day. I also heard something about my father. He was born in 1946. He didn't surrender, but was caught in the woods.

Many women who know that a loved one surrendered are reluctant to talk about it. Thousands of men surrendered; they were exhausted and despaired of reaching safety. There was talk of poison gas and hallucinogens in the springs, which drove the men to insanity.[41] Others testified to a combination of panic, exhaustion, despair, and hunger, which can cause hallucinations. But as long as Srebrenica had not fallen, one did not surrender, one fought on—just as the whole enclave fought to survive for years. The story of Sevda's husband follows the pattern: he has become part of the general mourning. His surrender, which was confirmed again and again, fades into the background and mourning eclipses everything. She realizes that he is dead.

> I simply can't believe or say that he is alive. So many years have passed. To say that he is in prison somewhere and might reappear. . . . No, I don't think so. He was murdered. I don't think he could have survived all of that. I don't know. So, after all these years, I've accepted the reality. I hoped for three or four years. I thought that he was in prison and that he would contact me. People say that in the past it took a long time to get information, but if six, seven years have passed. . . . Then I realized that neither he nor my father would return. I just don't have any hope left. . . . I would like to find him and to bury him. To know where he rests, so my child and I could visit his grave. You know, my whole family, except for my brother, is missing and I know nothing about them—that's all. I've accepted my fate, what else can I do? Worrying is useless, and I don't want my child to suffer because of it. I don't want her to have a difficult time in school. Life goes on. . . . I've been sad about all this; I'm still sad. My heart is [heavy]. . . . My whole family is gone.

Hazreta, whom I interviewed in 2004, suffered a great deal of abuse from her husband. Along with the death of her twin brother, the loss of her husband was one of the many disasters she survived, but her misery really began with her marriage. She described how she had been married off at age 15 to a family that exploited her. But everything was ultimately overshadowed by the cruelty she experienced at Potočari. She knew all too well how many men among her in-laws had been murdered, but did not want to talk about it; she had been too victimized herself. She and women like her tend to express themselves in a shrill confusion of grief. She was talking both about the father of her children and as a woman who does not know how to get on with her life. Whether her husband had been with her during the dark hours, or had gone through the woods, does not really matter; he is not coming back. That is now part of her general mourning, because she cannot psychologically integrate the horrors of those days in July. These are also the memories of the end of years of misery; those in Potočari had already spent three years under siege: people died daily from grenades, disease, and hunger. The trauma of the mass murder sits perched atop the nightmare of the period before, which sometimes seems to have never existed. But if one asks about it specifically, then the memories of those years before are there.

Too Much Lost to Remember

The trauma of murder and loss had cordoned off memories of the good times with the "others" (Serbs). The interviewees spoke about the Serbs in fairly general terms. Some, however, spoke of a special friendship. Sometimes, the sense of bonding was not lost, and that friendship was a part of what happened and is now mourned. It is not always possible, and certainly not easy, to acknowledge such a friendship, because one is also acknowledging positive emotions about people who did terrible things, which is confusing. Trying to forget exacerbates the confusion, however, because love and friendship are not easily erased, even after betrayal. It is much easier just to remember when everything was disrupted. All that went before is disturbing; that whole other side of the story is confusing. But time and again, it seems, acknowledging these emotions and these memories gives the women clarity about the present, their place in the world, their context. Occasionally renewing an old friendship stands in contrast to the rejection of old friends; most are too angry, or trying to protect themselves from the grief of what no longer exists. When feelings of love and friendship and old bonds still exist, this can be problematic, although I did encounter women who were able to renew old friendships.

One interviewee told me of her friendship with a Serb woman; they had been best friends since childhood. She was clearly pained.

> I dreamed about her in Srebrenica, but after all this happened, I was surprised to learn that her sons had been in the army, in a special unit that protected Karadžić. When I visited my village, I saw her in my mother's house and she wanted to hug and kiss me. I told her, "We can't be what we used to be." She began to cry and said that her sons hadn't murdered my son. But I told her, "They didn't do anything to save him." Deep down inside I still love her, but I will never admit that to her. I will not pardon her.

She and her friend used to attend church or go to the mosque together, it didn't matter which, but those days are gone.

The number of mixed marriages may have been small, but the friendships were deep. How is it possible to talk about these relationships without thinking of those who betrayed them? Not everybody can deal with such conflicted emotions. When so many murders were committed by people one was close to, there is too much pain to react with anything but rage. I regard the ability to begin new relationships as a sign of great emotional strength. It is dangerous; no one knows if these groups will be at odds again. It is emotionally risky, because there are real differences in experience. And sometimes it is socially risky to talk about such things openly. Yet there is another side to all this, the need to speak in terms other than bitterness and hatred. The kind of society that existed before is the only familiar alternative. Talking of the past is interwoven with thinking about the future; a number of women project their image of before, when things were good, onto their vision for the future. They long for a society in which close feelings for "others" are again possible. Realizing that makes talking about the past possible; otherwise, everything seems hollow and vacant.

Stories of Grief

When talking about the period between schooling and 1995, when the women worked and began families (20 years for some, only a brief span for others), the stories were fragmented. This agrees with earlier findings in oral history. After a major trauma, a relatively normal and routinized life is not much to talk about. In general, the women had led a family-centered existence. The American psychologist Steven Weine based his trauma therapy for Bosnian refugees on strengthening family ties, thus creating a new kind of crisis care.[42] Although such family ties do exist among Bosnian refugees in general, this is not the case for most survivors of Srebrenica, hence Weine's therapeutic model is not suitable for them. In the void after such a loss, discussing the daily ups and downs of one's marriage before the war becomes impossible. That time of normalcy is no longer imaginable. There are special moments in every life—marriages, births, moves—and those can be discussed. One hears about how good that time of the marriage was—albeit in nostalgic and general terms—about their travels and Sunday outings, how they worked the land, and how their lives were uncomplicated and happy. No one talks about the ennui and minutiae of daily life. In our stories, we gravitate to the special memories.

Seeing one's future spouse for the first time is such a moment. Behara disclosed to me that her choice of a partner was anything but spontaneous. Choices were made after a thorough review of the other's background and wealth. Then, during dances and parties, the behavior of the possible spouse was observed. Those dances and parties, which served as a "marketplace," happened often, and there one sought an appropriate spouse. The wedding was in its turn a chance for others to meet.

> A month after someone got married, there was a feast; that was the custom. It was called a *pilav*. We lived in Srebrenica and there was no transportation and no cars, and sometimes we had to go to a place that was farther out. Sometimes, it took us a whole day

to get to the place of the feast, where the boys and girls could be together. We walked three or four hours to get there, and the girls danced the *kolo*.[43] Sometimes, there were a hundred girls dancing. And the boys watched. If they liked a girl, they would approach her. But the family status was taken into account. "That girl is from so-and-so's family" was said, especially if the girl came from a well-known family.[44]

Zehta, who left Srebrenica well before the fall, had a horror story about staying in a refugee camp. She initially met with me in Srebrenica's town hall; she was trying to stimulate local entrepreneurship. The job suited her; she is well educated. Perhaps because she did not go through the hell of Potočari, she could give more thought to how things used to be. Her story was structured around the barrenness of the present. We wound up conducting her interview in an alcove behind a shop, where it was quiet. She smiled as she recalled:

> I worked for a bank for 22 years. What can I tell you? I come from a well-to-do family, and had a luxurious life before the war. I traveled all over Europe. I vacationed on the Black Sea and the Adriatic. I had a summer house on our lake. During that short time, the 10 years of my marriage, I had, as they say, everything. I didn't even know how much I had. I had three houses and room in this build-ing for businesses. We had a good time. . . . Years have gone by and I still dream that this didn't happen in my country, this didn't happen to my people. No matter how bad the wounds, and how painful, I see that dream.[45]

Grief separates and isolates feelings and desires from the past, which in turn hinders thinking about the future. The future is always uncertain, especially for the refugees, because so little has been settled. The saddest finding from my odyssey among the many women I interviewed is that a number of them are still frozen in the trauma; they can barely discuss it and can only think in terms of black and white. They cannot be blamed for this. Many would benefit from psychosocial help, but none has been offered. The need is enormous.[46]

Too little effort has been made to listen to the women's concerns and their condition. All too often, the survivors' need for extra care is not understood. The camps in East Bosnia are miserable, but not immeasurably worse than the camps elsewhere in Bosnia. There are individuals in all of them who have suffered enormously. There are the remnants of families that were torn apart, victims of rape, broken-down men who fled from a death that was waiting elsewhere for them. Survivors who live in the suburbs of Sarajevo are no more penniless than their neighbors. A great deal of money that was donated by states and charities has not reached the people, but money is not the same as learning the truth, which is the most important thing for the survivors. Of course, the truth about where their loved ones are is known in a global sense—they are probably in a mass grave—but where and with whom are not known. Sometimes, just learning that a father and son were together at the end and did not die alone makes a difference. But how did neighbors become murderers, and how could the world watch and do nothing while thousands were besieged in a small town and the men were butchered? The women ask: Why was the man I loved so much, who never hurt anyone, why was my child, my husband, my uncle, my father, my old friend murdered? Surely not because we are of another religion! A heart aches, the world seems hollow, and there is no tomorrow.

My interviews with the women were mostly monologues, interrupted occasionally by awkward questions or translation problems. It took time for me to understand that the interviews about the prewar period were fragmentary not only because of the trauma. It was enlightening to realize that almost every story was interwoven with reflections on earlier friendships and acquaintances and with a longing to return to that prewar era. That was a world of eloping, *ašikovanje,* wicked mothers, good and bad marriages; but it belongs to another time, the time of youth organizations in Tito's Yugoslavia and the country's decline, the time when there were no refugee camps and their villages were far away from the world.

In their stories about the world before the war, there are doubts about others' sincerity and rage at the betrayal on all sides. What happened has traumatized these women. At first, they thought that their questions would be answered. Now, they are bringing lawsuits, while their memories of "how he was, how he talked" are fading, along with "how things were when he was still there." Their children are growing up without knowing or remembering. What remains is a stump of a memory that slowly becomes more confused; there are too many open questions and inexplicable riddles. Official memories are beginning to take form, but the survivors are seen as marginal. Srebrenica has become a symbol, but not the symbol of its victims' suffering. They can be only occasionally seen—when they protest and when they bury their dead.

The multicultural society into which these women were born is the only model they have when talking about the future. To remember that society requires unearthing mountains of incomprehensible grief. Unearthing that grief is important for the future of the entire Bosnian society. The prerequisite is listening to them and taking them seriously, even though they are angry and demanding, even though they seem confused. Who wouldn't be after what they have lived through?

CHAPTER THREE

WAR IS COMING

I t became clear early on that many of the women had led sheltered lives in their little towns and villages before the war. Once it began, they knew there was a war, but they did not expect it to reach them, nor did they expect it to be so violent. The war reached East Bosnia in 1992; given its course in other areas, people knew in theory what could happen to them. After the victory of the nationalist parties in 1991, political factions in the municipalities had become more rigid and strident.[1] Relations between the groups were so strained that interaction was possible only at the personal level.[2]

Despite the squabbling and political friction at the local level, the war between neighbors was unexpected. Suddenly, there were watches, usually instigated by the village leadership, and residents in the valley were worried. I asked Ćamila, one of the residents of Srebrenica, if she had sensed that war was coming: "I felt nothing. What can I say? The war broke out all of a sudden. We hadn't seen preparations for it; the war broke out in the region in two, three days. A couple of days before it started, people began to talk." Ćamila worked in a factory at the time, and discussed it with her Serb co-workers.

> They said war was coming. I asked, "What kind of war?" The Serbs said they were in danger. How could they be in danger when we took the same bus to work, ate together, worked together, and did everything together? How could they be in danger? . . .
>
> Everyone was confused; suddenly, people talked openly about the war. They wanted to run away, they wanted anything and every-thing. Fires were built in front of houses. We sat outside, Serbs and Muslims, and we talked about the war. The Serbs claimed that the Muslims would start the war. One man said, "Good people, why war? In the last world war, there were lice and bedbugs, the floors were dirt, and life was difficult. Now, there's central heating,

everything is fantastic—do we really have to destroy all that, kill each other, and mutilate a lot of people? . . . And in the end we'll go through the same nonsense, talking about reconstruction. What's wrong with you—are you crazy? Do you want a war?" No one wanted that, but the rumors didn't stop. That's how it began. And it began on Bajram [Muslim New Year]. I went with my mother as usual to have lunch with our family. On the way home, my Muslim neighbors called out, "Ćamila, they have weapons." "Who?" "The Serbs. They have weapons. The war is coming." "What war? That's nonsense." . . . In the first few days, I wasn't scared of them, even though they were armed and had become nationalistic.

Ćamila could not believe that her neighbors would harm a hair on her head. She had a close relationship with them; they exchanged baked goods and loaned each other things. Then, a Serb neighbor, Džerka, sent her children away, but would not tell Ćamila why. Finally, she did tell Ćamila that she was afraid the Muslims would murder her child; Džerka believed the propaganda that was being spread. Ćamila found that unthinkable; she would have protected her friends with her own body. Apparently, Džerka did not want to frighten Ćamila, so she chose to say as little as possible.

Despite the war, Ćamila did not lose faith in the possibility of different groups living together. She remained in her old home in Srebrenica, where she died in 2007. New neighbors had come into her life, and she gave the future a chance, even with her despair and doubt. She was also involved in the memorial museum at Potočari; she used her deep grief regarding the past to work on commemoration and on education for the future.

Those I interviewed from Bratunac were more struck by the unimaginable cruelty in 1992 than by what happened in 1995. Today, Bratunac is considered as always having been a Serb town, and is even claimed as such, but in 1991 its population was more than 64 percent Muslim.[3] The little town is the link to the outside world between the Drina Valley and the valley in which Srebrenica is located; because of the stream of refugees through the valleys, its residents were more aware of what was happening elsewhere.

Early in 1992, the Serb population deserted a number of villages in the area, and there was also a brief exodus from Bratunac itself. At that time, the interviewees did not understand what was happening and why the Serbs left. Those who stayed behind isolated themselves from the "others," but on an informal level ties remained. These ties made escape possible for a few individuals, and led to a certain hesitation during the great roundup that began in 1992. Some Serbs were reluctant to murder old friends; despite propaganda that the Muslims did not deserve to live, the memory of their past coexistence remained.

The Serbs in Bratunac wanted to be annexed by Serbia, and would have liked the Muslims to go along with that, but the Muslims had no reason to. Šefika Begić told me:

> Our people didn't like the idea. You know, I'll tell you the truth. They did not agree to joining Serbia. They wanted to stay with their Bosnia. And that caused a break. My husband always said that things would turn out badly. He went to the meetings. He said, "If we are divided, there will be war." When we asked our Serb neighbors what would happen, they said that there would be something, but it wouldn't last long. Heavens! It lasted so long, and there were mass murders. But up to the last day, they didn't tell us what was going to happen. We were good neighbors, we lived on the same street. . . . I still remember clearly how it began. I had gone to the doctor in Bratunac. I've had high blood pressure for 20 years. After that, I went to the town department store. . . . Bratunac had already been taken. I saw soldiers arrive, but there were no familiar faces among them. They all had automatic rifles. People called out that it was the Serbian army, straight from Serbia. I will always say that. They came and stood in a row.

According to Šefika, at first the Serbians and their Serb allies were afraid of Muslim resistance. "But we didn't have a single bullet or weapon when they came."[4]

Bratunac: The Trauma of 1992

The first aggression in Bratunac in 1992 is not as well known as the one in Srebrenica in 1995; fewer people were murdered and no agency or organization had promised protection. It was a different kind of murder in Bratunac and its surrounding villages than the one later in Srebrenica; it was more personal, a roundup and slaughter of people the aggressors knew. It also happened suddenly, while the siege of Srebrenica lasted for years. The fact that many of the aggressors knew their victims exacerbated the victims' trauma. Through one of the NGOs I worked with, Women of the Podrinje,[5] I heard stories about the first days of war in Bratunac. Many women from Bratunac ended up as refugees in Srebrenica, and from there they followed the same path to Potočari; others were evacuated from Bratunac to Tuzla. In the interviews, the women felt it necessary to emphasize the murders in 1992, because it was the first time that neighbors had murdered neighbors; it was also the first violent confrontation.

Bratunac was taken on April 17, 1992; the main aggressors were Arkan's Tigers, a paramilitary group infamous for its cruelty. The group leader was

Željko Ražnjatović, a one-time bank robber and later a freelance agent for the Yugoslav secret service.[6] Ger Duijzings and many other authors have noted that they were ruthless in the extreme and, because they were at the vanguard, enjoyed first choice during the plundering.[7] From that point on, Muslims were considered fair game. This worsened after the death of Goran Zekić, a local Serb nationalist, on May 8; most Serbs believed he had been murdered by Muslims (his murderers have still not been identified). Duijzings described how on Sunday, May 10, "thousands of Muslims from Bratunac and several surrounding suburbs and villages west and north of the town" were rounded up.[8] The women and children were ultimately deported to Tišća. Before that, they were herded into the stadium, along with a group of men. About 600 or 700 men were driven into a school gym, where they were tortured and murdered. In the 2002 NIOD Report, Duijzings estimated that 500 people were killed during the month of May 1992. More recent research has shown that during the entire year of 1992, counting both civilians and military, 911 Bosniaks and 339 Serbs perished. The majority of the victims died in May and thus 500 seems a low estimate. This is interesting, because the higher figures come from the Information and Documentation Center in Sarajevo,[9] which has been accused of systematically keeping the number of victims too low.[10] Muslims were being terrorized on all sides; after that, most of the Muslim survivors fled Bratunac.

Šuhra Sinanović, president of Women of the Podrinje, told of her first jolt of horror. I had asked when she first sensed there would be war: "In 1991. I was in my garden when I suddenly saw that my next-door neighbors were agitated about something. These Serb neighbors were leaving with their women and children. I went to them and asked what was going on. Someone had told them they had to cross the Drina by boat." But it had begun earlier. "In 1988 or 1989 my husband and I were invited to a farewell party that the [Serb] neighbors were giving for their son. He was going into the army. We were invited and we went. There was music and there was a meal. After the meal, they began to sing nationalistic songs." Šuhra and her husband realized they did not belong there. According to her, it became obvious in 1992 that there would be war. On May 11, she saw the Serb army and the Bosnian Serbs coming. She was going from her village to her parents' house in Bratunac when she ran into a Serb barricade.

> A real bunker, with sandbags on top, about two meters, or maybe more, high. . . . We stopped. One of my neighbors, who was armed, asked to see our identification cards. They had started checking IDs about a month earlier. But I said, "Hey, neighbor, we know each other!" He looked in the car I was in and asked M, the driver, to step out. He took him to the other side, embraced him, said something to him, and then let us go. There were maybe 10 cars ahead

of us at the barricade; we were the only ones allowed through. We drove farther. It was about two kilometers from the barricade to my parents' house.

The telephone was not working, so she visited her infirm parents as often as she could—sometimes every day, sometimes every other day. The man who had driven told her not to take the bus back, but to wait for him to give her a ride.

He stopped at the fence, but the gate was closed and the shades were pulled down. I felt a pain in my stomach, and wondered what was going on. When I opened the gate, my cousin came outside, crying. Her father, my uncle, had been murdered 15 days earlier. He was the first victim in Bratunac. She asked me what I was doing there. I said I had stopped by as usual, and I asked her what was going on and where my parents were.

Šuhra's father, brother, uncle, and a son-in-law had all been murdered. She had heard that her mother was on the other side, with Serb neighbors; the man had worked with her father for 32 years. She went looking for her mother, who asked what her daughter was doing there. The mother was crying and barefoot; she had been to the police station.

She told me, "You see what has happened, go to your children." I asked her about my brother and father, and about what happened to the others. At the police station, they had told her to go home, because she had given birth to a *balija* [Muslim hay- seed] who would murder Serbs. She told me to go home and take my children and myself to safety. She had to bury her husband's brother, my uncle.

Šuhra did not wait for her ride; she ran toward home. Again, she came to the barricade, now on foot and in tears. The same neighbor as before stood about 10 meters in front of her. "He already knew that my family was in the gym at the school and that my uncle had been murdered that night." She passed the barricade and reached her family; they fled to safer terrain. Her brother and father survived the slaughter at the school, but they had been badly beaten. "They laid my brother on the floor and put my father in a chair so he could watch as they thrashed him. Sometimes, they put him on his back, sometimes on his stomach, while they beat him all over his body and his head with sticks." Serb neighbors offered to transport her uncle's body with their car, but the family buried him themselves.[11]

Theft and Murder by Friends and Acquaintances

The story of Bratunac is about broken trust and broken relationships. All the accounts tell of neighbors who behaved badly and also of neighbors who tried to help but usually did not succeed. I interviewed Binasa Sarajlić, the daughter of the almost legendary Zejneba Sarajlić, who ran Women of the Podrinje in Bratunac with Stanojka Avramović. I had met Zejneba in 2002 in her office.

As in so many offices of women's organizations, one room had walls filled with photographs. Zejneba had a remarkably friendly face, understood immediately what I was about, and offered me her full cooperation. Her office was located close to the beginning of the road to Srebrenica. In 2002 I had to pick my way through clutter and rubbish to reach the entrance. In 2006–2007 things were much neater, and the town itself looked better. Houses had been restored, Muslim residents had begun to return slowly, the streets seemed clean, and there was little to remind one of the time when one half of the town had chased down the other half.

The memories, however, are still there, and they are a hindrance to peaceful coexistence. In 2001 and 2002, stones were thrown at survivors in Bratunac who were returning to their homes in Srebrenica. Bratunac was also the site of repeated conflicts between returning Muslims, who demanded their homes back, and the Serbs who had taken them over starting in 1992. There has been constant struggle. The Serbs built a church in Konjević Polje on land that originally belonged to Muslims. The Muslims demanded that it be torn down, and the opposing party protested that this was a threat to religious freedom. Tensions increased in 2004, and since then have been on the brink of getting out of hand, although there are Serb Bosnians who want peace and admit that the church should not be there.[12]

Binasa's office was at Women of the Podrinje in Ilidža, a suburb of Sarajevo. Binasa was born in 1967, and was still young when the war broke out. At that time she worked as a hairdresser in Srebrenica, but returned to Bratunac often. Her family had close ties with their Serb neighbors. She talked about her shock: "We lived together. They didn't start the feast for their patron saint unless we were there, and we never celebrated Bajram without them. That's just how it was. What hurts the most is that during the war these people betrayed us and conspired against our lives." She told about a neighbor with an automatic weapon who was there just before the soldiers:

> A half hour later, Arkan's men came to our house and searched for
> an automatic weapon. After they left, he [the neighbor] came over

and asked if they had found jewels. "How do they know we have jewels?" I asked him. He said, "If they didn't take a sack of jewels with them this time, they'll be back." From that time on, he came every time Arkan's soldiers searched our house. And every time he asked what and how much they had taken. After their third visit, my mother went to the police station. They gave her a pass, and said she could use it to travel freely.

Her mother did not like the situation and wanted to leave. She was right. One of the men at the police station warned the family to leave, because something bad was going to happen.

Why did people we trust do that kind of thing? I don't know. My mother really trusted this one man. She went to him with that pass and asked for his opinion. He told her that we shouldn't go anywhere, because then they would kill us. In fact, he was the one who had reported my father and my father was also murdered. . . . If you have nothing to do with politics, and my father didn't, then why did Arkan's men come? We didn't know; we were confused; we didn't know what to think.

Binasa now thinks it was because her family was well-to-do and the neighbor was after their money. Shortly before, their relationship had been good. The neighbor had a daughter who was a good friend. There was also a younger girl, Vesna, with whom Binasa liked to play.

[In January] Vesna said, "Bet you don't know what I know—we're going to fight the Muslims." She was three and a half years old. I was dumbstruck, it was a real shock. Rade [the neighbor] and his wife, her grandparents, looked at me. Then his wife said, "Binasa is also a Muslim," and Vesna replied, "I know. But Grandpa, she'll be on our side." We had never thought about a war. My heart froze, I didn't know what to do. I put the child down and left. To this day, I get tears and cold chills when I remember that.

Binasa's house was on the road from Bratunac to Serbia; she could see all the military supplies that were headed to Bratunac, including 200 tanks. "We counted them, we were deathly afraid. We didn't know what was happening or what was going to happen." The family remained shut up in their house for a month, as though under siege. It was a long month; they passed the time by keeping watch. Life lost its purpose; there was nothing to do, nothing to talk about. "All I can say is that I didn't have a chance to say goodbye to my father." Her father was picked up and murdered. She feels the family's problems stemmed from a betrayal by their neighbor. "Everything was planned in advance. . . . it was all planned."[13] There was a deliberate policy to murder the elite first. The men in her family, just as with the others, were herded together at the school. When her father left, he asked if he should take his jacket. The answer was, "If you think you'll need it." The women were bused to an area controlled by Muslims. There were six or seven buses full of crying women; they were afraid of being murdered as well.

Binasa left her brother behind, with a couple of his friends. They were standing at a wall. After her brother had seen how their father had been murdered, he tried to hang himself, but his friends stopped him. In the Vuk Karadžic school, indescribable scenes took place. Hasan Nuhanović, a former DutchBat interpreter, has brought together in a book accounts of what happened there.

Report 12, by HS from Mihaljevići, a municipality of Bratunac, is such an account. HS was taken to the stadium in Bratunac after his village was captured. There, he was stripped of anything of possible value, even though he had been searched before. The school was crowded; there were Muslims from a number of surrounding villages. HS was brought in during the evening; the school was in complete chaos.

> One officer, whom I did not know, ordered all those on the floor to get up and to line up in front of the wall with their hands up. At that moment I noticed they had sustained severe beatings. The Serbs began to beat them again. The gymnasium was so packed that we felt like sardines.
>
> I think at that moment there were around 1,000 men. When we finally entered the gymnasium, members of the military unit called "Arkanovici" began entering the gymnasium. They began to call the roll of people by their names and family names. They were killed on the spot. The Serbs did not use firearms; they used metal bars, batons, and people were beaten so severely that the beating was lethal.[14]

The report continues:

> I want to say something more about that terrible time in the gymnasium. I will never forget how they sometimes selected victims to be tortured and killed. After they killed all those whose names were on the list, they threw a ball above the heads of those civilians packed in the gym whose names they did not know. The man hit by the ball had to bring the ball, and they killed him. . . . The imam of the mosque in Bratunac was beaten up. They tried to force him to drink alcohol and to show three fingers [the Serb salute].[15] Since he refused to do it, they began

to beat him up; the ritual was repeated. Then the imam was forced to climb a rope in the gym, and the Serbs made him fall. He was brought back to consciousness by splashing beer in his face. Again he refused to hold up three fingers, and was beaten to death. That is how it went for many.

Ambivalent Murderers

The torturers and the murderers knew the people they were dealing with; sometimes, they respected them, or at least felt that they should not treat people that way. Even direct orders and fierce propaganda were not always sufficient to convince everyone that Muslim lives were worthless.

Mirsada Bakalović, who was interviewed by Ger Duijzings, confirmed this.[16] Her story, like many others, shows that robbery was a major motive during that time in Bratunac. She felt the main goal was to strip the richer Muslims of their goods and then to drive them out of the area that the Serbs regarded as theirs. As people entered the stadium, the Serbs did not hesitate to cut off fingers when rings could not be removed. Agitated Serb women from Bratunac took part in both the thievery and the torture. According to all accounts, the slaughter had been well planned. There were lists of names, and those with the most possessions to confiscate and the elites were the first to be murdered. What happened followed the standard pattern for ethnic cleansing. During her stay in the stadium, Mirsada often recognized the people who were guarding her and asked them for help. She could not believe that she could not rely on their former ties of friendship. One man did escort her to her home and told her how shocked he was. He behaved respectably and helped her to collect some belongings. She decided not to return to the stadium.

After several days, Mirsada was caught and forced to sign a document giving up her apartment. From that point on, she tried to leave the town by obtaining a permit similar to what Binasa's mother had been given. She received a number of small favors from Serbs she knew, who were threatening other Muslims at the same time. The situation was so confused that a Serb friend of her daughter, who was with them, recognized them and greeted them warmly with hugs, while threatening the family with an automatic rifle. A member of the Serb crisis team visited the family "in hiding" and wanted to rape her in exchange for keeping silent. Shortly before she left, Mirsada tried to give her friend Desana a small parting gift, because their sons used to play together. Desana did not want to accept it, because it would remind her of their friendship and that was too complicated. After a grueling trek, Mirsada did succeed in reaching safe territory.

Raped and Abandoned

Bratunac was not yet accustomed to such horrors, although what had happened in nearby Foća, for example, was known. Foća was the site of a mass rape[17] and other atrocities. Although Bratunac had been isolated in May and was far from the war, its residents knew of those events and found it inconceivable that something similar could happen to them.

But similar things did happen in the villages around Bratunac, as Edina's story shows. She told of what she witnessed as a 15-year-old girl when the war broke out. I interviewed her in a shabby house on the edge of Tuzla, where she lived at the time. She had already told her story a number of times in public. She had been raped, and had testified as an unprotected witness at the Yugoslav Tribunal. She chose to speak out publicly and courageously about what happened to her.[18] Edina did not go through Potočari, but her experience was also horrific. What happened to her is an example of why the events of 1992 in the Podrinje are not called genocide, although they were more than a mere prelude to Potočari.

Edina noticed that Serb families in her village were departing; the integrated village was no longer integrated; only the older men and the men fit for army duty remained. The village came under fire, so her family decided to hide in the woods. When things calmed down, they returned home:

> On May 15, my sister, brother, mother, father, and I were at home. We were asleep when the shooting started, around midnight. It sounded like our house was surrounded. I was wide awake. I was so scared that I couldn't breathe. I had never been that scared in my life. The shooting lasted 15 or 20 minutes and then stopped. I went back to sleep and woke up around 5:30 because the shooting began again. At 5:30 a grenade exploded, but at that time I didn't know what a grenade was. It was a terrible explosion that rattled the windows. I ran, as did my sister and brother, to my parents' room. We stayed very quiet and didn't dare to leave the room. That morning, my sister decided to go into the woods. Muslims had fled there from all the other villages, but we hadn't wanted to. We thought that no one meant to harm us, because, you know, they were our neighbors.
>
> That morning, we packed some clothes and food and went into the woods. There was a hill in that forest called the Bar. We found other Muslims—men, women, and children. They were

living there in tents. They had made a kind of tent from pieces of plastic, and we joined them. There were a number of people from my mother's family. We also made a sort of plastic tent and stayed there 10 days. I remember that it rained every night. I'll never forget it.

On occasion, the family went to their house to fetch food and other necessities, and to feed their cow. One day, while they were returning, she, her father, and an aunt were captured by a Serb neighbor. He told them that they were to be part of a prisoner exchange. They wound up in a large building with a group of 40 prisoners—men, women, and children, old and young all thrown together. After a while the commander came, although they did not know he was in charge. He advised them to give a statement. He also told Edina that she, her father, and her aunt were prisoners. The Serbs wanted to know where the other Muslims were. The next day, her father was ordered to tell a nearby village that it had to surrender. If he did not succeed, then Edina would be murdered.

At this point, the interview became difficult, but Edina persevered; she was determined to tell her story. "He left. I didn't know how much time he had to return. I stayed with the other prisoners after he left." That evening, the former neighbor demanded her death because her father had not returned. The next day, she was taken with another man to be killed. "They took us out of the building. We were in front of the building and walking toward the fence." Nearby was a pile of sand with six bodies on it. "So I thought they were going to kill us. I wasn't afraid, I just hoped they would shoot me in the back. When we got close to the sand pile, a soldier yelled at me to go left. I went to the left, and nothing . . ." They kept walking in the direction of the health center. A soldier and a woman doctor were sitting in the area. Both were in uniform. "We had to sit at a table. The man and I sat down and I began to tremble." They sat there the whole day. Around 5:30 the commander came and told them to return to where they had come from that morning. When they got there, everybody was surprised they were unharmed; they had been told the two were dead. The same message had been sent to the village where her father had gone.

They stayed there a couple of days. Then the commander came with two soldiers. "One of the soldiers was my neighbor. He gave me, two other girls, and five boys work orders." The group had to clean his office. Other prisoners came to relieve them. Nine names were not on the list, including hers. All were females; the others left. After their departure the girls were chosen for clean-up work. She and two sisters were chosen and taken in the direction of Bratunac to a deserted house. They were told to sit down. Their captors' intentions quickly became obvious. "We said nothing and bowed our heads. The captors agreed among themselves who would take whom to a room." She was ordered to undress; she refused and he tore off her clothes.

I began to scream; I shrieked. He pushed me in that room onto the bed. He raped me. Because I was shrieking, he stuffed a piece of paper in my mouth. Later, I didn't have the strength to scream or to do anything. He took his weapon and aimed it at my forehead. He told me he would murder me if I yelled. I didn't have any strength left. I tried to wiggle loose as best I could. He kept going until deep into the night. I don't know exactly, I lost any sense of time. When he wanted to sleep, he stayed on top of me. He was always there. He didn't want to sleep. There was a table with handcuffs; he cuffed me to it so I couldn't escape while he slept. He was on top of me; he had a gun that he hid under the pillow.

The next day, a neighborhood watch began. Two days later, a group of men (including her neighbor) arrived with 11 or 12 soldiers. They were told that they were going to be taken back in cars.

We came to a house; we had to get out of the car and go upstairs. There was a kind of waiting room with a bed. My neighbor pushed me on the bed. The other girls were taken to other rooms. He pushed me on the bed and began to tear off my clothes. I started screaming. I don't know what happened to me. My neighbor attacked me again and began pulling my clothes off me. I yelled. The whole time, he asked me why my father didn't come back. I didn't know where my father had been taken or if he was still alive.

He raped me there. I was scared, I cried. After he raped me, he pulled my hair and kicked my back. He pushed me against the door to the other room. I fell. The soldiers brought a girl out of the room and dragged me to the bed in that room. Someone else raped me. I don't remember his name. He raped me there. When he finished, another one came in and raped me. And when the second was finished, a third came. They bound my hands and stuck a cloth in my mouth because I kept on screaming. Because I was crying, I couldn't breathe through my nose. I passed out because I couldn't breathe. I was out of it. When I woke up, I saw that I was wet and my hands were bound.

Her neighbor, who had started it, came back and raped her again. When day broke, she and the other girls were allowed to go to the toilet; they had to walk naked through a room with about 20 soldiers in it. They were ordered to find some clothes and then to peel potatoes.

Edina's story takes an unusual turn here. The commander of another group of soldiers began to take care of them. He let them fetch water to wash, and said he would take them to Bratunac. There, they stayed a couple of days at police headquarters. The commander then took them to an empty house; from there, they were moved to a house where a Serb military policeman hid them for eight days. They had to remain quiet and could not even make a light. Military police brought them food once a day. They were told to make a statement about where they had been, without reporting anything negative; after that, she and the other girls were taken to Serbia. They landed in a refugee camp in Šepak.[19]

They had lived together, Serb and Muslim; they had been neighbors. Residents of Bratunac had married spouses from the other group, and a few Serbs ultimately felt "forced" to murder their spouses and children. Such deeds formed the backdrop for the events in the stadium, where Serbs did not shrink from killing people with their bare hands. Something had snapped; the usual norms and boundaries no longer applied. Murder and torture were now applauded as proof of manliness.

Mitko Kadric told Ger Duijzings how he was both attacked and saved by friends. Both types of behavior are evident in the following. He addressed an old friend in the Bratunac stadium.

> I asked him, "Can't you help me?" He said, "Well, about the only thing I can do is to see that you get out of here. Then go to one of the burned-out villages, and take it from there." . . . We left the school, it was dark. I saw soldiers; they yelled, "Don't move!" We stood still. I saw R in uniform and with the soldiers; he was an extremist. He ordered, "Don't move!" My companion answered, "Leave us alone. I'm taking Mitko out of here, so he can escape." R called out, "Go back; the orders are that nobody can leave the school." We had been friends up until then; I couldn't make sense of it. I tried speaking to R as a friend, "Are you crazy? How is all this possible?" He shouldered his automatic rifle, and then again, and said, "If the two of you don't go back, I'll shoot both of you dead." My friend said, "We have to go back." We went back inside. My friend said, "Go sit by the door, and I'll come to get you as soon as we can leave." . . . He came back later, gestured that it was arranged, and that he would come and get me.[20]

Mitko survived. There are a number of such stories.

Muslims who were being pursued found it unthinkable that their old friends and acquaintances now belonged to the murderers. This was true throughout Bosnia. The interviewees emphasized that they considered those friendships to be valid when the war erupted. That sense of connection and of living communally now seems almost impossible, given the violence that was used by neighbor against neighbor. Yet trusting one's neighbors seemed a self-evident—even natural—first reaction. Some of that trust endured as the war dragged on, even in Potočari.

Srebrenica 1992

Those same days in May were not as violent in Srebrenica as in Bratunac, mainly because the population fled almost immediately. On April 18, Sabaheta looked out her window and saw that her Serb neighbors were armed, in uniform, and standing in the street. She had not believed that the bickering between the Muslims and the Serbs would reach Srebrenica, even though some had predicted that. She lived in a part of the town where many Serb families lived. One night, the women and children from those families left the town. After that, many Muslim families left as well.

> On April 18, 1992, after getting up I stepped out on the balcony of my apartment. I saw all my Serb neighbors in uniform and with weapons marching in the street. I went back inside and told my Šaban, "Look, Šaban, look at what is happening." We went to the balcony and watched in amazement. But we weren't afraid. They were our neighbors, so why should we care if they were armed? I didn't have a clue, it just wasn't obvious to me. And then, after maybe one or two hours . . . a horrendous racket of vehicles and shouting began; it was terrifying.

From her balcony, she could see that guns were being fired from the vehicles. And then she saw it was the White Eagles, the elite forces of Arkan, the much-feared murderer. "They began immediately plundering and slitting the throats of Muslims. My Šaban and I were terrified. We went in the hall and waited for someone to come and murder us. But that didn't happen in 1992."

Neighbors Become Murderers

In her study of ethnic violence and boundaries, Cathy Carmichael examined the rituals used by groups to distance themselves from one another. The goal of the Serb aggressors was political victory, and the military helped to achieve this. In such situations of violence between neighbors, Carmichael feels there is something else in play. She argues for studying the rituals that go along with the psychological distancing,[21] and in this context she has reviewed information from the proceedings of the Yugoslav Tribunal.

Carmichael's view is that for a long time there were few cultural fault lines between Serbs and Muslims. The fact that there were so few boundaries between the two groups made it necessary to create them with force, making the shock even greater for the victims. The Serbs' nationalistic feelings created a desire to change the status quo with its vague territorial and national boundaries, and they wanted their own national territory. In order to accomplish their goal, they used unexpected violence in a world that did not know how to respond. The disruption was enormous, both for the Muslims, who lost everything, and for the Serbs, who lost their sense of human decency. And both the Muslims and the Serbs were confused by what was happening.

An explanation also must be sought in the power of the past. Historically, there had been differences, but those cultural boundaries were denied or (more optimistically) unguarded. Often, I was told that the "others" began to act and behave differently. This could mean that a subtle difference became more obvious, a process that is usually reciprocal. The Muslim inhabitants of East Bosnia had gone through a long period in which they transitioned into being Bosniaks. That happened on many levels and was reinforced by the failed politics of Yugoslav unity and the frenzy of Serb nationalist expansion. The Muslim inhabitants of the region may also have laid down borders and staked out their cultural attitudes and territory. Things the Bosniaks found innocent and non-aggressive may well have been interpreted by the Serbs as just the opposite.

How people remember things is also problematic. I have noted how difficult it is in the present to comprehend fully how the two groups interacted in the past. Even those who can do this probably will not remember with ease the phase of cultural marking and separation. It is even more difficult for individuals to remember their own possible contribution to this separation, which ultimately led to murder. Acknowledging the cultural marking that took place might be seen as a suggestion that the Muslims are themselves guilty of what happened to them, although only the still-active Serb propaganda machine makes that claim. How the boundaries are drawn between two groups is one of the core issues in wars involving people who knew and lived with each other.

The unconscious separation between the two groups was apparent in an interview with Šuhreta Mujić. When I asked if she saw the war coming, she replied, "We could see it in 1991, 1992. It began in 1991. Our young people were normally together, Serb and Muslim. All of a sudden, the Serbs were down there somewhere and the Muslim youth were in the upper part of the village. There were barricades, there was one just down from my house. . . . Our neighbors knew that war was coming." On the surface, she is talking about 1992, but in truth she is saying that she felt the distancing well before the war's outbreak.

Abdulah Porković has a small restaurant in Srebrenica and worked for Doctors without Borders during the war. I asked if he sensed the war was coming. He assured me that he did not; otherwise, he would have left. "I thought everybody was like me and nobody could hurt someone else. Because of that, I was stupid enough to think there wouldn't be a war. I did not think there would be a war. I still think, even now, if they hadn't brought in outsiders, there wouldn't have been a war." According to him, panic grew in the weeks before the war, because the Bosnian Serbs had fled. They had been deliberately scared off by political propaganda, scandal-mongering, and frenzied stories in the media about the war elsewhere. That fear also provoked a reaction among the Muslims, who began to protect their houses. No one felt safe any more, and the Muslims also began to flee. Such flights were improvised—for example, in cars with foam rubber mattresses and a few belongings—because of a sense of urgency. "There was something ominous in the air," Abdulah said.[22] He also said that parties were being delineated, but it was not yet clear that they would oppose each other. Things were definitely changing.

Without realizing it, Vahida delved deeper into those gradual changes. I interviewed her in May 2005 in Camp Živinice. That refugee camp is one of the worst places I have ever visited; it is marked by poverty, filth, and especially stench. At that time, Vahida lived with her daughter in a room she had decorated as best she could. Since then, the family has returned to their original region, where their old house is being renovated. I asked Vahida about the war coming.

> We felt it. It happened slowly, bit by bit, but if you were clever you could see it. They started doing everything in their own way, using their own expressions and stories, and making remarks. You could feel it in the bus, but it wasn't that bad. You know, it changed gradually. Tito died in 1980. A number of changes began then, but not in our village, where they were our neighbors. Our people worked for them, and they worked for us. Our boys commuted with their boys of the same age to work in Belgrade. They took a couple of days off work around the weekend, and worked on the house of one of the neighbors. . . . Our boys said they could feel that something had changed after having a couple of drinks together. They felt it.

Vahida was concerned and discussed it with others. Then, there were nationalistic television programs and nationalistic parties. "We did feel something, but we didn't believe it. We thought something might happen, but it was just speculation."

During that time, Vahida said, children were pestered at school. Serb children gave the Serb salute, holding up the thumb and the index and middle fingers.[23] "Things looked and sounded bad. Some said we should prepare for a war, and wanted to get weapons, but younger people didn't believe what the older folks were saying. People who were older told stories about the last war." Young people swore that they were mentally prepared, and would not let anything happen.

> That's how it was. There was friction; some people hung out flags. If a couple of them were in a car and they saw a group of us, they yelled at us or made certain gestures. There was so much in 1989, 1990. . . . I felt it, but couldn't believe it. I watched all the programs on TV, I watched the negotiations and I knew.
>
> And people began to leave. First the people with more education and those who were close to the local authorities sent their families away like refugees. You heard that so-and-so had left, and that another so-and-so had taken his wife and kids elsewhere. We couldn't do that. And we didn't believe that things would go so quickly. There was an occasional skirmish or fight. For example, they would take a Muslim for a ride and give him a nasty beating. They were insulting and threatening. They would insult anybody—man, woman, or child. They wanted us to see that war was coming, that they were counting on it, that something was going to happen. . . .
>
> When the war began in Croatia in 1991, we realized it would come here too. They waited until 1992; in their minds, there was 1942 [when Serbs and Croats fought around Srebrenica],[24] and then 1992. So the war began in 1992, when the Serbs held military training in the hills. You could hear them shooting in the hills every night. . . . March was cold, and April too. It was Bajram when it began, first in Sarajevo. When things started on April 4 in Sarajevo, we got together and set up sentry posts around the village. . . . In March, the police were divided in two; the town government had split into two groups.[25]

All this still does not explain the reversal from warm personal feelings to a world of hate and violence. The historian Ben Lieberman describes what he calls the two groups' "cognitive dissonance"—behaviors and attitudes brought about by holding two conflicting ideas, or behaviors that go against one's convictions.[26] This internal conflict can be resolved by regarding the others as outsiders. That becomes problematic, however, when the aggressors are well known to the victims. How could good neighbors kill each other?

Lieberman considers the mass murder at Foča to be an excellent example of cognitive dissonance. A young Muslim woman testifying at the Yugoslav

Tribunal said that all the murderers were known to her; all the witnesses testified that they knew the aggressors. The man who appeared at her door with a machine gun was the neighbor with whom she had drunk coffee the day before. Lieberman gives examples of other rape cases in which the rapists were known to the victims, and he also refers to testimony given by a physician who had been in solitary confinement for trying to steal bread. The physician was questioned by a military officer he knew from the town. When the officer entered the cell, the physician expected to be punished. Instead, the officer began talking about the physician's brother, whom he claimed to know well. He said the brother supported the Ustaša, a Croatian nationalist movement, and was currently in Sarajevo. The physician told him that was nonsense. What happened next was rather remarkable. The officer took the physician to the kitchen and gave him a plate of beans and bread. After the physician had eaten, a guard escorted him back to his cell. The physician had no explanation for this strange sequence of events. A military officer in a barbaric prison gives his neighbor a plate of food, and then has him locked up again. It is an often-repeated pattern—friendship is acknowledged, yet cruelties are carried out.[27]

Lieberman demonstrates that a neighbor can change into an enemy if his thoughts turn to the long-term history of nationalistic conflict. Stories about the "close relations between neighbors typically recall scenes of everyday life, of individuals as friends, classmates and colleagues,"[28] but stories about ethnic rivalry show the same people in a hostile light. Lieberman feels that the normal mental framework becomes a crisis framework that is based on myths of violence in the past and the role of the victim, in which neighbors and friends become part of the enemy nation. Furthermore, stories of personal relations fall within the chronology of everyday time; those of ethnic hatred are part of a much longer time trajectory, in which enemies have fought for centuries. The two stories are bound together in a destructive process in which they become accusations of betrayal and violence in the present. The neighbor or friend is now part of the evil group and must be destroyed.[29] Nationalistic stories can stir the fires of hatred;[30] once they take root in popular consciousness, they can lead to destroying each other.

Lieberman shows how the past and the present melt together; adversarial images from the past make today's friends and acquaintances seem like threats, thus erasing the personal histories of relationships. The good relations from the recent past now seem incomprehensible. This psychological process should be studied mainly at the microlevel. A preliminary study of Vukovar, a town divided between Serbs and Croats, shows the importance of doing such microstudies. In 2002 Dean Adjuković and Dinka Corkalo interviewed 48 Serbs and Croats;[31] they emphasized the sudden democratization of Yugoslavia and the creation of a number of political parties (which in turn made nationalistic parties possible) as a key factor. According to them, the problems began during the elections in 1990. The inhabitants had "feelings of helplessness, fear, lack of comprehension of what was happening, and unease about the future."[32] Their interviews are full of little details from daily life, such as a class at school that became divided. From 1990 on, things did not go well. Even good intentions were regarded as hostile, the low point being when a former friend offered no help in a time of need. Ultimately, Adjuković and Corkalo feel that the preeminence of the nationalistic story explains the nationalistic behavior. I find this unsatisfactory. Lieberman's cognitive dissonance seems a better explanation of how betrayal and cruelty are possible among acquaintances, friends, and neighbors. But that still does not explain the war and the violence in Yugoslavia.

The social psychologist James Waller examines this question, which concerns me and so many others, in *Becoming Evil*. How do normal people become murderers?[33] He distinguishes a number of moments in such occurrences.

In the first place, there is the *actor*, or perpetrator. According to Waller, the potential for evil is present in every person; what is crucial is not to activate it. Being capable of evil does not mean doing evil, and indeed the majority of us do not commit evil acts.[34] In his research, he looked for the context in which a person loses self-control, thus allowing the potential for evil to develop. Waller feels this can happen in a society that has lost its cohesion. Under those conditions, a "culture of cruelty" can arise, in which people become perpetrators. A prerequisite is the construction of the "other," one who gradually becomes the local victim and disappears from the perpetrator's world. Only then is murder possible.

When does a person lose his or her boundaries, when does the kind of behavior shown in 1995 and also in the years before become almost normal for a group of people? It is striking that, in Bratunac, when the victims saw what their friends and neighbors were doing, they appealed to their common past. To reject that appeal required a lot of energy and a major psychological deviation, which were aided by excessive amounts of alcohol. When all restraints have been loosened, the "other" becomes less than human and in need of extermination. In turn, shame exacerbates the situation. Proof that the "other" is less than human is required, and General Mladić set the example; he treated the Muslims as though they were dogs and showed not a glimmer of sympathy. Mladić modeled the behavior, and many Serbs emulated him.

The chaos of the aggressors' group violence is matched by the chaos of the victims. In the spring of 2006, Anna Albers interviewed Muška, who talked about how as a student she had experienced the division between the population groups:

> I watched informational programs on TV, programs dealing with politics. . . . Really threatening language was used—against a certain people or a part of the population. You realized that a government was talking like that, and that you could expect anything from people like that. So I was aware of everything and followed the developments. You attend school, you go there, also with kids from Serbia . . . and all of a sudden every incident becomes a threat; it's seen as rebellion.

She liked to go to the Serb cafés in town, but she no longer felt welcome there. "The atmosphere was palpable, so you left as quickly as possible. Everybody knew everybody there. It is such a small area, everybody knows everybody, even if they come from Serbia." According to Muška, everyone knew to which group a person belonged, but that was not a problem for her. She did her homework with Serb children. "And then it just changed . . . everything. I noticed that the attitudes of my school friends changed. You come to school and they say on television you have to be careful, this is a Serb country, and when you hear that kind of talk, you become very quiet. You don't want to be noticed. Because that's what it's all about, not being noticed."

It did not take long for her to realize that her Serb classmates had a different view of history, one that she could never imagine. She became increasingly aware that she had to be careful. This concerned her, and she talked about it at home. Her grandmother said that the time before the Second World War was also one of difficult relations between the population groups. "You heard it was a touchy subject—on all sides, I think. Every story has two sides." She felt the war coming closer; she expected it to be horrible. "You know your next-door neighbor is going to do something; you aren't part of a republic or another land—you're talking about your neighbor. That's what is so creepy. You didn't know how or when. The pointed talk out of Belgrade was clear; they would only protect the Serb people and Serbian minorities in other republics."

Her father worked in Belgrade, where he heard belligerent talk, a great deal of propaganda, and announcements. It was difficult to believe "that everything can get changed around. That you can't find a recognizable word or sentence. I was aware then that it had begun in Bosnia. . . . You know you should flee—but to where?" The war came, her communist youth ended abruptly, and her illusions were gone. It had been a good time. Her mother was at home with the children. On her 12th birthday Muška took the oath of solidarity as a pioneer:

> That was a kind of ritual. All that was happening in communism back then was fun. Children were made aware of their land from an early age. You took the oath with a cap and a red scarf. . . . You took

the oath and it felt like a party. All the celebrations, like liberation days and Day of the Republic or Day of the Country were huge events. That's how you grew up, you were aware of your country. I am Yugoslav, I am communist. That's how you felt. You're happy, you're a child. You're part of those things, you sing in a choir, but only songs about Yugoslavia and "The Internationale." That's the kind of thing you sing. I have to say, it was a pleasant and happy youth.[35]

Nothing remains of that happiness. Zejna, in an extensive interview with Arieke Duijzer, summed it up well:

> I get wrapped up in my story and sometimes I get lost in it, and then there's something in it that causes me so much grief and pain, and I don't know if that's important to you. We were concerned with the everyday, not that we were crying, but we had our worries. Srebrenica was one large concentration camp. People went crazy. You lost your will to live. You couldn't see any future. Every morning, every night was a nightmare. There were noises everywhere. There was shooting, and grenades were launched. Every day was full of grenades; you're awake and you're someone who just lives in fear.[36]

Two Stories

Despite the magnitude of the slaughter in Bratunac and the murders in the surrounding villages in 1992, the trauma of 1995 overshadows those events, and they may eventually fade from memory. Bratunac was the beginning, and Potočari brought to a close years of hunger and misery. For some, however, 1995 was only a temporary end to the misery (their lives have not improved much since then), and for a few it marked the beginning of even greater misery. Every story transects other stories, forming a chain of traumas. In oral history, following the experiences of one family and comparing the stories told by parents and children can yield new insights. The same event has different contexts and meanings for different generations.

On rare occasions, I had the opportunity to interview more than one generation in a family. The most remarkable contrasts were in the stories of Sevda and her mother, Šefika. I interviewed them about their lives before the war. Although both had been in Potočari, Sevda talked about how bad life had been before 1995, while Šefika talked mainly about how good things were then and how bad they are now. Both women tried furiously to show how they had moved beyond what happened at Potočari, albeit with great difficulty. Both had lost their husbands. Šefika also lost a son, one of Sevda's brothers. Both had lost many other family members.

The Daughter

Sevda talked lovingly about her early childhood; she had felt sheltered even though she was unhappy. Her mother had been cold and distant; despite that, Sevda felt protected.

> When I was a little girl, I went to school in the neighborhood. It was perhaps three kilometers farther up in the village of Bjelovac, close by. I went to school there, eight grades. My childhood was fine, but not like it is for kids today. I had to help my mother with everything. In the evening I studied, so I didn't have much time to go out; sometimes I could on Saturday and Sunday. My younger brother was with me when I went out. He was a year younger than me, so I could go to town with him or to gatherings.
>
> The house was big, big with two floors—a new house with two floors. Everything was in good shape; it was a new house. That's how I remember my childhood.

Her mother, who was a strict homemaker, taught her how to do household chores such as washing dishes, cleaning, and baking bread and pies. Her father worked in the mine at Sase; he rode the bus to work. The top floor of their house was rented out to people from Sarajevo, so there was not enough space. Sevda slept often with her grandmother, especially after she was too big to sleep in the same room with her brothers. "My grandmother lived nearby and was alone. She was my mother's mother. I went there to help her and then stayed overnight. Her house was next to ours." Sevda did housework for several of her relatives—her mother, great-grandmother, and aunt. She also attended middle school: "Other women asked why she let me go to school. I was late getting home from school. It just didn't seem appropriate. Girls who went to middle school were considered whores. But my father was good; he insisted that I go to school." He also wanted Sevda to work outside the home. She attended a civil engineering school, but stopped after she became interested in boys. Sevda's mother kept the boys at a distance and ranted about decency and propriety.

Going out on Saturdays and Sundays was a regular pleasure for Sevda:

> There were a lot of parties to attend, for example if boys went into the army. I took the opportunity to see a friend and have fun.

Bratunac was nearby and we could go out there. That was only possible on Saturday, because I attended school the other days. I didn't go out that much; I didn't ask my parents for permission, and I didn't whine about it. I knew what they thought, especially my mother.

Sevda stayed within the social norms; the most that happened with boys was a handshake. After the civil engineering school, she took a course in ceramics, and then a typing course. She tried to find a job. She dated her future husband for two or three months. "I didn't know him well, but I married him. I had met him at a party in the neighborhood. We were sending a fellow off to the army. I was there with my brother. He was a distant relative and we began chatting. He wanted to know whose daughter I was, and where I came from. So we chatted and got to know each other. He asked me to go out with him, and I accepted."

Her future husband was somewhat older than she was; like her father, he worked in the mine at Sase. He wanted to get married quickly. I asked Sevda about her dreams for the future. At that time, she had dreams; now, we were sitting in a shabby but comfortable apartment in Tuzla. She was a refugee who had succeeded in rebuilding her life, of which she was justifiably proud. "You know, when I attended middle school, I thought I was going to work. I've always loved to work." But her husband forbade her to work; she acquiesced and stayed at home. She kept house, washed dishes, and crocheted tablecloths, which she sold. Today, she would not marry her husband again.

She ran away with him. She had hidden some clothes in the outhouse. Her mother was shocked, especially because she considered her new in-laws to be unacceptable; she didn't care for him either. "I really don't know. He was just a bad seed, that's all. I had a difficult life with him. It was a dog's life. I came from such a good family, a peaceful family that didn't fight or carry on. And then I was in a big family and didn't know who was in charge or who did what. They all did as they pleased, and my mother didn't like that. Later, I didn't like it either. But how was I to know?"

Sevda wanted out of the home and the marriage, but her new family was tough and dishonest. "I didn't know them very well. They were neighbors, but I didn't know what went on in their home. I knew they worked, that they had jobs." Her mother also didn't know the family. "I didn't know what was going on until I had been in their house for a month. He hit his sisters and called them sluts; they didn't dare say anything to him. And if I said something, he'd hit me as well. He even hit me when I was pregnant."

The biggest trauma in Sevda's life—her husband's abuse—took place before 1995. Despite all she has been through, she has managed to build a new life for herself. She may be poor, but at least she does not suffer from anxiety attacks.

She has had much help, and is now capable of caring for her daughter. She is young, proud of her resilience, and wants to make something of her life. She can and does talk about what happened. The trauma of 1995 is appended to the trauma of her bad marriage. Since 1995, she has shown admirable strength in rebuilding her life. In my opinion, her youth was a key factor in her success.[37]

The Mother

Šefika, Sevda's mother, is about 20 years older than her daughter; Sevda is her eldest daughter. In contrast to Sevda, Šefika was keen to tell me about how good her life was before the events of 1995 and how desolate her life is now. The disturbed relationships between the Serbs and the Muslims still cause her distress. She also found the interview stressful, which led to complications with her diabetes. There were many interruptions. Sadly, the interpreter was too young to cope with the situation; although she tried, the gap between her life experience and Šefika's was too great. The interpreter could not understand the need for patience with an elderly woman who has to search for the right words to describe the unthinkable. Šefika lost her husband, a son, and a brother. In 1992 she lost a sister-in-law, and her son was one of the victims of the 1993 soccer field shelling in Srebrenica. Before the war, she had been a woman of standing. Losing her sheltered environment caused her great anxiety.

Šefika had learned about hate from what her mother experienced in World War II. Her mother's first husband was suspected of belonging to the Croatian Ustaša and was killed by the partisans. Šefika's story is intertwined with resistance to the idea that you can judge people by their origins. In the touristy village on the Drina where she rented rooms, Muslims and Serbs lived together. "Everyone prayed in his own way to God, but otherwise there was no difference. We were together when someone died or got married." In her mind, her life story is about her neighbors' violence against her and the memories of her life in Bratunac. That is the most important. Her husband was important in an Islamic religious organization, and she was a well-respected woman. During the interview, she clearly wanted me to understand this, despite the humble housing (a little row of cottages built by the Dutch) where she now lives. Šefika's poverty is painfully obvious, and she still finds it incomprehensible that she knew some of the executioners in Potočari. It was a nightmare.

> People heard that Mladić had announced he was going to kill us all, and no one was going to leave alive. And you know what happens when people panic. They were screaming, running, no one knew. . . . I also didn't know what I was doing when I left my house. . . . We never thought our neighbors would do something

like this. We thought they would save us in Potočari, that they would do something for us. . . . We recognized several neighbors. They came to us and asked about certain people and certain things. . . . We believed they would help us and also those who went into the woods. Srebrenica had fallen, that was a fact. We would leave if we had to, and of course there'd be a lot of screwing around with possessions and property. . . .

   When I see them now, I ask them, "Why didn't you help anybody, at least my brother? He was also your brother. . . . We all loved each other." They say, "We didn't dare. There was an order from Serbia, from someone, we don't know who." But I think a neighbor can help a neighbor.

Today, she still speaks to her old neighbors, "but I feel like they have blood on their hands, and wire to bind my hands or slit my throat." After the war, Šefika was beaten up in Bratunac by Serbs; the violence has not come to an end for her, and a new trauma has been added. Her world remains shattered and dangerous, although she thought that she would always be sheltered.[38]

   It is clear from the stories of mother and daughter that they have experienced the same history. They have both lived through the explosion of ethnic violence, the nightmare of nationalism, and the horror of genocide. The days in Potočari are prominent in both women's stories, as are the murders of the men in their family, and both women are justifiably confused and sad. Once we look beyond the main themes, however, we see two individual histories. The mother watched her sheltered life disappear and became caught in a spiral of downward social mobility. The incomprehensibility of what happened was amplified by paralyzing trauma, which made her confused and ill. Currently, sitting passively day after day wears on her, although she feels that her life is hectic. Indeed, it is hectic in her mind, where the images refuse to settle down. The daughter is attempting to move up socially. She realizes that she must put the misery behind her if she is going to prosper and give her own daughter a good upbringing. Forgetting what happened is impossible, of course, but Sevda's interview gives little indication of her traumatic history.

   There are many histories of Potočari, as well as many prehistories. What happened both before and after Potočari determines each narrator's vision of what that history is. Meaning is given to what happened in different ways, but all the stories end with the question of why a most satisfactory way of life—a world in which individuals might have been unhappy but which was still a good world—had to be brutally disrupted. And that disruption came at the hands of people they knew (even though it is clear that not all Serbs turned against the Muslims). Couldn't things have been done differently? Why did people let themselves get dragged into it? Had they forgotten how good things had been? And how can good friends change so radically? These questions spur a search for answers which might lead to clarity and perhaps even to peace.

Fazila, a seemingly ordinary story

Fazila found some of those answers in her faith. By becoming religious, she feels that she is living as her mother taught her to live. This has helped her to get through the difficult years. She now lives a tranquil life in Potočari and has opened a flower kiosk near the entrance to the cemetery where hundreds of men are buried. When I interviewed her, the kiosk was not yet open; she had just started a small greenhouse in which she was growing vegetables and flowers. Snaga Zene, the survivors' help organization in Tuzla, had arranged for her to use the greenhouse. Fazila's story is that of an ordinary woman living an ordinary life, but that was not the case before the war. She was married to Hamed Efendić, a leader in the Muslim SDA (Stranka Demokratske Akcije) party, who endured much in those difficult times.[39] Her story began uneventfully; it was about a woman who grows up, marries, and has children. She looked back on her youth in a solid and well-to-do environment.

> I can't say that my childhood was really happy, but I lived with my mother, with my parents. We were a happy family, because we were together. My father had a job and my mother was a housewife. I was their first child; as the oldest, I had to take care of the younger children. I was also the first child to earn money through working. Just imagine, when I finished the eighth grade, I took a two-month sewing course. I began sewing and gave all the money I made to my mother. We lived in the town, which meant that we didn't have another source of income, like farmland. . . . In that era, girls usually didn't go to school, at most primary school, but my father said, "I want my girls to be educated, so they can do what they want to." I think it's important to tell you that. I finished the eight years of school in 1967.

Her father died right before the war, and her mother at the beginning of the war:

> I came from a mixed marriage. Although both of my parents, Adila and Salih, were Muslims, my father was a communist. He grew up and went to school in an orphanage, because the Chetniks killed his father and brother in the Second World War. He never found their

graves. My mother's family accepted him, because my grandfather was an educated man who went to school in Brčko and Tuzla. I don't know exactly where he graduated and where he worked.

My mother grew up in a wealthy family. . . . Compared to my father, my mother lived in luxury. . . . My mother had a wonderful personality. She was brought up in a religious environment and was skillful. Although she didn't go to school, she could read and write. She knew many Islamic texts by heart and often we had to read to her. We read the texts to her. And when she was so sick, we read to her. We, her children, thought reading to her would make her better. That's how things were then.

Fazila was aware that her mother's discernment and prudence formed the hub of the family. "If people wanted to buy something or travel, they came to my mother for advice. They were all better educated than she was, but still they went to her." Fazila's parents disagreed about her father's enjoyment of going out, hunting, and having a drink. Her mother objected because Islam did not allow alcohol. "When we got older, my mother wanted my sister and me to marry into families that abstained, the members were religious, and the head of the family was a good man who had his affairs in order." Her first suitor was rejected because he was not sufficiently obedient to his father. Her mother encouraged her to go out with the man whom she ultimately married. Fazila's memories of that time are happy ones:

> I had a lot of friends. Talking about that past makes me cheerful and happy, because I enjoyed that time. I went to school and after school I went home or I went for a stroll. Back then, there weren't any cafés, so we would go for a stroll. We promenaded up and down, while the boys stood around and made remarks. It was delightful; I wish things were like that now. . . . I didn't know other people's religion. It didn't matter to me. . . . It did matter to me if someone was a good person. I never thought there would be a war, that we would fight with each other. I did think we might be attacked.

She married a man from a religious family and began to realize how uneducated she was.

> I really didn't know anything. I knew how to pray, but I wasn't accustomed to do so. May God forgive me, but I must be honest. My father-in-law asked me where I received my religious instruction. I answered, from my mother. He never asked me that again. My

spouse knew more about it than I did, because his father had taught him, but he usually didn't pray either. Just sometimes. During my marriage and while my children were growing up, I realized I should pray to God and fast during Ramadan. No one said I should, but it happened and came to a head before the war.

Fazila took a moment to reflect on her growing consciousness of Islam during the 1970s in Bosnia. She bought books, studied, and learned new things. That was important to her during the time before her mother's death; now, after the mass murder, religion is a way for her to survive.

Her husband's family milieu was an obvious influence. She had met him by chance. She was working in a shop after school; a young man entered the shop.

> Heavens! I had never seen such a handsome man. He was tall, slender, and good-looking. He asked for shaving cream and cologne; that was what men usually bought. I put them on the counter. It was an ordinary shop, not self-service. There were no adding machines then; I used to write out things in groups of 20 on a paper bag and calculate them. [But] I didn't have a pencil to write up the purchase. He took a yellow pencil with a lead point out of his pocket and gave it to me. I figured up his bill. I wanted to return the pencil to him, thinking I could do the math without a pencil. I had just started working in the shop, and he was my first client. He told me to keep the pencil. I looked at him—what a guy! And I kept the pencil.

When Fazila got home, she told her mother about the incident. Her mother was upset. Who were his parents? Was it a good family?

The young man did not return to the shop. Fazila didn't understand. Then one day, when she was cleaning the shop, she stepped outside to throw something away and saw him. Other boys were congratulating him. He had a new Fiat. She walked over, congratulated him as well, and shook his hand. Owning a car was unusual in those days.

> He invited me to go for a walk. I wanted to go with him, but I didn't accept. "No, I'm too busy," I said. I really wanted to go, but I couldn't, I just couldn't. I didn't know how it would go, so I made an excuse not to. It used to be that it wasn't a good idea to let a boy know you liked him or wanted to see him. That only made them vain, and then it was just a game to them. So I went home, and he was all I could think about.

A meeting was arranged. Because it was Ramadan, a prayer had to be said first, and he had to wait. Her mother did not find him particularly suitable, but Fazila saw him almost every day for the next nine months. I asked about the difference in lifestyles. Did things change when they married?

> My husband's family was wealthier. They had a great deal and they wanted to hold on to it. I found that somewhat unpleasant. In my father's house, if a dish or a glass was broken, it wasn't that important—can't be helped, so just buy another one. In my husband's family, that was considered major damage. They were critical about wasting things. We had to be frugal; you had to know where your money went. If you had to impress others, then it was done. My husband always had money, but he spent it only on what he thought was necessary, and never on going to a café or for things he didn't consider necessary.

Her father had always been generous, and spent money with ease. Now, money was something that had to be earned. Yet Fazila was content, despite the frugal lifestyle. There was enough of everything. They traveled, they were well dressed, and she was especially proud of her husband, who behaved impeccably, worked in the garden, and did not smoke. Admittedly, he did not help with the housework, but he did help to keep the house in order. That would change radically.

According to Fazila, the years before the war were not unusual—she had children, she had her own house, she made a career for herself. She went from the small shop to a large business, where it seemed that nothing could stop her success. In those same years, however, her world became troubled when her husband got involved in politics. He became a leader in Izetbegović's SDA. The party's importance increased as Muslim nationalism and opposition among the different groups grew. She did not approve of his involvement in politics: "I was also involved, but as a member, nothing more. He gave me a membership card; I kept it because his signature was on it. I don't like politics. I am who I am, and I don't like politics." His political activities began to dissipate their savings.

> He just handed out money while he walked around. He gave out the money and if I asked him why, he said that it was his fate in life. I consoled myself by saying that God had saved me from a drunk, but he hadn't saved me from this. I tried to comfort myself. You know, when things go wrong with someone, they just get worse. He just loved to help people as best he could. Everybody thought we had a lot of money.

For Fazila, politics stood for evil and in opposition to religion, which represented good. "If you are religious, if you believe in God, then you should stay out of politics. Politics means lies, shamelessness, and all those things that take hold of people. Religion does not allow that."

I asked about relations within their family, knowing that her man was under enormous pressure during 1991–1993.

> It was difficult. The most disturbing part was that he neglected our home, his children, and me. He only thought about other things, other people, about their situations and what happened to them. But what was my situation and that of the children? He didn't think about that at all. I had to care for the children all by myself. It hadn't been that way in the past. I had to make sure they ate, and that they had what they needed, this and that, . . . everything.

The region's official history confirms that Hamed Efendić was an important man. His status played a role in the entire interview, just as it did in other interviews with women who were married to "important" men. Being the wife of a well-known politician was difficult during the increasingly antagonistic politics of the early 1990s. Fazila's view of politics as evil is understandable. Her story does not include details of political events, but rather focuses on how her relationship with her husband changed. "Actually, I wasn't interested in his salary; I had no idea where the money went. Before he entered politics, I know for certain he didn't spend a dinar on anything but his family. He could handle money better than I could, but once he got into politics, I didn't know how much money he had and what he did with his salary. I wished I had money, so I wouldn't be hungry, so I could buy things for my children."

Along with the changes in her marriage came the slow march toward war. She and her husband realized it was too late to flee. "Too late, too late," she says now. Her story tells of a world of politics and public life, but within that world is her own small, private one.[40]

Much research has been done on gender differences in memory. But it seems that the differences between how men and women remember are sometimes fewer than those between women.[41] Male memories of the trek through the woods are obviously different from female memories of Potočari and the time before. (Only a few young women went through the woods and survived.) Mothers were often alone, caring for their children, during those dark hours. At some point, they were separated from their husbands, and they have been alone ever since. Memories of the prewar years and of how the war came are different for everybody. Those living in villages were suddenly confronted with a war they had seen raging elsewhere on television. Those living in town or in one of the villages where the Serb-Bosniak conflict was heightened felt the war coming a couple of years before its arrival. The memories of children who were in school at the time are different from those of the women who were older than 30 in 1990.

Can commonalities be found through all these memories of the prewar era? I believe they can, and they are delineated by feelings of betrayal by friends and neighbors and the resulting confusion. Such emotions are quite common, because nobody seems to understand how it all happened. People of different ethnicities began to exclude each other. Muslims watched Serb television programs with bewilderment, realizing they reflected a reality different from everyday life. That their neighbors might buy into that reality and distance themselves, or even take part in the crimes committed later, was quite a shock. People in mixed marriages left the region or—in the most appalling instances—some murdered their spouses and children at the appointed hour. (Most researchers today think such occurrences were rare.) All this was followed by the international community's betrayal and abandonment, which compounded the confusion.

The loss of meaningful relationships remains the most problematic. People one truly cared about suddenly went to the other side, scrambling one's emotions in the process. This remains a major preoccupation for the survivors, and overshadows the past history of the everyday. It is a critical theme in the disruption of their lives and is what they invariably tried to tell me. How was it possible that their good lives—lives in which women went through the normal ups and downs of marriage, had children, and, especially, grew old together with their spouses—had been so dramatically overturned? Why did this happen to them? Where is that lost world, that good world in which they wanted to watch their children and grandchildren grow up? Or should the cause of what went wrong be sought in that earlier world?

CHAPTER FOUR

LIVING ON THE RUN,
LIVING IN DANGER

*In most wars refugees flee because of the fighting. In Croatia
and Bosnia much of the fighting aims to create refugees.*

—Economist (May 23, 1992)[1]

I n 1992 it was not yet obvious that the flood of refugees was going to be so
large. The situation in Srebrenica deteriorated gradually from 1992 through
1995. The town became the final destination for thousands of Muslims,
because it was the only area where they thought they would be safe. They were
being driven out of their villages while Srebrenica was becoming overcrowded,
and food supplies were dwindling. Yet the refugees chose to head there, especially after Srebrenica was declared a "safe area."

Closing the door to one's beloved home while it was still standing and
while the Serbs were just a threat was difficult. In 1992, when Srebrenica was
taken by the Serbs for the first time, large groups of people hid in the forests
on the surrounding hills. It was a precarious, hand-to-mouth existence, with
no provisions and little or no shelter from the elements. Often, they were too
frightened to make a fire, because the enemy might see the smoke and start
shooting. Most people slept in the open air; many of the children became ill.

"Closing the door" should not be taken too literally; some had to jump out
of windows to save their skins. Escaping while the house was on fire—or while
being shot at—was yet another matter. At first, one might think that fleeing
one's home is the same for everybody, yet there are great differences among
the stories of those who wound up in the multitude of refugees in Srebrenica.
Having relatives to stay with in Srebrenica made a difference. For some, arriving
there was an enormous relief; for others, it meant camping on the street in the

rain and snow. There simply was not enough space in the town; every house was bursting at the seams.

Where to sleep was the major preoccupation of many women. Moving in with someone added to the overcrowding, and often household relationships were already strained to the breaking point. Those who had no family in the town knew they probably would not find shelter; if forced to go there, they were aware that they faced an uncertain future in the short term. Those who arrived in Srebrenica penniless and without relatives or friends in the town lived at the bottom of the social ladder in ever-worsening conditions.

In hindsight, Srebrenica was not the most obvious refuge, even after it was declared a "safe area." There was a growing awareness in the surrounding hills that the town was overrun with refugees. Several outlying villages were still accessible early on; town residents foraged there for food and talked about hunger in the town. As word spread that there was not enough shelter and food in Srebrenica, people tried to stay in their villages as long as possible. The fields around the villages were deserted, and some people planted crops there. As long as there were no land mines, the refugees could work the fields during twilight or at night.

In the interviews, many told about their first flight to Srebrenica or their temporary flight out of the town in 1992. This information is available only from oral accounts; there are hardly any written reports. This orally transmitted history was later overshadowed in their memories by the mass murder in 1995 and its preamble, the years of slow death in the ghetto. It is only through such narratives that we know about those first few weeks or months of being on the run, the first year in the woods, and how the women were not aware of what lay in store for them. They had not yet become inured to giving up everything.

Some of the villages were far away from Srebrenica; those refugees covered distances of more than 50–100 kilometers to flee threatened areas and to make their way via detours into the town. Such journeys were fraught with danger. Women walked for days carrying babies or with small children in tow across enemy lines. The weather made a difference. Snow meant that one left tracks that the Serbs could follow. Rain penetrated everything, and the children were soaked through. Often, there was no place to get dry and nothing to eat. For some, the flight went quickly and smoothly, and leaving home was the saddest memory. Most accounts, however, told of wandering through the hills of East Bosnia. Many women who were interviewed no longer remembered their departure; everything was overshadowed by how it felt to be afraid and exhausted. Having family with them made a difference, for example, if mothers and sisters were there to help with the carrying. Guidance from Bosnian soldiers also helped but was not always available. Most important was whether the family was still intact at that moment, for then there was hope of coming through it with all of one's loved ones and seeing each other in Srebrenica.

Anyone who interviews the women survivors needs to realize how important these details are, and how these variations in memory help us to understand the refugees' current existence. Individual suffering has its own history; it recalls moments other than those in the general historical picture. Accounts are no less important because they are individual. It is painfully sad that the experiences of all these women—who wandered back and forth, with children and sometimes with animals, usually with little baggage and no food, and who ultimately wound up in the town—are not mentioned in the historiography. Their "little" sorrows were not deemed to be worth listening to.[2]

This chapter is based on a combination of general information about the region, the accounts of many survivors, and an understanding of what it means to flee.[3]

Šuhra, whom I interviewed in a miserable barracks in a suburb of Sarajevo, was pushed farther and farther by the advancing Serb army. The soldiers began to dig trenches in the fields around her village.

> There were soldiers everywhere. We didn't understand what was going on. The soldiers invited all our menfolk to come to the school. Our neighbors from the village there were suddenly all in uniform. Whoever was Serb was in uniform. . . . The Serbs began to set fire to the houses of Muslims in the hills. . . . We couldn't go anywhere else, so we had to go into the woods. For three days, we ran away again and again and returned. On the fourth day, shooting began in our villages, and we ran away and never went back. We left our home for the last time and never returned. We took some belongings with us. We wandered here and there and stayed 20 days in the forest. My brother-in-law was carrying about 40 kilos [88 pounds] of flour. I made some flatbreads on an open fire. I built a fire and kneaded the dough. I had two tablecloths that I put the dough on. I rubbed oil in the frying pan and baked little flatbreads. Everybody got a half. We only had 40 kilos of flour and we could live off of that for 20 days. We also made a bathroom. We used sticks and covered everything with earth, so that people on the outside couldn't see in when you washed yourself or used the toilet. That was how we lived in the woods.[4]

They slept in the open air until they eventually improvised a small hut as protection from the raw weather in May 1992. When the food was gone, they had to leave. There was another place that seemed safe, and Šuhra's parents and brothers were already there. But the lines shifted and the next village was set on fire. There was no other option than to go to Srebrenica.

In *Returning to Nothing*, the Australian historian Peter Read examined what it means for an individual to lose his or her place in the world.[5] The loss of a home, familiar building, or village (e.g., by destruction) is incomprehensible to an outsider who knows nothing about the complex network that surrounded it. Leaving one's home means giving up a way of life—including its web of relationships —for the solitary existence of a wanderer who has no ties. Taking flight is a beginning; when that beginning has no end, it becomes a major milestone in one's life history. The misery of being on the run was shared by many displaced persons in Bosnia; incomplete families and overflowing orphanages are still common there today. In the case of Srebrenica, being on the run for long periods, combined with an extended stay in the "safe area" and later the massacre, led to a specific kind of traumatization that can be triggered repeatedly. After the 1995 massacre, all other memories became secondary. What happened has not been mentally integrated; it remains an enigma that no one understands.

Histories of refugee flight are usually written by observers. Few accounts have been narrated by the refugees themselves, except for the occasional interview with a journalist. The American historian Benjamin Lieberman noted that all modern accounts of refugees' stories seem similar; since the end of World War II, they have become a specific genre.[6] In any given war, one deportation tends to resemble the others. The end result is a massive displacement of people—by foot, on tractors, on donkeys and horseback, sometimes burdened with possessions and sometimes with nothing but the clothes on their backs. Only those who have experienced such deportations can describe what they were really like.

The best-known deportation accounts in Europe concern the forced marches of concentration camp prisoners in 1944–1945.[7] The Germans did not want their prisoners to fall into the hands of the advancing Red Army; the death marches were part of the attempt to kill people systematically through exhaustion, malnutrition, and shooting. The prisoners were already weak when they set out through the snow-covered fields of Poland in the late winter of 1944 and the early spring of 1945. But those marches cannot be compared to the refugee stories about Srebrenica between 1992 and 1995; the conditions were completely different. As the Serb army approached, the residents panicked and fled, without knowing how long they would be gone or what they should take with them. Everyone knew that the Bosnian Serb army had committed atrocities in the Drina Valley; when the army advanced on Srebrenica in 1992, inhabitants in the area feared for their lives. Murder was not the goal, but a tool. The goal was to rid the land of those ethnicities whom the aggressors felt had no right to be there. The ethnic cleansing in Bosnia was particularly vicious.

In the historical literature, there are numerous refugee memoirs from different wars, and several have been published about the fall of Srebrenica.[8] Such memoirs are usually written by educated people who find other matters more important than trekking from village to village and from one unsafe place to a seemingly safer one. There is also the genre of immigrants' stories, books about how it was to arrive, to acclimate, and to miss one's former land.[9]

Jasmina

Jasmina's story is one of the worst that I have heard. (Sometimes, though, I do not fully comprehend what words such as *worst* really mean. The image of a mother and a baby being without shelter for days in the snow haunts me.) She is not the only one who told of fleeing farther and farther repeatedly. All the women fled; once on the run, it could take a long time for them to find a place where they could stay for a while. But Jasmina is still camping out, because she has yet to find a permanent residence. She lives in Ježevac, the refugee camp I wrote about in an earlier chapter. Her position in the camp is worse than that of other inhabitants, because she was forced by circumstances to move into a small house with strangers. Nothing belongs to her; she is a guest. She lives in a tiny little room. She has a roof over her head, but nothing more. She has no chance of employment, even though she is a healthy, strong, and capable woman. Because she has no job to go to, she is cooped up when the weather is bad. Sitting with the other residents is not always an option.

A common problem for all Ježevac residents is that job possibilities are too far away or nonexistent. Doing nothing is even worse when one lives in a cramped space. In the summer, when the weather is pleasant, one can sit outside on the grounds around the little houses. The residents have lived without hope in close quarters for so long that there is no sense of privacy, yet the need for privacy is great. The residents cope as best they can, but there is little or no desire for social interaction. When Jasmina fled, she lost her home and her family. Her life came unglued; she is no longer a settled housewife, she has lost that identity. Now, she is a single mother, a widow, and a person with no permanent residence. When I interviewed her, her life had been that way for 10 years.

It was September 2005. Jasmina and I had met before, when I visited the camp in April of that year. At that time, she sat on the floor in her new living quarters; she had just moved in. The other residents were not pleased with her arrival. Their little house was already full (the camp houses truly are minis-cule). If a new family moved in, the already inadequate kitchen and bathroom facilities had to be shared with even more people. In March, the Grab Potok Camp, located a little farther up the mountain, had been evacuated. Only those who were elderly and ill were allowed to remain behind. (Given the drizzling rain, that may have been a kindness.)

The evacuation was done in phases. At the time, I wrote for a Dutch newspaper that there were "women in open trucks, sobbing children—emaciated because of the hard winter." They could only go to where the trucks took them, which was to the camp below.

> Return to Srebrenica has been possible since 2001, but the women and children, like so many others, are too traumatized to go back, or they no longer have a home there. The international community's policy is that return is the top priority; this is called "repatriation to the region." The policy does not take into account whether this is actually possible. Many refugees have psychological problems with the idea of returning, or cannot survive in a town where there is nothing to do.[10]

Some told me they were afraid there and suffered from nightmares; others did not even want to hear the name. They wanted peace and a better house somewhere else. Because those wishes were not in line with the official repatriation policy, usually nothing happened and the refugees were forced to continue living as they were.

Living conditions remained shockingly bad during the years that I traveled there. I often wondered why nothing changed. Even before the evacuation, it was difficult to imagine Grab Potok as habitable, if only because of the filth and the stench. Every time I went there, I was immediately surrounded by a crowd of children who apparently had too little to eat and never got any treats. The entrance to the wooden barracks was a smelly hallway; the doors of the individual living quarters opened onto it. Some of the units were decorated as pleasantly as possible, and sometimes they were comfortably heated. Others were bare and filthy. It all depended on the coping skills of the individual residents. But even the well-maintained units were rather dirty, and everywhere it was miserable. Some problems defy solution, and fighting the filth was a losing battle. The communal bathrooms were an invitation to a dreadful epidemic. Ironically, Grab Potok is located in a beautiful nature reserve.

In 2002 the former Dutch prime minister, Wim Kok, and the minister of development cooperation, Eveline Herfkens, visited Srebrenica. The Netherlands acknowledged its responsibility for the victims of Srebrenica, and agreed to take measures to help them. More hygienic conditions, stimulus for income-generating activities, and medical and psychosocial care were promised.

There would also be projects for the many children. However, as I wrote in 2005: "Up until now the people lived in barracks next to the main building in degrading conditions, without money and in tiny rooms. Depression is common and can lead to behavior ranging from suicide and psychosis to neglect or emotional damage to the children." The main building was intended for geriatric care, but no one wanted to go there; Grab Potok was at the end of the world and there was no real desire to help these people. They were regarded as a threat to the labor market and to the social order in general.

The reality in 2005 was still ever-present filth and traveling during rainy weather in open trucks. This was not good for those who had not yet recovered from a previous forced deportation; as I wrote then, the complaints were the same. Over the years, I noted that the Netherlands had not met its responsibility. In 2007, something finally did happen for the remaining 10 geriatric patients. They were moved to a different camp and are now being cared for. However, for the former residents who were forced to live in Ježevac during the time of my research, nothing has changed; indeed, nothing has changed for all the inhabitants of the camps. Ježevac is certainly no worse than many other places in the canton of Tuzla.

When I returned in September 2005, Jasmina was still dogged by bad luck. She and her daughter lived in a tiny room that was too small for two people. We could not sit outside, because it was drizzling. Jasmina just sat around, because she had no work. Her freezer was broken, so she could not freeze summer vegetables for the winter months. If she kept the room warm, then the food spoiled. Even the frozen chicken that I brought was a problem, because she had no place to keep leftovers. Jasmina had worked her entire life; her family was poor. As a child, she was not given affection and she was not coddled. She made a doll out of a scarf; there were no other toys, an indication of how poor her family was. Yet Jasmina never suffered as much hunger as she has in Srebrenica.

From the age of eight, she worked after school in the fields. She never had time to play. If she didn't work hard enough, she was whipped; the blows were aimed mainly at her legs. In the summer her dark hair reddened in the sun and her face was dark brown. Even now, Jasmina has a swarthy complexion—probably because she is of Roma descent. She didn't think that her life would ever improve or that she would marry. Life was nothing but work; there was only today's drudgery, no dreams of tomorrow.

When she had had enough, she ran away from home and married a divorced man who needed a wife. He had two daughters, whom she helped to parent. In the beginning, she was satisfied with her life, but then her own first child died. A long depression followed, which ended in 1991 when she became pregnant again. She gave birth to her daughter, Enisa, in the hospital in Zvornik. Jasmina gives Enisa the love that she never had, and Enisa gets all the love that Jasmina has to give. During her pregnancy, it was obvious that war was not too far away, but what could she do? Waiting seemed the best approach, because where could she go? She was happy with the baby and wanted to give her child a peaceful and healthy start.

In 1992 the family ran into the woods when Jasmina realized that the Serb army was coming. "I picked up my Enisa, she wasn't even a year old, and closed the door behind me. My mother-in-law was ill and stayed behind." In the evenings, they went into the forest, and they came back in the mornings. That was too dangerous for her husband, however; he stayed behind in the woods. The Serbs had already left the village and it didn't seem sensible to remain behind with the Muslims. However, "we couldn't leave, because of my mother-in-law." The Serbs threatened to burn the village to the ground, so the family moved into the hills, where they stayed for a year. There was nothing in the hills. A makeshift hut provided some shelter, but basically they lived in the open air. The family—Jasmina and her baby, her husband and his two daughters—lacked even the barest necessities.

"You're asking me how I felt? I had nothing to eat." Sometimes, the men fetched food from their old village, but that ran out. In return for food, Jasmina did some digging for people who hadn't yet been forced to flee. On occasion, she got some milk for the baby. It was a sorry existence.

> When there was fog, you could work the land. But if it lifted, they could see you immediately and they shot up the field. You had to run fast. . . . That's how I survived. Sometimes I went to sleep hungry. Sometimes I had nothing to eat for two days, and I gave Enisa the only piece of bread that I had. I worked, I plodded along. I had nothing, nothing at all. I looked like a skeleton. It was difficult; I had no coffee, nothing. Sometimes I didn't eat for a couple of days and I couldn't sleep because of hunger.

Of course, there was the baby: "The whole time I was thinking, I can die, but don't let her die. It was really difficult." Despite everything, the baby grew like a weed; she was lucky.

After living outdoors for months, Jasmina found a shed that the owner let her live in. She scrubbed it clean and whitewashed the walls. She chopped wood to heat it; the stove came from her old home. But that village also fell into Serb hands. "Cerska fell, Konjević Polje fell, all the villages fell. They captured all the villages. Then, messengers came and told us that we had to go to Srebrenica. I began to cry. Enisa was barely a year old. And I had to carry her. I took Enisa in my arms and picked up my backpack. I followed the Bosnian army. All the people were leaving, it was 1993. In January." Her husband, who up until then had been on the front, accompanied her.

> I walked for two days and two nights. I went with others through the woods. We came to Potočari, we came to the school. Soldiers were waiting for us. They saw that I had a small child, and so they gave me a plate of beans for her. There was no bread, only beans. I fed them to my child and we stayed there and slept. The next morning, the soldiers said that we had to go quickly to Srebrenica. Because where we were, we could be seen from Bratunac by the "others," and certainly from the Zvijeda mountain, and then they would begin shooting.
>
> We started toward Srebrenica. I think it was seven or eight kilometers, and we were on foot. I had to carry my little Enisa and the backpack with her clothes. When we got to Srebrenica, there were so very many people, I can't describe it. At one spot on the street someone had built a fire, somewhere else a person was busy trying to get warm, and at another spot there was a dead man. And so it was. I slept with Enisa for four days in the snow. No one wanted to take you in. . . . I had no place to go. Everything was full. There were so many people, it wasn't just us. There were people from eight different villages.

According to Jasmina, during her first days in Srebrenica there were at least a thousand people in the snow. People chopped wood and made fires on the street to warm themselves. Jasmina couldn't gather firewood; that would mean leaving her child with someone, and she didn't know anyone.

Mother and daughter found shelter in a school; at first, they lived in a classroom with 80 people. Things were a bit better there, but the windows had no glass and the thin plastic sheets covering them let the cold in. But it was dry, and that was good. Later, the Red Cross intervened, and they were moved to another location; the refugees were given mattresses and some help. I asked how she kept her child clean. She made a fire outside and boiled the clothes. Jasmina got up at three in the morning. At that hour, it was safe to fetch water in the dark as she could not be seen and shot at. She carried the water in jerry cans. She also washed her own clothes outdoors. Jasmina has a strong constitution, and apparently her child does as well. They had already lived in the hills for a year. In the middle of the Bosnian winter, her situation was precarious—as it was for many others as well.[11]

When I interviewed her, Jasmina was still physically strong, but her social position was not. She belongs to the lowest level of Bosnian society, where there is little possibility for improvement. Those still living in the camps in 2005 were the weak and the truly destitute.[12] They were different from the women I interviewed in the towns and the cities. No one can claim that the people in the camps are poorer—everyone is poor—but the degree of displacement is much greater there. The feeling that one's life has not settled down in any sense dictates the tone and the manner in which the story of the journey to Srebrenica is told. Being harried began more than 10 years before our interview and had never let up; every attempt to take control of her life had failed, and there is no future because there is no clarity. What happened—and why—remained incomprehensible to Jasmina, except that, like everybody else, she knew the Serbs were dangerous.

The villages were guarded by the men. Soldiers came and gave orders and everyone knew what had to happen. At some point, it was decided that the situation was too dangerous, and the women and children had to leave. But it was almost never obvious where they should flee to. If the men were physically strong, they went somewhere else to help with the military defense of the territory. It is apparent from most stories that the women and children were watched over by the soldiers and protected as much as possible. But does protection matter if the only sensations are fear and freezing cold? Even worse, these women were caring for small children who were often starving. It is almost unimaginable, a woman with little ones in the Bosnian winter—yet the lives of refugees are almost never imaginable.

Ramiza had heard that people were being killed. "We were ready to leave. I went back to the house briefly to get some food, because I knew that my little girl would ask for something to eat. But they were already surrounding the houses." Ramiza slaughtered a chicken and packed some provisions that were already cooked. "I did not know where we were going. Suddenly, there was gunfire, but you couldn't tell where it was coming from. At that moment I wasn't sure that we could escape without being wounded. There was a wooded slope above our house. They shot at us, but missed. Maybe we were just lucky." She succeeded in reaching the woods. "My child wanted to eat. I had to hold my hand over her mouth, so no one heard her crying. We had just started to eat something when a bullet hit the birch above us. We had to crawl away, and I dragged my child along with me."[13]

Variations in Poverty and Misery

Housing in Sarajevo and its suburbs is often poor. I have visited many former barracks that were not suitable for habitation; people lived on top of one another, without comfort or privacy. To have a bit of privacy, some slept in the attics, where there was almost no heating. Downstairs, there were apartments; depending on the location, some had their own bathrooms. Residents who lived in those apartments were the lucky ones. Usually there were two rooms, one for living and one for sleeping. Often, they were occupied by large families or by several single women with their families. There is also the threat of eviction, or at least a perceived threat. The Bosnian government wants to close these centers; it encourages the residents to return to their old homes. The government conveniently ignores the fact that most of that housing no longer exists, and money to rebuild is slow in coming.

There also seems to be a deliberate policy of renaming the refugee problem in the hope of defining it out of existence. When the refugees arrived, they were housed in buildings, or collective centers, that belong to the state. These buildings (e.g., schools and barracks) were needed again for their original purposes, and "collective lodgings" were built, mainly by foreign NGOs, specifically to house refugees; Ježevac, Mihatovići, Tišća, and Karaula are examples. Some were large camps, others were small-scale projects, such as the one in which Ramiza lived. Some refugees landed in houses deserted by Serbs. However, many of them lived under threat of eviction, because the previous owners could legally reclaim their property. Most collective centers have been closed. As a result, the idea that all the camps have disappeared seems to have taken root among a number of Bosnians. They listened to me with disbelief when I explained there had been only a name change.

One problem at all these centers is that many residents do not know how to apply for the various funds that are available. This is not unique to the survivors of Srebrenica. Evictions and not being able to return are the order of the day in Bosnia. What is unique is that a number of the women would not choose to return to Srebrenica even if they could do so. The memories are too horrendous and the difficult living conditions in the villages surrounding the town are well known. Also, it would mean returning to a completely displaced community.

Some are in a better position to cope with the situation. There are societies and organizations of survivors in the Sarajevo suburbs who help each other.[14] Many (especially among those from Srebrenica) are reasonably well educated, and their cultural attainments did not disappear after the massacre. They are not just a mixed group of people from rural areas; there are teachers, skilled medical personnel, and engineers among them. In their collective fight for recognition, honesty, and return of their property, these people have acquired new skills. And they have become a new group, which is engendering social and cultural cohesion. That is certainly how I would describe the associations of women survivors. Despite their traumas and painful poverty, these women have taken the opportunity to undergo a rapid intellectual and political metamorphosis.

A myriad of social patterns are intertwined, yet poverty and dislocation run through all of them. It is possible to have a discussion with a well-groomed woman in the offices of an organization, and then learn that she lives in the greatest misery. I met families living in lovely new houses close to Sarajevo, yet their lifestyle was still that of being on the run. I also visited families who have succeeded in building new houses on the edge of the city or in one of Sarajevo's suburbs. They plan to stay there and have made peace with the fact that they can no longer live in Srebrenica. They would never feel safe there, because the place calls up too many memories. They are coming to rest and building a new existence. Sometimes, the new house has a bit of ground that is used as a vegetable garden.

This does not mean that the survivors now live contented lives. They are mainly families without men, or families whose men escaped through the woods. Perhaps there is a son who was young in 1995 and is now in his late 20s or older. Tensions abound. The refugees have not found peace; in a sense, many are still in transit. The house and the land that they once owned in Srebrenica might still exist, but the fear of returning to nothing—an unknown nothing—predominates. Once, there was a place where they belonged, but that place is now gone. Beginning in 1992, people lost not only their material possessions but also their sense of belonging. Leaving home has meant giving up much more than a house.[15]

Devleta, life as a refugee

Devleta, who lived high up in the hills for a year before joining the masses in Srebrenica, told of this loss. I interviewed her in Ježevac, where she lives with her mother-in-law and her children. She is an energetic woman who cares for her elderly mother-in-law. She has no choice, because there is no one else who can help.

The little house in Ježevac where they live is a variation on all the attempts to make a refugee camp cottage into a home; the pleasant space is a credit to Devleta's boundless and admirable energy. She is also able to look back on her life without bitterness:

> I had a good life. I had my own house. I had a good marriage. I never thought that I would witness all this and that these things would happen to me. I lost my mother when I was little. I was poor. And precisely at the moment when my life began to get better, when one of my sons was three and the other five, rumors about war began. My husband worked in Belgrade. He came home for the weekend, but then he wanted to return to work. He was stopped at the Ljubonski Bridge and couldn't go farther. When he came home, he said: "This is the end. There is no life for us here

any more." Panic crept into people. People in the village became worried and looked for hiding places. My husband dug a trench where the children and I could hide. We spent one night in it, but it was unbearable. Around three in the morning I went back home; by then I didn't care about the danger.

When day broke, I went to check out another village close by and saw that a lot of people were pulling out, one after another, in tears. My father-in-law felt that I needed to take the children and leave. I cried, my children cried. Where should I go? What should I take? I really didn't know what I should take with me. Of course, I would take the children, but what would they eat? Where could I find shelter at night? I didn't have anything to cover them. I couldn't take everything. I only took a blanket, a piece of bread, and some eggs that were cooked. I was in tears when I took my children and left. I joined other people on the road. We went up into the hills. We got to the top and spent the night there. In the morning, my husband came and brought me a backpack with clothes for the children and some food. From that time on, occasionally I went down to the house. My father-in-law remained behind. He hid when the village was set on fire. . . . He made sure that there was food for me to take to the children. That was a hard time, really hard.[16]

After a year in the hills, Devleta wound up in Srebrenica. She had a miscarriage there when she heard that her brother had died at the front.

To the Town: Srebrenica Fills Up

The structure of the stories is similar; the refugees could not hold out in the woods and hence went to the town. Magbula, who now runs a nice restaurant in Srebrenica, also ran away. I interviewed her in 2004 in her restaurant. She is very active in trying to improve the economic life in Srebrenica. "We went into the hills, to the woods. We went to villages that were hidden away, far from the border of the river Drina, far from Bratunac. Then, a month later, we walked to the old town of Srebrenica."[17]

Mejra was also in the woods: "Yeah, we were in the woods. We didn't dare stay in the village. Later, the village was burned. The Serbs walked around every day, plundering and setting houses on fire; they destroyed houses with forklift trucks. Some people had binoculars and watched. There was a gigantic forest above the village that belonged to the state. It was so large that you couldn't walk through it in a month." She went there. Her husband worked for the forestry department; he knew the way. She told how the livestock in the villages were burned alive and how she could hear the bellowing and screaming. "We went into the forest in April, before the village was destroyed. The snow came up to our knees. We stayed there until the fall. But later, we had to come down. We couldn't stay there any longer, because winter was coming. It was too cold for the children to sleep under the birches. There was no food. No one had brought food, because we left in such a hurry."[18]

Srebrenica was often the end of months of flight from the surrounding villages via other villages. Mothers were always looking for shelter and something for their children to eat. There was too little of both, and people went hungry. Improvised huts in the forest and shelled-out houses in villages were pitiful hiding places to sleep in. Some also slept in constructed trenches covered with plastic sheeting. The surrounding Serbs were relentless and shot wherever they suspected that people might be living.

In the stories about the war around Srebrenica, and also in those about the siege of Sarajevo, sitting cooped up seems to plays a major role. Families with and without children sat in the shadowy darkness of a house with nothing to do, waiting in fear. Would they or wouldn't they come? Would they start shelling or shooting at the house? The refugees sat in a house—preferably one that offered protection against grenades—where there was no electricity, so they sat, deathly afraid, in semi-darkness. (In the woods, it was worse; they could not make a single sound.) The children also sat; they could not go outside. If a patrol passed by, they had to be still.[19]

Mejra Hodžić hid above her village with a small group; she told about walking and sleeping in snow that came up to her knees. Later, when winter began in earnest, they had to leave the hills. The children could no longer sleep under the trees, and there was not enough to eat. It was too dangerous to return home, so she went to Srebrenica. She had taken little with her because she had left home unexpectedly. The same was true for Šuhreta, who had suddenly seen soldiers approaching. Her son recognized Arkan (the feared leader of a Serb paramilitary organization)[20] in one of the vehicles, so Šuhreta ran into the woods. To this day, "it breaks my heart to look at the forest." She trekked from hamlet to hamlet.

> We were refugees, hungry and without clothes, without shoes. Everything was still at home, the livestock, our food supplies. You arrive at someone's house and they give you supper, but never breakfast. We trekked on farther in the night. . . . We foraged in the night. When the wheat was ripe, we harvested it in the night. Sometimes, we walked the whole night long with our belongings on our backs.[21]

There are no exact data on the number of refugees. It is generally assumed that between 35,000 and 40,000 people were in the Srebrenica "safe area" between 1992 and 1995. Not all of them came in 1992, when the Serbs retreated after conquering the area. In that year, Srebrenica was a place of war and violence; just like elsewhere in East Bosnia, it was a place to be avoided. But even then it was miserable because of the influx of refugees; there were simply too many people. In 1993, grenades hit children playing on a soccer field. Images of the incident showed the world what was happening there, and Srebrenica was declared a "safe area." After that, the stream of refugees swelled.

In March 1993, *Le Livre noir de l'ex-Yougoslavie* was published.[22] It was the result of a collaboration between *Le Nouvel Observateur* and Reporters without Borders; the proceeds went to *Oslobodenje*, the only remaining newspaper in Sarajevo that still defended the idea of a multiethnic society.[23] The volume brought together what was known about the region, assessed the state of affairs, and described the misery two years before Srebrenica became famous as the scene of a massacre. At the time, world attention was focused on the siege of Sarajevo. According to reports, more than 850,000 people were in flux,[24] but in July the estimate grew to more than 2 million. No one knows the exact number; counting is impossible when so many persons are in transit.[25]

A World Is Lost

Fleeing while being shot at is rather common in war; one leaves in a dreadful fright. While on the run, some were probably aware that, if their homes had not been burned or shelled, other refugees would probably move in. A home is a part of one's identity; often, it is a significant part of the family heritage and is on land that was acquired through hard work. The livestock that grazes on it are also of great personal value. In agrarian communities, assets are not portable and are closely tied to place and tradition. Stories that are woven around the land and the house create the fabric of a family's culture. To give that up is to give up one's identity as the person who lives in that house, on that street, in that village, and the status that goes with it. To leave all of that behind is a complex psychological process; it also begins a downward slide in social mobility and the refugee usually ends up at the bottom of the social ladder.[26] A refugee goes from being a respectable citizen to less than stateless,[27] a penniless wanderer who is dependent on the charity of others.

Zejna, who was interviewed by Arieke Duijzer in the Netherlands, regretted that she did not realize she would never return when she left her home.

> I was at my sister's house in a village near Srebrenica; then the war came there as well. It progressed from village to village. We fled on

foot, about 30 kilometers, maybe it was 50, with a bag of clothes and nothing more, with another woman and her children. When we locked up the house, it felt like we would be back. We didn't say goodbye. If I had known, I would have looked at everything one last time and said goodbye, perhaps taken something with me. You didn't think it would come to this, I saw no reason to.[28]

Neither did they know where to flee to; they just left. The idea of going abroad (where many ultimately wound up) never occurred until later to those whom I asked about it in interviews. Many had never been abroad before; they were in shock and wanted it all to stop.

What remained was the daily fight to stay alive, and that fight is not over. Many interviewees live on approximately €30 per month and still suffer hunger on a regular basis. Comparisons are difficult because price levels are different. It is sufficient, however, to look into their faces, for example, at the embarrassment of a woman who cannot offer even a cup of coffee to a guest and immediately uses whatever her guest has brought her. Bosnia is a land where hospitality is shown by offering food. I did not mind if there was nothing to offer me, but the interviewees often did mind. Everything revolves around food, both then and now. The hunger began in the early days of war, and it began with fleeing.

If one could stay overnight where there were provisions and get something to eat, or if one could stay overnight with family or acquaintances, then one was far better off than those who were truly adrift. Nura, who lived in the Mihatovići Camp when I interviewed her, had gone to her mother's house when the war broke out.

> When I got there, she had a supply of food, so we didn't have to buy anything. I ate with them, I slept in their home and sometimes in my sister's home. She helped me a great deal. I stayed there for a while. But the days passed and there was no shooting, nobody threatened us, and nobody came. We still had electricity. I felt no danger there. After about 20 days, we saw smoke. My village was burning. You could see it from the hill. People kept watch, even if there was no danger. People made rounds here and there. They saw that my village was burning. A nephew came to tell me that. I was concerned about my husband and his family, but three or four days later he came and stayed with us.[29]

Her in-laws were with her the entire time. But when the food ran out, they had to leave.

We went to a house farther up in the region. We lived there by ourselves. My sister brought me food and prepared meals. She brought me flour, clothes, and shoes. I didn't have to carry anything. I don't know how long that went on.

I had gone to fetch water when the men began shouting that the Serbs were getting close to us, just past the nearby village of Goden. They started shooting, so we had to go up on the mountain, to land that we had above the village. Everybody in the village had some land on the mountain. We made huts with conifer branches, to hide in and to sleep in. My husband succeeded in bringing a cow and a calf, and I believe five or six sheep as well. But we had to slaughter them, because we had nothing to eat. We remained on the mountain for days, but we quickly ran out of food. We hadn't been able to bring anything else with us and we had to look at our situation realistically. My husband had a hunting rifle. He was a hunter, but he had to sell the rifle for food. So he didn't have a rifle any more. While we were there, the army ordered us to leave, so we went down from the mountain. . . . I carried the child; she was so small and almost died during the trek. My husband led a horse, which was carrying the few things we had and our remaining food. He didn't want me to walk too close to him, so that there was less chance we would both be killed—that way, one of us would survive for the children. That was how he thought. We traveled for eight hours. There were lines of people, but you didn't hear anything, not a word, nobody spoke, nothing. . . . Soldiers went out scouting and came back. All of a sudden, we heard dogs barking. We were afraid and thought that someone was there. Luckily, we could continue. There was nothing. When we arrived in our area [the enclave], we sat down and rested a bit, but we didn't really dare stop. It was a narrow path and we had to walk in single file because of the land mines. You couldn't leave the path. . . . Finally, we arrived at my sister-in-law's home in Srebrenica.[30]

Rich or poor, leaving one's home and not knowing what the future would bring was a disaster. I interviewed Kadira in Ilidža, a suburb of Sarajevo, in the office of the Women of the Podrinje. Kadira has a place to stay now, but that is all. According to her, the survivors of Srebrenica no longer have a place in society and make up its lowest level. She has not found a permanent residence. When the war broke out, she was pregnant. She gave birth at home, because the local hospital was in Serbia and she could not get there. Kadira was warned of a coming attack, so she fled into the woods. Later, she started toward Srebrenica with her husband, brother-in-law, sister-in-law, and mother-in-law:

> First, we went to a village that was already barricaded. There was a large hill, so I asked my husband to leave me behind in the woods. I had just given birth, and it was difficult for me to walk. I asked him to take the baby with him, and to leave me behind. But they didn't want to leave me behind. They waited a bit and that night we passed the barricades. We reached the village of Poloznik, where our people were and where the Chetniks hadn't yet arrived. My husband asked a woman to take me in, so that the baby and I could sleep there. There were a lot of people, and the village inhabitants couldn't take in too many. But a woman let me spend the night in her house with my baby. We stayed there a couple of days. Our men had to go back to our village to get food, because the people who gave us shelter couldn't feed us. In a couple of days, they began shelling the village and attacking it. We fled to another village, Petinići. A man gave us shelter. There were 17 of us in a room no larger than this one [approximately 16 by 20 feet]. We stayed there a couple of days. Again, our men had to forage for food in a nearby village. They usually went to our old village, because there was plenty of food there. We were farmers, so there was enough to eat. Some went and never came back; they were killed . . . some of them. . . . It all depended on your fate. We were extremely anxious about whether the men returned or not, because they had to go through enemy territory.[31]

They had to set out again; this time, the journey was more difficult, and many of them died. It took 22 days to reach Srebrenica.

Kadira lost her husband, a brother-in-law, and other relatives. When she arrived in Sarajevo in 1995, she moved into a house abandoned by Serbs, which seemed a good solution at the time. Her story was structured around her eviction from that house years after the war was over, and how difficult it was to make ends meet. She also complained bitterly about how local and regional officials in Sarajevo dealt with the refugees, although she knows that others were also evicted, and that such occurrences were common. It took a long time for her to find shelter after the events of 1995; the first time was in Tuzla, and she talked about the wretched circumstances that she encountered there. Although the core of her story is the trauma at Potočari, it is shot through with feelings of displacement. She still does not know what the future holds for her, and this causes her anxiety. Any feelings of being at peace do not last long.

Running for Your Life

Although men were not the only victims of violence in 1995, they had reason to be especially apprehensive throughout the war. They were responsible for defending the region and they served on the battlefront, whether they wanted to or not. In *Postcards from the Grave,* Emir Suljagić recounts how there was little choice in the matter; men were rounded up and taken to the front lines. He tells of a small bus that stopped in the center of Srebrenica; men were forced to board it.[32] I have been told that in the early days it was impossible for an able-bodied man to refuse military service. And in 1992 it still seemed possible to fight back; men felt that they could defend their villages and homes, and could stop the opposing army's advances. They briefly succeeded in 1992; months before Srebrenica and its surrounding areas were declared a "safe area," it was retaken by Bosnian soldiers. Naser Orić was the local warlord associated with this.

Being on the run was especially dangerous for men, because they could be taken prisoners of war. In a book of testimonies regarding Srebrenica published in 1999, Witness 16 tells how he fled in April 1992 with 101 men and 3 girls. It is one of the few accounts of the bitter trek through the snow, and it was written by a man—no shivering children were involved. It took approximately 30 hours to reach Srebrenica by foot. At one point, the group had to cross an asphalt road: "But then we were spotted by a watchman from the road maintenance station. We watched as he examined the place where we had crossed the road with a flashlight. We went further. The snow cover on the ground got deeper; we were already far into the Birač mountains. . . . I realized that we had begun to walk in a circle, probably because of the cold and the heavy snow." The refugees scattered after being shot at, yet managed to regroup. However, they had lost the trail.

> We began to ramble around in small groups, while the Chetniks brought in reserve troops, transport trucks, and dogs. Luminescent rockets streaked through the heavens. There was machine gun fire all around. My toes were frozen, I couldn't even feel them. I hallucinated; I thought my mother was bringing me pancakes. Some froze to death during the trek; most were taken prisoner by the Chetniks. I continued to wander around with eight other men for five days and nights.

They succeeded in reaching Srebrenica. But for months after that, "I lived through the heaviest days of hunger and enemy attacks in Srebrenica. I couldn't walk normally because of the frostbite I had suffered."[33]

Of course, it was not only dangerous for men. Vahida[34] narrowly escaped after her village had been encircled. She tried to save some belongings. Not all the houses were set on fire at once; the intention clearly was to chase the inhabitants out of the villages. Finally, the women and the frail also left. About a thousand of them gathered on the banks of a small river. Several soldiers joined them, some of them armed. Under their leadership the refugees formed columns and set out for Srebrenica. When crossing asphalt roads, they had to watch for vehicles and wait until the road was deserted. Half crossed over while the other half waited. They also had to get past the Serb trenches.

> The soldiers ordered us to be very careful, and told us that not a single child could cry. There were a lot of small children, and a couple of older ones. Sometimes they were carried. There were also three-day-old newborns. My own grandchild was five or six days old—but you didn't hear a single child cry. We were in between the trenches when God sent the wind and covered the moon with clouds. It got dark and the wind blew, saplings bent to the ground. As soon as we were past the trenches, the moon came out again.

A bit farther up, the group was threatened with gunfire.

Vahida did not make it immediately to Srebrenica; she landed in the nearby village of Milačevići, where women with small children and babies were given shelter in homes. The men were sent to stay in school buildings. Again, there was shelling, and many people were killed. There was no food, there was nothing. "All we had was what we could carry in a bag. We had to leave our provisions, everything, behind. The houses were burned, the stables were in ashes; all that was left was the livestock, cows and sheep. Everything was left behind. . . . We had nothing. We had to depend on the compassion of others in order to survive. It was May when we arrived, and we stayed there until June." She reached Srebrenica via a number of detours.

People ran in order to save their skins. Sevda[35] told me: "They shelled us with grenades. When they attacked during the day, I picked up my child and ran. But we came back that night." The men watched the village while the women fled.

> I carried my Alma and had a bag in my hand. I was on the banks of a stream when a grenade landed nearby. It was such a blow that my child fell out of my arms and landed in the water. She was only a year old. When I got to the next village, she was blue from the cold. But there was no real harm done; she survived it okay. The grenade landed so close and scared me so badly that I let her slip

out of my hands. But I caught her. It was not a large stream, so there wasn't a lot of water. She just fell into the water. I picked her up, wrapped her in a little blanket, and kept running. We ran along the stream, because it was easier to avoid the grenades there and it was the shortest way. In the little village that we reached, there were more women and children, but everybody shunned me. If you have a small baby, it cries, and if they hear it they throw grenades. We arrived in the village; we were hungry and thirsty. We came to a house and went inside to eat something, but we didn't dare make a fire. If they saw a light in a house, they began shelling immediately. Everything was always so close; they could see everything that was between the hilltops. When evening came, we hid in the cellar. It was not a bomb shelter, but we wanted to be together. I don't know how many of us there were. Women and children from an entire village hid in that cellar.

In such cases, there was nothing to do but to sit during the day; closed up in shadowy darkness, often unwashed and uncomfortable, the sitting seemed endless. It turned out to be a prelude to the waiting in bomb shelters in Srebrenica. Since then, waiting has become a way of life for some; they still wait for the husbands and the sons who never return.

Unwelcome Visitor

Hanifa came from a small village located high in the hills and now resides in Ježevac.[36] She related the following:

We hadn't decided [what to do], but their soldiers came to our hill and chased our army away. . . . Their army was stronger and they came to our hill. First, they set fire to the village of Tumače, then it was Cerska's turn. Our army, or rather the commander of our village, ordered us to go in the direction of Kravica, where some from our village were already. He said that we had to go to Pervani and that the following night the army would come up with a solution. So I started out, without shoes. I only took a bit of food with me—it was Ramadan—a bit of bread. We had made coffee, but we left it on the stove, where everything stood ready for our evening meal. It was dark. We had received orders to go. There was shooting; we went along the river and didn't dare to take the asphalt road. Those who took the asphalt road didn't get very far. We were going to Srebrenica. Some were murdered en route, but my family survived; only my son-in-law, my daughter's husband, was killed. We went from door to door and asked if we could spend the night. Darkness everywhere. But people did not let us in. They asked why we hadn't fought back.

Hanifa continued to be refused when she asked for shelter. Even a school that was being used as temporary housing did not let her in.

> Snow and ice, it was March 10. No one wanted to let us in the school. My daughter, her child, and I sat in the snow. And I was expecting. I was pregnant in 1992. So we sat in the snow, my two girls and me. An old woman came up to us and said that we could come in, but we could only sit; there was no room to sleep. So we were allowed to spend the night in the school. We sat in a room, the teacher's room. The old woman was there with her two grand-children, her daughter, and two other people. We sat there in the same clothes we had on when we left; we had no evening meal. I had brought my cow, and I milked her. Yes, I had brought a cow—I still had a small child! We drank the milk.

There was constant bartering for a place to stay while they were in the village. That got worse once they were in Srebrenica and there were fewer and fewer items to swap for shelter.

From Hanifa's perspective, we can see the coldness and inhospitality of the people who turned her down. She is still justifiably angry about it. But there is another perspective; the inflow of refugees was immense, and this woman had a cow with her. People had to draw the line somewhere; there were so many outside in the cold and the snow. This was true both in the villages and in rapidly expanding Srebrenica. In such a situation, of course people took care of friends, family, and themselves first. Sometimes, I asked those who had homes in Srebrenica about this. Then I realized it was not fair to judge those who knew their provisions were being depleted.

"Why didn't you defend yourselves?" was the question asked over and over again. It was a way to keep the needy refugees at a distance. Later, the question became "Why didn't you flee sooner?" Well-meaning Serbs asked this of the refugees at Potočari. It put the responsibility on the victims and allowed the questioners to disengage. While fleeing from Sase, Šuhreta was asked time and again why she hadn't defended herself:

> So we were submissive to the people who took us in. We had to keep our mouths shut in front of those who allowed us to stay in their homes, but we were grateful anyway. When all the hills and

the villages in the hills had fallen, when the whole area around Srebrenica fell, we had to go to Srebrenica the town itself. I was lucky; I had livestock with me. I had a cow, a few sheep, and a horse. I milked the cow and each of my children got a glass of milk. There was also a piece of cornbread, but no wheat bread. [But] it was enough to give you something in your stomach. While we were in the villages, I slaughtered my sheep and we ate them. But when I was in Srebrenica, I had nothing. Nobody had anything. Those were hard times.[37]

Fleeing from Ethnic Cleansing

Some refugees ended up abroad during that time. Although they were no longer in danger of being killed, there were problems adjusting to a different culture. Some nations (Germany, for example) had a good reputation among refugees. It was better not to wind up in Hungary, where the warring Bosnian ethnicities were put in the same refugee centers.

Some Bosnian Muslim refugees who were sent abroad were treated like second-class citizens. Zehta no longer remembers how the war began,[38] but she does remember how shocked she was when she landed in Slovenia. When I interviewed her in 2004, she had recently returned to Srebrenica. The town hall where she worked had been stripped bare; the plan was to refurbish it in the coming years. She started crying early in the interview, when she remembered how she had left the town. That was when her normal existence ended.

> That day, all my illusions fell like a house of cards. I couldn't believe that a war we saw on film had begun right here on my doorstep, right before our homes. We tried to say that war could begin anywhere, except in Bosnia, because we lived with each other. One home was Serb, and the other home was Bosniak; for 50 years we had lived with each other without problems. And all of a sudden, someone had to move out of the area, because he was Serb or Muslim.

She could have taken a bus, but that would have meant leaving her two older sons behind. She ended up in a camp in Slovenia.

> It was dreadful—three families in one room. There were seven people and four beds. Can you imagine what it was like with seven people, including a baby, living together in a small area? That was difficult for those of us who had lived comfortably before. Srebrenica was a wealthy area, and we didn't know what it was like to have nothing. I had a lot of money, but at that moment, on that day, money became worthless. I couldn't buy a thing, not even

bread for my child. You realize that you don't have anything, and you don't know what to do. Those were difficult moments.

The former residents of Srebrenica were treated as though they were uncivilized peasants: "The manager of everything there—I don't know how else to describe it—who was later replaced, used us as a target for insults. He abused the children—at least I consider what he did as abuse. He brought candies and threw them down; the children fought for them on the ground. Then he took photos and sent them to others to show how the Bosniaks behaved." He called them Gypsies or Kurds.

Nothing went right, everything was unpleasant. "Food is prepared totally differently in Slovenia than in Bosnia. In the beginning, there was not enough to eat. Meals were prepared in a group kitchen and then brought to our building. There was a dining hall, because before the war this had been an assisted living facility. Before we arrived, Croatians had been placed there." She explained how small the food portions seemed to a Bosnian, and how a number of things were new to her. In particular, she was not used to eating beans with pasta. In Slovenia, peppers are eaten raw, but in Bosnia they are cooked. Her greatest fear was of inadvertently eating pork.

She had left in April 1993, but in November she was back in Tuzla, where she took an English course. She was aware that things were worse for her children in Srebrenica. "The thought of my children living in that hell, that they had nothing to eat, no shoes, that my home had been burned to the ground in 1992, it was enough to make a mother imagine just about anything. I am well aware that my experience of the tragedy of Srebrenica differs from those who were there." She had known that something was going to happen, but had not imagined that it would be such a tragedy.

> Years have passed, and I still have the feeling that I am dreaming. This didn't happen to my land and my people. No matter how great the wounds and the pain, I see it all as in a dream, a mystery, something that I cannot explain. Nobody wants to restore this town. We get angry when we hear that a lot of money is sent to Srebrenica. I say that Srebrenica is not Tuzla, Sarajevo, or another town. Srebrenica is Srebrenica. If someone wants to send money, then it should be done in the proper way, because it is nasty when people donate and nobody knows where it came from and who got it. We were promised things, and we trusted that they would happen. We are still living on promises that were made to us.

Stories of living on the run are about more than moving from one place to another. They are also about the meaning that is given to the events and about the psychological consequences. In contrast to what usually happens to refugees, many of the women I interviewed did not move from one land to another in the beginning. In this war, people fled within their own land and culture to an area where their group was dominant, so the usual adjustment problems were not present. Although they all experienced downward social mobility, the same language was spoken. Even though the refugees were not welcomed at the end of their flight (and no one can deny that too many died during flight), being on the run within one's own land is different from fleeing to a land with strange customs. Traditional ties were not completely broken. Those who fled to Srebrenica in 1992 and 1993 were going to a "safe area," an enclave that was temporarily designated for the Muslims in the region. The hostile reception was the result of overcrowding, although some had family and friends in the town to mitigate this. However horrid the situation was in 1992, refugees then were in a different position from those who fled in 1995 after the fall. The shock and trauma were not the same. The fall in 1995 ended years of decline into poverty and misery. In 1992 and 1993, one could not have foreseen this; although the social network had been damaged, the context and the ties had not disappeared completely. In 1995, everything was lost.

Living on the run before the events of 1995 has almost faded from the collective memory of the survivors, even though the history is now known far beyond the region. All of Bosnia seems to have a story to tell about fleeing, and this fits with the kind of war that took place there. The stories about trekking to Srebrenica are overshadowed by what happened later, which was so horrible that everything else seems to have fallen away. Still, whoever interviews survivors hears almost immediately about what it was like to be afraid and outside in the snow, after having left home without a proper farewell. "I became lost," Devleta's mother, Šida, told me. She was one of my oldest interviewees.

> I also lost my sanity. . . . I know nothing any more. I don't know what I am doing. How could it be otherwise? My only child, I so wanted to have a boy. . . . We never got any help. What can I do? I'm an invalid. Nobody gave us money or anything else. What can you do? Nobody cares if you can't work. What am I supposed to do? A living person can't go lie in a grave. If they had just given me a bit of money. I haven't received anything since I came here, and I'm an invalid. A person has to eat and drink. I have nothing. People are surprised that I live with my daughter-in-law. I'm grateful to her. She takes good care of me. But what else can I do if I have nowhere else to go? She doesn't have any money either! . . . Nobody wants to help us, to send us something. Nothing. Not a single package, not a bit of money. So here we sit.[39]

Why is there no help for these survivors?

CHAPTER FIVE

A HUMAN SHOOTING GALLERY

Srebrenica 1992–1995

The massacre in 1995 tends to make us forget the period between 1992 and 1995, when life in Srebrenica gradually became unbearable. All the interviewees talked about how difficult life in the town was during those years. After the Serb capture in 1992, the Muslim population fled into the hills; when the town was "liberated" from the Serbs later that year, there was a massive flight to it in the hope of finding safety. The original residents were flooded with requests for shelter and help; people from the villages camped out on the streets and were regarded with suspicion. The years 1992–1995 were also years of tension between the two groups of Muslims. The *opstina* (town government), which consisted of original residents, had to find ways to deal with the flood of refugees. As more villages fell, more refugees arrived in the town, destitute and looking for help. But that was not the only major problem: the shelling of the town caused ongoing chaos.

After Srebrenica's liberation in 1992, the Muslim residents returned to a ghost town. Looting had been rampant, and for the first time houses had been set on fire. That would happen more frequently, until the town was almost reduced to rubble in 1995. There were many dead on both sides; the death rate for 1992 was high.[1]

Those who were residents of Srebrenica before the violence and slaughter of 1995 are now almost invisible. It is difficult to imagine them as average people with normal feelings and values who enjoyed a good standard of living. Even after being driven out in 1992, they were not yet the victims of genocide, but people with futures, hopes, and aspirations. During the war, they adjusted their values and lifestyles, trying to preserve what they considered to be good. Old values do not simply vanish in a war.

The behavior of Sarajevan residents as they adapted to the norms of war while attempting to preserve what was good has been studied by the anthropologist Ivana Maćek.[2] She regards adaptation as a method of survival and suggests that inventiveness is a form of resistance.[3] People created a new "everydayness" and a new normalcy with infinite variations. The story of Srebrenica in the years before the fall is similar to that of Sarajevo. In both cases, the local populations suffered a lengthy siege, but things ended differently in Sarajevo; although many died, there was no genocide. The world's attention was focused on Sarajevo, while the people of Srebrenica felt abandoned and wondered why no one came to their aid. They watched the skies, hoping to see planes that would bomb the Serb positions.

The United Nations' decision to declare Srebrenica a "safe area" made the original residents and the refugees feel protected. The inhabitants lived with their UN "protectors." They welcomed the strangers into their homes and helped them when they could. They considered that to be one of their duties. Even when certain soldiers behaved badly, the residents were aware that their protection depended on them and thus tried to maintain good relations. At that time, the inhabitants could not have known that the UN guarantees were worthless and they would not be protected. That is why there is such disappointment in so many of the interviews.

Besides the NIOD and NGO reports, there are many eyewitness accounts of how life in Srebrenica was during 1992–1995. The reports vary, and many firsthand accounts are diametrically opposed. I have deliberately chosen to focus on the perspective of the survivors of Potočari, and on their problems with their memories of what happened.

The process of remembering at the time of my interviews was complicated by the legal process against the Muslim warlord Naser Orić at the International Tribunal. Many surviving Bosniaks remember Orić as the liberator of Srebrenica in 1992. As a leader of raids for food, Orić was accused of atrocities committed when the raids got out of hand. Furthermore, according to the charges, atrocities against and murders of prisoners had also been committed under his command. He was found guilty of only the latter offense; as commander, he should have stopped the violence. In defense of Orić, a number of survivors testified about how dire the situation was in the overcrowded town. The trial transcripts contain harsh descriptions of starvation and of rape and murder by the Serbs.

It is the responsibility of the International Court of Justice to judge both sides for the atrocities committed; this book does not deal with such matters. One of the NIOD researchers has a list of all of the known incidents committed by both parties.[4] There were victims on both sides, and some of the murders were too brutal to recount. It is indisputable that both sides pillaged and committed unconscionable deeds. The Bosnian army could not control the starving mob. Hunger was a motive, but the archives also reveal revenge, hatred, and blood thirst. There was something more going on, something that had gone wrong much earlier.

Looting (but not murder) was a tradition in that region of the former Yugoslavia. In feuds between neighbors, it was common for one side to plunder the other's property. It occurred in every war and even in overheated conflicts; it was considered "normal" behavior in such circumstances.[5] When the inhabitants of Srebrenica were being starved as part of the deliberate strategy of ethnic cleansing, their only options were to loot others, or to find provisions in a more legitimate manner by making the dangerous trek through the surrounding hills. People also occupied abandoned Serb residences in the town. "Some people wound up in apartments that were full of things. The owners had closed the door and left," one woman told me.

In the following, the memories of the women and the problems they currently have with those memories are examined. It is important to remember that the women are not impartial—no one was. It was war; there was an "us" and a "them." People's memories also differ due to their individual social circumstances, for example, their age at the time and if they had already lost loved ones before 1995. Not everyone in the town was equally miserable; neither did everyone regard their neighbors as the enemy from the beginning. Indeed, the old ties made it possible to smuggle messages to the outside world, and in the years 1993–1994 there was trafficking in food (although there wasn't much food to be had) with the Serbs. More problematic is remembering that both sides committed atrocities in the war. Everyone is aware of this, but even today there is still a division. "It was unavoidable, so there's no point in regret" stands in opposition to "It was unforgivable, and we can't go any further without admitting this."

Especially in the stories of younger women, the earlier period was not as miserable as the one that followed. It was a time when many marriages were intact and the men in the families were still alive. It was a horrid, cruel time, during which many lives were lost, yet some people still experienced everyday happiness. From early in the war, the new state of Bosnia regarded the crimes of the Serbs as genocide, precise criteria for which had been laid down in 1948.[6] The Bosnian state submitted a complaint to the International Court of Justice in The Hague as early as 1992, and in 1993 a complaint regarding Srebrenica was added to it, but the court ruled on it only in 2007, when it declared the events in Srebrenica to be genocide. Earlier, the ICTY had already judged Srebrenica in those terms. Before 1995, no one knew what was going to happen, although it was obvious things could go very wrong and a possible takeover of Srebrenica did not bode well for the town's inhabitants.

Writing the history of the years before the massacre requires extracting it from what happened in 1995. In the beginning, there were probably just as many murders in Srebrenica as elsewhere. Comparing the town with other places where the war raged does not reveal a significant difference. When Srebrenica was declared a "safe area," the situation changed because of the blockade.

Alma Mustafić, who was interviewed by Lara Broekman, was a child during that period. She told what it was like to be little in the overcrowded town:

> Everyone knocked on our door, asking if maybe we had a room for them. At a certain point, the house was overflowing, because my father couldn't say no—he was such a good man. . . . He kept saying, "Yes, come on in, come in." It came to a point when our whole family was living in the living room, even though we had more rooms upstairs—one large room and two smaller ones. Originally, the smaller rooms were for my brother and me. There was a big family in the large room, and two smaller families in the other two rooms. Then my mother said, "That's enough," because my father wanted to take in even more people. He said something like, "Come on, we have a huge living room; it can hold a lot of people." But my mother told him, "No. I gave up the whole house to other people. I want the living room for us, for our family." And that was a good thing, because . . . you can't offer everybody shelter. And then . . . people began knocking on our door and asking if we had something for them to eat. I thought it was dreadful, opening the door and them asking, "Do you have something to eat?" And we never sent anyone away. . . . Especially when children came, I found it awful. There was a little one, a little boy; he was quite chubby, and he came every day. My mother always had something put aside for him; he was her favorite. We didn't even know his name or who his parents were, but my mother had a soft spot for him.[7]

Many opened their homes to family members, as did Ajša, who now lives in Srebrenica. She cannot imagine herself being happy anywhere else. She came from a small village to the town to get married. Those were happy years. When her family from the village fled to Srebrenica, she didn't think twice about taking them in. "My house was full. You couldn't move; the living room was packed." Unlike many others, in 1992 her family stayed in the town. "We stayed, because we thought nothing would happen. We were here the whole time." She did flee into the hills behind her house during the first days of 1992, but she remained focused on the town and got her food from there when possible. She returned to the house with great caution during the nights for food and to milk the cow, so the children would have milk. But she could not continue living in the woods; she still becomes emotional when she talks about camping out there with her small children.

Ajša remembers how conditions in the town deteriorated. People lived in every available shed; stovepipes were stuck through windows in order to have fires without chimneys. They ate catnip mixed with flour. I asked how she managed to find enough food for all the people in her home.

> We shared. What else could I do when all my family came? I didn't have enough rooms to give all of them shelter. One of my uncles lived in the room upstairs. . . . Another uncle lived in bad conditions in the garage. I tried to give each family a room. They cooked for themselves, but I tried to help. I did what I could. I had a garden and I told them they should grow some things for themselves, that they should plant something. But I didn't cook for them. I gave them what I could, of course, when they had nothing and I had something.[8]

When her father-in-law's house was shot to pieces, Ajša took in his family, which included small children; they stayed with her for one night, but it didn't work. She still becomes agitated and sad when she remembers the two youngest children, whom she could not help.

The growing filth and worsening conditions irritated her. "There was no water, no electricity, everything you needed was broken. If you wanted to do laundry, you had to fetch water from somewhere else." The Serbs had undermined the water reservoir, so there was no running water. Fetching water was just one thing that had to be done; there were countless chores, including gathering and cutting firewood. Foraging for food and standing in line for water were signs of the times.

Images of Misery

The situation in Srebrenica has been extensively studied by the researchers of the NIOD Report; that material is based primarily on reports from a number of NGOs and interviews with NGO members in Srebrenica. The inhabitants were helped by Doctors without Borders (Médecins sans Frontières, MSF), the Swedish Rescue Services Agency, the Norwegian People's Aid (Norsk Folkehjelp), the Movement for Peace Disarmament and Freedom, and the United Nations High Commissioner for Refugees (UNHCR).[9] I was able to review some of these organizations' reports. They all had the same goal: to alleviate the most urgent needs of the refugees, many of whom were homeless. The Norwegian report gives the impression (perhaps because of its reporting method) that their aid also focused on preserving what I would describe as a "civil society." The Norwegians not only built houses and provided the basic necessities, but also seemed most sensitive to the refugees' daily lives. In 1995, the authors noted, the town's original inhabitants tried to bathe and stay clean and to lead relatively normal lives. "They looked down on the refugees who lived from hand to mouth, didn't bathe every day, stole, and suddenly had become very religious."[10] The refugees (especially the women) were less educated. They were less "civilized." Refugees had approximately one and a half square meters (less than five square feet) available to them in a world without electricity, water, mattresses, and the like.[11] It was not uncommon for 10 people to live in a room that was only four square meters. The NIOD Report noted that the town government and the help organizations estimated there were 43,000 people in the enclave, most of whom were from the surrounding villages. It might have been a couple of thousand more or less; the figures are only an indication. Especially in the town proper, there were proportionally more refugees than original inhabitants.[12] The Swedes were especially active. In just a couple of months, they built Novi Sveskigrad (New Swedish Town) close to Srebrenica. Thousands of refugees found shelter there.

Control in Srebrenica was in the hands of the original residents, who had more access to relief supplies. That control was tainted by internal divisions and power struggles between council members, who belonged to a new Muslim elite that had acquired political power in the years before the war.

Reports from Doctors without Borders show there were periods when the average daily calories consumed per person amounted to approximately 1,000; the lowest point was in the autumn of 1994. In 1995 this increased; approximately 1,500 calories per day per person were dispensed by the government.[13] Salt was a serious problem; the Serbs made certain it did not reach Srebrenica. Doctors without Borders seems to have been the most knowledgeable regarding such needs. It distributed food and, later, seeds for planting. The organization had direct contact with the local government, the *opstina,* but its success was mixed.

In 1993 an opportunity arose to evacuate children from the town in three convoys organized by the United Nations. Negotiations went on for weeks. Trucks were so overcrowded that suffocation was a threat, but between 8,000 and 9,000 women and children were evacuated;[14] the men had to remain behind. Parents sent their children to unknown destinations, and the great heartache began. Local authorities worked against the evacuations, fearful that they would contribute to ethnic cleansing in the enclave. As a result, the original residents of Srebrenica were not allowed to leave.

In 1992 photos of severely emaciated men behind barbed wire at Omarska in West Bosnia had stunned the outside world. In 1993, before Srebrenica was declared a "safe area," photos of the miserable conditions in the enclave shocked the world again. The images of Omarska were stark and had been manipulated to make them reminiscent of the concentration camps, ghettos, and mass starvation in World War II. But the conditions depicted in the photos are assumed now to be true. In 1993 the French general Philippe Morillon penetrated the Serb blockades around Srebrenica to check out the conditions firsthand. Morillon stayed in the town a couple of days, but then found it impossible to leave. The townswomen had organized a human barricade to stop his departure; if Morillon left, they feared, they would be sitting ducks for the Serbs. It was the women's first action as a group; after the war, they would form a variety of survivors organizations. The women allowed Morillon to leave after he promised the town protection, and they trusted his word. His guarantee gave them new hope, which lasted for some interviewees until the summer of 1995.

At the time of our interview, Hafiza Malagić lived with her family in a suburb of Sarajevo and was active in Women of the Podrinje. The women who had fled Bratunac knew each other and created a network, just as many others did. Hafiza told how she fled the region around Bratunac and wound up in Srebrenica as a refugee just as Morillon arrived. Understandably, in her memory the events are a tangle of stories.

> Morillon was in Srebrenica then. Later, he wanted to cut and run. One person said to sit in the road so he couldn't go forward. I don't know exactly what he wanted. . . . We were told Morillon wanted to scram, and if he did, we'd be left behind and murdered. So women and children took to the streets. We stood there in shifts, one group during the day, another one at night. We relieved each other, but I don't know what happened then. I didn't know if he stayed or how he left. I stood in the street, because if you're scared you don't have a choice. It meant that, if the Chetniks came, they would kill us all. It was a large group of women—everybody was scared, so everybody went.

In the follow-up to her interview, Hafiza talked mainly about her bad memories:

> It was frightful in Srebrenica. It was frightful to live there. It was unlivable. Fear and hunger. Four or five families lived in one

apartment. It was frightful; I don't know how to tell you about it. We were scared. And when they started shelling the town, we hid ourselves. We were afraid to walk around. But the worst was not having water. We had to search for water and sometimes walked three, four, or five kilometers. And when we found water, it was so crowded that sometimes you had to wait two hours to get two half-buckets of water. We had to stand in line. In the evening, we left our buckets in the line, and then waited the next day for our turn, because sometimes you only got your turn the next day.

There was food in the beginning. People brought food with them from elsewhere; people had planted gardens in the villages and sneaked out during the night to fetch food. Some people had so much food that they had enough until the food convoys came. But even when the convoys came, there were people who had and people who didn't. . . . In 1993 we could get by because we got some food from the villages, but at the end of 1993 and in 1994 there was no food anywhere and the convoys couldn't get through. The biggest problem was the lack of salt. You can't eat without salt. And it cost 80 marks per kilogram [2.2 pounds] when it was available on the black market. Who could afford to pay that? Nobody. . . . It was especially a problem for big families. At times, my brother's children went without bread for three days.[15]

Even though everyone was poor—including the original inhabitants—and it was difficult to keep one's head above water, not everyone descended into beastly behavior. Many chose to try living as normal a life as possible and to maintain at least a modicum of social dignity. It is noteworthy that in such situations there are always people who try to maintain the infrastructure needed for a civil society, which watches over the affairs of daily life, including the needs of the weakest. Srebrenica was not unique in this.[16] Education was arranged for the children, so the town would have a future after the war; classes were organized for various groups in the mornings and the afternoons. There was a makeshift hospital in the town (admittedly, without medicines and cleaning supplies), and there were also a number of primitive electric generators. According to the interviewees, many tried to retain their self-worth despite the prevailing misery.

Rukija sat shivering in her cellar. She is one of the older interviewees and now lives on the outskirts of Srebrenica.

One night, I was in my house when a shell hit the bakery; it broke out my windows. I screamed in fright and ran into the cellar; I stayed there for two years. My neighbors usually came to my house for protection when there was shelling. I had a little stove in the cellar for making tea or soup or something else. If I wanted to bake bread, I had to go upstairs. I mixed it quickly and baked it, if I didn't bake it in the cellar. I baked it quickly upstairs and then took it to the cellar and ate from it for a couple of days. We used up all our supplies, there was not enough of anything, we were hungry. That's how we lived. . . . People used to say that a person could hide in a mouse hole, but we couldn't hide ourselves—not in concrete, not in a mouse hole, nowhere.[17]

Many of Srebrenica's original inhabitants tried to help, but often they were taking care of family members who had come in from the villages. It was a strange world: a void surrounded by danger, a world in which there seemed to be nothing to do. "Walking up and down was the most important activity for men, children, and boys; the only change in that pattern came when a convoy arrived or the International Red Cross brought mail. The women were often the only ones who worked; they tried to keep their households in order."[18]

Because many of the men were on the front lines, the task of organizing a civil society fell mostly to the women. They did not try to replace the men's world of local government during the war, nor did they take part in the strategic defense of the town (although there were women on the front). The tasks they took on were a natural extension of traditional women's work. They were quite busy trying to cope with the new conditions.

Sabra remembers the beginning of the various women's groups and especially the need to keep the town livable. Today, she is active in the Sarajevo branch of Mothers of the Enclaves of Srebrenica and Žepa, which is where I met her. In the first interview, she told me about her background and her work for the soldiers who lived in the compound. In the first part of the second interview, we discussed the attempts to keep the town reasonably habitable. The first action was to set up a schedule for fetching water to clean the stairwells in public and apartment buildings. Elderly people also had to be helped. It was not just about the necessities to survive. They attempted to offer people in the town a life of some sort, because having nothing to do can lead to depression. After the library was destroyed by shelling, a small group of women rescued the books damaged by water, and cleaned and dried them in the sun.

It was the library. I lived at the end of the town, near the hospital and the post office. When I heard the library was in rubble, we went to work there. Other residents saw how we managed to save a part of the library and how we got more done as a group. We women, as a group, kept our houses clean and also the surrounding area. Other people saw that and did the same. We also helped at the hospital. We fetched water for it, changed the bandages for the wounded, we washed sheets that were brought to us. We cut those sheets into pieces, washed them, and made bandages from them. . . . The hospital had been looted. They took everything, bed linens, everything. Nothing was left in the hospital. A group of us women organized, and collected some bed linens from our homes. We also went door to door asking for similar articles and we helped in the hospital, because there were only three doctors. Sometimes, 50 or 60 people went to the hospital at the same time. . . . Later, more people came to the town. There were shacks next to the embroidery factory with older men who had no one to help them. We visited them, washed their clothing, and cooked food for them. We tried to help them a bit.[19]

After the Serbs left in 1992, there was an enormous amount of rubbish. More than 80 houses had been destroyed; cars and trucks had been stolen; and there was constant shelling. What was built one day was destroyed the next, and every day there were sick and wounded. Help had to be offered in an organized way. The NGOs supported these activities by what would later be called Zene Srebrenice, and praised the organization in their reports. Sabra told me: "We all contributed something. We tried to keep the street in front of our house—the area where we lived—clean. We tried to normalize life. The problem was that we didn't have anything to clean with, no soap, no detergent for dishes and laundry. There were older people who had survived the poverty of the last war, and that had been even worse." Those survivors taught the women the old ways, such as using ash with hot water as a disinfectant. "That killed all the bacteria."[20]

Efforts were made to restore the town's social cohesion. People had to stop loitering on the streets and start doing useful things. The streets needed to be clean in order to restore public services. The doctors in the hospital and at the front needed a great deal of help. All in all, it was an enormous task, causing many differences of opinion on how various things should be done. The *opstina* did not want to cede its power to the NGOs, but wanted to decide who did what and who helped them. At first, those who helped were not paid in money, but in food or supplies. During previous times of war in post-communist Yugoslavia, that had led to labor unrest and work stoppages. The NGOs found Srebrenica's government to be a legacy of the former bureaucracy in which politicians knew how to turn an emergency into a political advantage.

Individuals can also try to uphold the old norms and not give in to the despair and maliciousness of war. Razija is such an individual. She is an older woman (b. 1937) who has returned to Srebrenica. She had dressed up for the interview; I was glad that she was happy with the attention and my visit. I found talking with her a pleasure; perhaps by that time (December 2005) I also had become used to the interviews.

For Razija, being well-mannered is synonymous with finding ways to live with each other. Before the war, she enjoyed good relations with the town's Serb residents. She believes people should help each other. She lost her husband, who was 60, early in the war. Her life had been good until that time; her children had grown up respectably. Her husband had been a shoemaker and her son helped his father in the shop after he finished working at his regular job. Shortly before the war, Razija's son started receiving his salary in goods rather than money.

> Just before the war broke out, he brought home a lot of packages of chicken, which I froze. He also brought soup, biscuits, bags full of many things. He said that was now his salary. I told him it was wonderful, because we had to buy those things anyway. As long as we had that food and flour, we got along quite well. . . . We managed to survive. [Later,] we suffered hunger until the air drops started. Life got somewhat better later. There was ready-to-eat food in the plastic packs, some coffee, salt, sugar, a bit of everything— just enough to survive. Later, we received humanitarian food aid; then things really got better.

The real misery for Razija began in 1992; understandably, she began talking about it early in the interview. That was when her husband was so frightened by a shelling that he died the same night. Her memories of that period are important because those were her last days and weeks with her husband. Together, they had watched as an entire row of houses was set on fire. Her memories of the beginning of the war have not been covered up by the horrors of 1995. His death was the great rupture in her life—for her, the memory of the war is not Potočari, but his death. Since then, her life has changed in ways that she still cannot fully comprehend.

No one was left to care for her. Her son had left the town before the war began, and her daughter lived in Sarajevo. Although Razija's house was not burned, when she went outside, she saw smoke from other houses on fire, and she couldn't bear to look.

> People were scared. You fought just for yourself, you didn't get mixed up with anyone else. I was especially afraid of being hit by grenade shrapnel. What would I do? I thought, people have relatives, but I have nobody. What should I do? My husband was dead, I had been left behind. I was surrounded by strangers, people from the villages. None of my people were there. I couldn't count on anybody. Later, when the UN soldiers came, people living abroad

sent money to their families. My brother sent me some money, and my sister's daughter-in-law and a cousin. So I could buy flour, salt, and coffee. When I first got the money, I decided to buy coffee, no matter what the price. There were people who brought coffee from Žepa and sold it. I bought some and invited my neighbors over. They said, "Wouldn't it be better to make coffee for yourself every morning? It will last longer that way." But I thought, as long as I have it, I will share it. I can't drink it alone.

During the entire siege, she had nothing to do. Her existence became monotonous; all she could do was hide and wait.

I didn't dare build a fire during the day. They could see smoke from the chimney, so I only made a fire when it was dark. There was no electricity. It was like in the films I watch now sometimes, with the electric poles on the ground and the wires in the street, a terrible sight. And nobody walked in the streets. It was dreadful. And when they began shooting, I was paralyzed with fear. They were shelling at four in the morning, so you couldn't sleep well. All we did was hide. We went from one house to another, from one cellar to another.

Razija had running water in her house, because she was connected to a local creek. She did not mind sharing the water with others and letting them in her house. "I let everyone use it; I refused no one."[21] Occasionally, she also helped with their laundry; in return, people sometimes gave her soap or fabric softener. Being single, her rations were tiny, but that was no reason to deny people the use of her bathroom, even though it was a great deal of work to keep it clean. It was her way of showing respect to others and earning their respect.

Razija's story (and there are others) counterbalances the claim that the many refugees were brushed off by the original inhabitants. But sometimes, working for one's own survival was difficult enough. Magbula, a woman who now works energetically to rebuild the town, was glad when she could return after fleeing the Serb capture in 1992. She and her husband had been warned that the town was not safe, but the longing for warm food and a bathroom was too great.

We were filthy and the children had lice. After a month in the woods, I wanted a bath. We came down the street [from the higher part of the town, Stari Grad, which means New Town], where everything had been destroyed by fire. It was raining dust and ash. I will never forget the smell of that smoldering fire. We went down into the town to our home. It was still intact, and there was also electricity; it hadn't been shut off yet. We had electricity for 10 days. We bathed and I deloused the children; we did this and that. It was difficult, and we were starving.[22]

The NGOs noted time and again the tension within the community and the hopeless situation caused by the flood of refugees from the villages. Because the original inhabitants had their hands full with their own families, the argument was that extra effort was needed from third parties. The desperation of the refugees and their alienation from the original residents may have been exaggerated in reports and letters. The survivors were aware that they were all in the same boat, and many remember moments of solidarity.

Eyewitnesses from the Ghetto

The residents of Srebrenica experienced periods of great famine, but it was not the same for everybody. Some had secret stores of food or managed to grow vegetables. Hunger was seasonal; the valley is fertile, but the winters are long. For the years 1992–1995 we can rely on eyewitnesses such as the Pole Tadeus Mazowiecki, a special reporter from the Human Rights Commission of the United Nations.[23] His reports give his perspective on the former Yugoslavia; Srebrenica at that time was one of the "safe areas," but it was not regarded as important. Mazowiecki was more concerned with what was happening in Croatia to the west, and gave much attention to Gorazde, another protected enclave. Later, after the fall, he resigned; he felt responsible for what had happened under the eyes of the international community and felt he could no longer function. The other official observer who reported specifically on Srebrenica was Diego Arria, the UN ambassador from Venezuela, who represented the Security Council in that area. There are also reports from that period by journalists who succeeded in reaching the town despite the Serb blockades, for example, the German Phillip von Recklinghausen.[24] Another important source of eyewitness accounts regarding the situation in Srebrenica is the Yugoslav Tribunal, and in particular the trial against Bosnian warlord Naser Orić.

Eyewitnesses and Judgment: Testimony with a Purpose

In 1993, Diego Arria visited the enclave with a group of observers. Their mission was to determine if the situation was as bad as the rumors indicated. He later testified for the defense of Naser Orić, as did Srebrenica survivor Kada Hotić. Of course, Arria's testimony was treated differently than that of the survivor, whom the judges felt did not follow their guidelines. The court assumed that Srebrenica had been under siege and suffered from famine; that did not have to be established. Arria stated that, besides starvation, the residents lived with the constant threat that the defense lines might fail.

> What happened in 1995 might have happened also in December 1992, in January 1993, in February 1993, at any point in time. The people living there were with their backs to the wall and the only possibility they had was to flee below the ground. . . . The greatest mistake one can make in describing the situation is to consider it to be merely a background, as if starvation, a refugee crisis and disease are only scenery, scenery behind the stage, immovable, whilst actors tread the stage.[25]

Arria was of the opinion that conditions in Srebrenica even before the fall amounted to genocide in slow motion. The question was not whether the refugees would die, but when. He reported this to the United Nations, calling Srebrenica an open prison.[26]

Arria arrived in Srebrenica on April 25, 1993; the town had already been declared a "safe area." According to his testimony, the inhabitants had become like hungry animals who lived in the forest, and he warned of a human tragedy. The UN Secretariat and the most prominent members knew what was happening. Arria remembered the looks on the diplomats' faces after ABC journalist Tony Birtley entered the enclave and showed on television how grave the conditions were.

Arria was shocked at what he saw in Srebrenica. "You only see devastation, burned houses, only women and old men and children in the streets. No water, no electricity, no gas, no doctors."[27] When he arrived, the evacuation had just begun. Serb doctors chose those who could leave town with the convoy, thus aiding (according to Arria) the UN in the selection process. It was "exactly what happened two years later when they took 7,000 people out of Srebrenica and murdered them in the same procedure. 'You get into the bus, you don't get into the bus.' . . . It is the coldest, cruel[est] experience I have seen, and [it took place] under the United Nations banner."[28] Of course, the doctors who took part in the selection process in 1993 did not know what would happen later. The real similarity is in the unresponsiveness of the party being addressed—the United Nations—in both 1993 and 1995.

Arria's testimony contained a strong message. The officers of the United Nations were more comfortable dealing with the Serb commanders, who were career military, than with the nonmilitary Muslims. He found the military affinity also to be an explanation for the later failure of the Dutch troops to protect the Muslims.

During the same trial at the Yugoslav Tribunal, Kada Hotić described what she witnessed when she returned to the town after the first capture by the Serbs.[29] Like Arria, she was a witness for the defense of Orić. No one can claim that Kada, who is also active in the Mothers of the Enclaves Žepa and Srebrenica, is an impartial witness. That organization regards the mass murder at Potočari as the finale of the drawn-out attempt to eradicate the Bosniaks of Srebrenica; in other words, the 1995 genocide began much earlier.

Kada, who was deeply affected by the war, has also spoken out in former U.S. ambassador Swanee Hunt's book *This Was Not Our War,* which contains discussions with women who were victims of the Bosnian war from across Bosnia and from all areas where women were affected differently than men. Hunt conducted the interviews meticulously, although she hesitated to ask precise questions of women such as Kada, who had lived through so much. Yet Kada, like all the other women, wanted to testify. The following passage is from Hunt's book: "We were hungry. We were shelled. We didn't know what was happening. I had to walk 20 kilometers carrying 25 kilograms [55 pounds] of corn seed, to feed my family. I couldn't let my son do it. He could've been taken by the Chetniks and killed."[30] She went to the fields of villagers who had fled to the town. According to her, the first year (until the food drops began) was the worst.

Violence from Both Sides

Stories about violence are always interwoven with other stories. If the violence was committed by the Serbs, then the story has to do with the gradual exhaustion from the siege and the massacre in 1995. If the violence was from the Muslim side (and we know this also went to extremes), then the story is bound up in explanations about how it was unavoidable because of the starvation. We tend to forget that there was violence on both sides, because of the extraordinary events in 1995. Serb propaganda (which is still active) uses the violence by Muslims to show that the violence of Potočari was not extreme. In 2005, the Serbian Radical Party argued that thousands of Serb citizens were killed. An example is the Orthodox Christmas night massacre in the tiny Serb village of Kravica. In 2006, Human Rights Watch observed that many people in Serbia believe that the murders committed by the Muslims during those years were just as brutal as the genocide in Potočari.

I work from the assumption that the violence on both sides was worse than has been acknowledged; too many parties benefit from remaining silent. Both sides stole and took over houses from the other. This is standard practice during war in the Balkans, and besides, the refugees needed shelter and other things to survive. Survivors see the world through a different lens than that used by academics who read about war in armchairs; that is especially true when it comes to memory. For many, it is still too early to acknowledge the suffering and misery of the "others," especially in light of what happened later. If an individual is able to admit what happened and to reflect on the fact that both parties committed crimes in the war, I regard that as a sign of great strength and success at growing beyond the role of the victim.

The unbearable living conditions are often used as an excuse. Džidža, who is active in an organization of women survivors, makes a direct connection between their starvation and the plundering and murder committed by the Bosniaks. She believes it was a matter of self-defense; misunderstood acts were committed in a starving world that no one now wants to understand. She does admit that many things which happened are not acceptable today.

> You know, there was starvation, and what happened in Kravica was the result of that starvation. You must know that. I would like to say that in The Hague. . . . The famine started immediately, the third of May, when we left. I was planting beans, digging. In our village, we usually planted beans. I was planting and I was nauseous from the smell of gunpowder and smoke from the weapons. It was cloudy.

Džidža[31] talked about how she saw refugees arriving from Zaklopača and, later, from other villages. The refugees were at their wits' end.

> Those people arrived with nothing, starving, and with only what they could carry. A mother from Zaklopača had already lost six sons and two grandsons. Only one grandson was still alive. Those people came our way. People from 11 villages passed through here. There was no way to control them. If you told them not to do what they wanted to do, they were capable of killing you. They said, "You're on their side. You're just like them. They murdered so-and-so from my family, so you're just like them." That's how it was, I swear it on the Qur'an.
>
> Help did come, I think, in 1993 after the French general Morillon arrived. If help had been able to come over the yellow bridge, if normal help had arrived, then nothing would have happened. But they didn't let the help through, and people were starving, so they were willing to attack anybody. If you're hungry, you can survive, but if the children are also hungry, then it doesn't matter who or what someone is. The lack of help was the only cause for Kravica and Jezero.[32]

She is referring to the times in the war when the Muslims made looting sorties into Serb-controlled villages around Srebrenica. From her perspective, the story is logical, and murder is understandable within the logic of frenzied, starving hordes, hence her constant reference to the motives for plundering.

Džidža planted corn, grain, potatoes, and beans.

> I planted double what I had planned for myself. Every day, people came asking for food. They came with bags and totes and asked if they could have something, because they had nothing to eat. What I want to say is that the famine made people go to Kravica, but they didn't go to commit murder. As far as I'm concerned, everyone who is guilty for Kravica should take responsibility, but no one went there to kill. Refugees went there because they were starving. Any normal person can understand that. I'm not trying to justify it, but nobody went there to lay claim to the place. They took the food and left.

In Kada's testimony at the Orić trial, she also insisted that hunger was the cause of the atrocities committed. She was testifying for the defense, whose argument was that everyone was fighting for food and at times it was impossible to control the civilians.[33] The defense also argued that the looters operated independently of Orić and that suffering in Srebrenica was so horrible that using violence to obtain food was justified.

Kada also testified about returning to Srebrenica in 1992 after the first Serb takeover.

> There wasn't a soul in town. There was nobody there. When we entered the town and we walked down the streets, we saw burned-down houses, some totally burned down, some only partially. In some cases half a house or a couple of rooms were left standing. But all houses had been broken in, all furniture was in disarray, whatever was of value was taken away, and it was a ghost town.
>
> And then we all went to our own places and we tried to make at least a little bit of those homes habitable. Only the apartment buildings next to the hospital were not set on fire.[34]

She continued with vivid descriptions of how another area of the town was still standing. The judge asked if she had spoken with someone who had seen the houses being set on fire. Kada described her contact with a woman who lived in the center of town and had not fled to the woods. That woman tried to put out the fire in her house and to protect her possessions.

Refugees could see from the hills that three people were starting fires. They watched in horror as a building where invalids lived was set on fire. Eight people inside were burned alive. Their screams were hair-raising. Kada must have been told about that because she was in the hills, but the judge did not acknowledge her perspective. According to Kada, the situation improved only after the UN came to Srebrenica (1993). She described how quickly the town filled up. "[P]eople started coming from Bratunac, especially people from Bratunac who had been chased away from there. And they told us they were betrayed there."[35]

Then the judge interrupted her, as was often the case at the tribunal. The judge was not interested in her story, but in testimony that could lead to a judgment about the looting parties in Srebrenica, who were looking for food under the leadership of Orić. Did the facts add up? When did she return to the town? The tribunal was writing history according to its methods; it distrusted witnesses because dates were difficult for them to remember precisely. Those hiding in the woods did not have a calendar handy, and hence cannot be specific. Furthermore, hard questions are needed during testimony to debunk fanciful stories; such moments show clearly how selective judicial witnesses must be. Kada had to prove that she had seen the arrival of people from Bratunac with her own eyes; she could, because she had seen them from her home in Srebrenica. Her testimony was detailed, although she could not be more precise about when she went out foraging for food. "It was autumn because the corn was ripe. Again, I don't remember the dates. We had taken the corn and the food from the houses and the storage rooms, and then when we ran out of that, we would pick the corn from the fields and along the road until we had picked everything."[36] After a couple of expeditions, it became too risky; they had left footprints and the Serbs began to plant land mines. In the end, there were also mines in the cornfields.

Other Witnesses, Perspectives, and Agendas

Foreigners working for NGOs in Srebrenica wanted to go beyond internal reporting and tell the world what they had seen. Their accounts of what happened reflect the perspectives and goals of their organizations, which in turn are linked to the participants' memories of their roles.[37] NGO employees tended to have limited views and responsibilities.

Thierry Pontus, a doctor with MSF, described not only the horrors of the makeshift hospital, but also his remarkable experience of a food drop.[38] He had followed a colleague to the site of the drop. It was pitch black when they set out. Pontus wondered if there was danger of being shot while looking for food packages. He quickly realized that the greatest danger came from competition for the packages. Groups had formed, and an unarmed individual had almost no chance of obtaining a package or, if he acquired one, holding on to it. The local government was powerless to stop such violence within the enclave. There was also the danger of being hit by a falling pallet of packages; in the dark, one could neither see nor hear the pallets as they were dropped. Darkness was mandatory; a flashlight made one a sniper's target. Pontus continued: "We made slow progress over the mountain road. The road was bad and quickly became a narrow and dangerous passage. . . . I am silent, the tension is mounting. We move even more slowly. To my left is a steep drop. To my right is a slope covered with impenetrable conifers." They had to proceed farther by foot. He was cold. He remembered stories about the night food drops in World War II; all those who were waiting for food were caught by the Gestapo.[39] He was scared. As the airplane approached, its motors stopped, then quickly started again. "All of a sudden the mountain across from me lights up. A small flame, ten, a hundred, a thousand tiny lights go on like little Christmas lights, little glow worms."[40] The lights began to move. Shortly thereafter, it was dark again. In the distance was the sound of an automatic rifle.

"On the road, which I thought was deserted, people appear carrying packets about the size of a pillow." They were all walking toward the town. "Something has changed in their movements, in their stride. They are not shouting for joy, but they are laden with packets and there is food. It means perhaps enough food for a couple of days, and it hasn't been that way for a while."[41] Of course, Pontus was not one of the locals; he went to the drop, observed it, and wrote his observations after the fact and in between his reports as an MSF doctor trying to justify his medical decisions. But he was writing about something he could not forget.

It is mainly the Bosnians who have blamed the world for leaving them to rot in their misery. Hatidža Hren's book *Srebrenica, het verhaal van de overlevenden* is a collection of survivors' stories, some of which I have cited in previous chapters.[42] Some of those accounts are difficult to forget; they were the first cries at a time when no one wanted to listen to the survivors. Bosnian journalist Emir Suljagić chose a more literary approach in his memoir, *Postcards from the Grave*.[43] He showed through his experiences that people in Srebrenica were capable of acting and making decisions. I was much impressed by his willingness to show the darker side of the siege era. That takes courage, given the current climate among the survivors; they are understandably inclined to veil the shadier side of their own party's behavior.[44] They are now regarded as the victims of genocide, but the massacre was only the closing chapter of a period of great suffering and hardship. People react differently in difficult times; the reality was raw and people were cruel to each other.

Suljagić described how people were self-centered and how a small group ruled the roost. He tried to avoid stereotyping people as victims. The persons he knew (most of whom are now dead) were not just victims, but real people with feelings, ties, hope, and despair. They had lived in a civil society and tried to preserve it, despite the siege. Suljagić did not succeed in focusing attention on the survivors; perhaps his tone was too disengaged and perhaps he made the victims seem too human, too fallible. That is now unacceptable in Bosnia; the victims are regarded as martyrs and hence have lost their human faces.[45] In Suljagić's book, the townspeople reacted sometimes well and sometimes badly to the war conditions. There were good people and villains, black marketers and starving people who lost their scruples and their sanity.

Suljagić described how the starving people he lived with could think of nothing but food while searching for packages after a food drop. He also, like Pontus, stood in the darkness wondering what he was doing and what awaited him: "In a way, it was our war within a war. During the day we fought against the Serbs, and during the night we fought against each other for every bit of food, for one plastic packet. For the nth time people lost all their scruples, went beyond all limits of human behavior, once again losing all dignity. The fight for survival had acquired yet another form."[46] Suljagić also pondered the word *enclave*, before comparing the town to a concentration camp: "This cold and precise word denotes all the differences between us, inside, and them outside. We never called Srebrenica an 'enclave,' because that had absolutely nothing to do with our reality. We called it [a] cauldron, world's end, appendix, probably because those words better described how we felt. What we were going through every day was inaccessible to the rest of the world."[47]

An Empty Town and the Stories Now: Perspectives on Being under Siege

Ćamila returned to an empty town in 1992:

> That's how it was. Nobody took Srebrenica, no one marched in. There was some fighting, here and there and at the same time. And then they left everything behind and ran. That's how Srebrenica was liberated. It was a deserted town, with no one there. There were more dogs and cats than people. It was peaceful, and we lived very quietly; no one provoked us and we did nothing to cause irritation. Until Cerska [a nearby village] fell. When Cerska fell and the surrounding villages began to fall, that's when the chaos in Srebrenica started again. People from all the villages around the Drina came to Srebrenica; it was chaos with such a concentration of people.[48]

These are all stories of people who were involved, and the person narrating determines the memory. As a diplomat, Arria saw a mass of people, and he did not stay long in the town. The account by Kada, who remained in Srebrenica, is much more detailed, and also more vulnerable; she is an average woman and not unbiased. Different stories emphasize different aspects. They show how diverse the experiences of those years were. The stories begin to resemble each other only in 1995, when all the narrators became victims. Then, it seems, the surface differences among the inhabitants' experiences disappeared.

Of course, the poverty was shared by all (albeit in a variety of ways), and every interview showed that something previously unimaginable happened. Ćamila talked about the misery and the poverty, but also about how she had a material advantage:

> We could survive one way or another. We all had a little extra in reserve. We didn't come from a rural area; it was industrial and we were used to buying what we needed. But we had supplies, because so many people had left; we had five or six houses in the family where we could get things. But then, all those people came, with nothing, and they filled every nook and cranny in Srebrenica. They spread out plastic sheets, they heated food in cans. . . . It was snowing, there was a snowstorm; the streets were muddy; every corner was occupied. People put down foam rubber mattresses and that was their place on the face of the earth, right in the middle of the street. The biggest problem in Srebrenica was a shortage of seed. And we didn't have a chance to get any. We could eat what we had from before. And more people kept coming into the town. At the beginning, we gave them some seed, but even if you only gave a handful, a hundred people meant a hundred hands, so you ran through your supplies.[49]
>
> In the beginning we were good hosts and hostesses, just like it should be. . . . But at a certain point we realized we were running out of food and that we couldn't buy it anywhere, so we became stingy. The living conditions were impossible, and we began to fight to survive. There was no electricity from the very first days, because the Serbs destroyed everything; there was no running water, because they had blown up the water supply. So there we were, without electricity, without water, without anything, but with a lot of people who came from all over the place. We were in a prison camp without the necessities of life. Then, people started arriving with livestock. But there was no food for the animals and no place to keep them. So they began to slaughter the livestock. The result was that you could get a kilo [2.2 pounds] of meat for a kilo of grain—or even 800 grams of grain, or two kilos of meat for a kilo of grain. That lasted 10–15 days, at most a month, until

everything had been roasted and eaten. We didn't have freezers and we couldn't smoke the meat, none of that, and people were starving. People slaughtered their livestock and ate them up. And when one animal was finished, they started on the next one. So the herds were ruined. There was no harvest. People went to Žepa and Luke to get food. They went there, hungry and exhausted, to buy something—they would give a necklace for a sack of potatoes. But you run out of jewelry, [and] you [still] want to eat, and there's no place left where you can buy something. It took people days to go to Žepa. Sometimes, the Serbs let them through, and sometimes whole groups perished. Occasionally, a man succeeded in bringing back 20 or 30 kilos of something, but he had to carry it the whole day, and a few times a man died under the weight. He couldn't take less with him, because he knew his family would starve to death if he didn't bring food.[50]

Ramiza was one of the women who went out foraging for food. I was surprised at her enormous strength. I began to realize that, besides money, physical strength was a resource for survival. In her little house in Tuzla, she told me about her experiences.

Humanitarian aid wasn't enough. We only got 1½ kilos of flour per family member; my father and brother were a family, so together they got 3 kilos. My husband, our child, and I got 4½ kilos—if they really did give out 1½ kilos per person. But we couldn't survive on that. You're not a mouse that gets enough just by licking flour. Occasionally, the Serbs let a convoy through if they felt like it. But sometimes they didn't let any through. There just wasn't enough food.

Ramiza was one of the strong ones who reached Žepa; it was a march across enemy lines and through forested hills. She had family on her mother's side in Žepa. Her aunt went there often and invited her to join her.

It was a heavy and difficult trek from Srebrenica to Žepa. It took us 24 hours. There were ambushes, and you never knew if there would be one. It took us a day and a night. We went through a forest with streams. There were all kinds of obstacles; it was a heavy and strenuous journey. There were 20 or 30 of us. Some walked alone, others in small groups. You stayed with the group you began the trek with. But some people didn't want to wait on you.

In Žepa, she looked up her family, who gave her enough food.

It was difficult, but once I was there, I asked about my mother's
nephew and we went to his house. He gave us all kinds of things
and asked why I hadn't come sooner. At that time, we had enough
rice in Srebrenica, but they gave me rice as well. My aunt and I left
to return to Srebrenica. It was both strange and sad. I hadn't dared
to tell them not to give me rice, that we had rice. So I took it. But
when we came to the first trees in a forest, my aunt told me to
throw the rice away. "Why should you carry it and collapse under
the weight?" she asked. She probably felt sorry for me because I was
carrying so much. And we didn't need the rice, because we had rice.
So we threw it away. We came to a copse and my aunt took the bag
of rice and placed it in the branches. That first trip was fine. After
a while, my aunt and I went again. . . . We began walking early in
the evening, so we could get by the Chetniks in the dark.[51]

One went with people one knew. One did not sleep during the journey. "It was
far away, we walked day and night. You can't imagine how far away it was." After
making it through the danger zone, there was relief. It was indeed dangerous;
once, they went through a field that was ambushed the next day.

Ramiza planted a small garden in Ćumanići, a village that had belonged to
the Serbs. She had to, there was no choice in the matter, but it was dangerous,
just as dangerous as fetching water. "I planted there. It wasn't that steep, but
whatever I planted, like the corn for my child, got washed away by rain. So I
replanted several times in different spots until I got fed up with it." At the time,
she thought she was just unlucky. In hindsight, she sees it as an omen of the bad
things to come.

In order to understand events in the besieged enclave and how those under
siege remember that time, one must consciously choose to shift one's perspective and try to see that world through their eyes. The survivors tell what they
have seen; that is all they can remember. They know how easy it is to judge the
actions of all parties at a given moment in a place of excess that was anything
but normal. As women, they made different choices in their stories than did
Suljagić. Because they were traumatized and have difficulty with the past, their
stories are dramatic and yet depict the history of the everyday. In contrast,
Suljagić the intellectual gives us images dominated by the victims' role. They
complain of betrayal and describe how they were abandoned; they tell the history of small events.

Srebrenica had become a wartime economy,[52] with all the corruption and
graft that a black market brings. People tried to feed their families, they fought
for their families' survival—and they were oblivious to what was happening

elsewhere. They stubbornly clung to their daily lives despite living in a criminal world. The women had their hands full with their homes, or they had nothing to do and hid behind walls that could stop grenades, or they did the first for a while and then the other. They are not the ultimate victims in their stories, and that is surprising. Within the margins of their little world, their stories contain a variety of perspectives, including most prominently that one should make the best of it and that one should remain a respectable and decent person. They told of how they worked at being decent people, how despite all the worries they tried to set a good example for their children, and especially how they wanted to take care of them—even in Srebrenica. But that was not always possible.

The term *concentration camp*—with all its hideous connotations, including murder—is often used to describe 1992–1995 in Srebrenica. The German journalist Phillip von Recklinghausen used it in 1993, because he wanted to rouse the public. But the history of the enclave shows another picture than the hopelessness of a concentration camp. The population was not simply suffering under their tormenters. Despite everything, they felt protected.

The Inhabitants and DutchBat

In 2005 *Herinneringen aan Srebrenica* (*Memories of Srebrenica*) was published in the Netherlands.[53] It contains the stories of Dutch soldiers who served in Srebrenica, who bear the marks of the massacre and what happened after. The soldiers tell of their confusion, their rage, and their inability to offer protection. The mirror image of their perspective (and of the official reports) is how the locals saw the troops and how they remember the soldiers.

There was enormous disappointment in the Dutch military, and feelings of betrayal are widespread. As soldiers of the United Nations, they were supposed to protect the residents. A number of my interviews came to a halt when the subject of the soldiers came up. Relations with DutchBat III (the soldiers who arrived after January 1995) were certainly problematic, but not in all instances. Some Bosnians knew the soldiers were Dutch, but they were generally regarded as part of the UN, which was protecting the Bosnians, and their nationality did not matter. Sometimes, friendly relations were established. It was only during the massacre, when they failed to give protection, that the interviewees seemed to be aware of the soldiers' nationality.

The negative feelings were strengthened by the population's inability to defend itself. The residents had been forced to turn in their weapons to those same soldiers; that did not always go well. The published collection of DutchBat memories shows that disarming the population was not completely successful. During the last few months, weapons were probably still being smuggled in.

Judgments on the military's actions are mixed. Although the NIOD Report exonerated the behavior of the DutchBatters during the massacre in 1995, the commentary regarding the period before was highly critical. For example, in preparation for their assignment, the military had been given prejudicial instructions regarding the "Balkan person,"[54] who, it was claimed, is accustomed to settling conflicts with violence. From the beginning, it was expected that the soldiers would have problems with the Muslims, hence the soldiers were advised to keep their distance. Within that context, Muslims were regarded as riffraff; according to the NIOD Report, stories caricaturing the Muslims were spread around. The soldiers were told that women in Srebrenica wore the veil, even though many women still talk about how modern their dress was. The report justifiably asked to what degree these stereotypes became "self-fulfilling."[55] The soldiers were made fearful and apparently were not capable of critically assessing the characterizations they had been given.

The NIOD Report noted: "Before the DutchBatters were sent out, they were already talking about a 'goat trail' instead of a 'path.' Children 'panhandled,' men 'were untrustworthy and told sob stories,' all Muslim women wore 'pajama pants' and headscarves, and had 'moustaches' and 'typically Bosnian teeth.'"[56] The report also noted that "introduction to the devastation, the wretched living conditions of the residents, including numerous refugees, and not forgetting the permanent stench meant a profound and for many DutchBatters shocking experience."[57] This led to the awful racist graffiti that was later found.

There is also an interesting paragraph in the report about the cultural confusion of the DutchBatters and their inability to put themselves in the position of the residents, who suffered from "the effects of physical and mental hardships. The results these had on the mindset of the population—the apathy, the depression, and the singular focus on survival"—were unacknowledged factors for which the Dutch soldiers were not prepared. Furthermore, there was the filth and pollution, about which nothing was done, according to DutchBat,[58] and amazement at the profiteering of the elites.[59] The report covered, justifiably, the issue of anti-Muslim behavior, although in my opinion DutchBat behaved no differently than other UN peace troops. Sometimes, things went well; when they went badly, it was big news in the Netherlands. There is general agreement that the soldiers were not well prepared.

More shocking is the fact that in 2005 a number of DutchBatters were still trying to defend actions that were clearly unacceptable and thus justify their poor behavior. For example, one soldier was charged with racist behavior toward his fellow soldiers, and his racist attitude was also visible in how he spoke about Muslims. Ten years after Srebrenica, he still said: "I called them stinking Muslims. That is true. First, they smelled bad. Second, they were Muslims. . . . I feel screwed over by my buddies, the judiciary, and politics. But I can understand why some people were offended by my choice of words."[60] Another example involved children asking for candy and food. Apples, sweets, cans of soda—these were treats they had not had in a long time. "I was fed up with the kids standing around the gate and whining for food and candies," one of the others wrote. "I asked a soldier to make a drawing. He sketched a large UN soldier who was screaming *Nema bonbons* [No bonbons] while wringing a little boy's throat with his large hand."[61]

Managing the misbehavior of a number of soldiers and keeping it behind closed doors was a major chore for the military leadership and, later, the Ministry of Defense. The *Feitenrelaas* (lit. "account of facts"), or case statement, had reported right-extremist views among some DutchBatters. This was leaked in May 1995; the statement itself was not made public until December 1999. The editorial team of the television news program *Nova* called on Dutch legislators to ensure that such serious facts not be hidden from the public. In May 1995, the complaints against the military were investigated by the military. Naturally, the military leadership denied that children had been paid to search for mines in trenches.[62] Here again, the NIOD Report gave a reliable account,[63] and raised the question that was the subject of ongoing discussion: had the battalion leader – Commander Th. J. P. Karremans—fulfilled his responsibilities?[64] Karremans is the same officer who became famous for fearfully raising a glass with Mladić in 1995 while the massacre was taking place. Before then, he had been invisible; he was not often at the compound, and was stiff and rather awkward in social situations.

In the Netherlands, the question of the soldiers' behavior became lost in the need to exonerate the Dutch for the events of 1995. It has always struck me that the formal investigation was conducted by members of the military.[65] Clearly, it was not an independent investigation, although it needed to be thorough and unbiased. The rules of engagement for international peace missions are there for a reason; hardly any peace mission has been free of complaints. Furthermore, the Dutch soldiers sent to Srebrenica were a new sort of professional, non-conscripted military, and it was not yet certain if this group had coalesced into a disciplined force. The rules were therefore even more necessary for them.

Distance and Ambivalence

There were many rules regarding the soldiers, and rules are not always sensible. Munira Subašić, president of the Mothers of the Enclaves of Srebrenica and Žepa and one of the people who talks without hesitation about betrayal, told me: "We were starving. And I went to them and asked for food. But if there was a mouse in their storeroom, they threw all the food in a garbage dump and covered it with earth. They didn't give it to the people. You know, that kind of thing."[66] Even more serious were accusations that DutchBat was involved in the black market and that soldiers accepted money to be given to family members of the inhabitants and then kept it.

Munira pointed out that, even so, the enclave could not have survived without the continuing supply of goods from the soldiers. Some DutchBatters asked people on the home front to send them goods, which they then distributed to town inhabitants they knew personally. Other soldiers sold what they received on the black market. The stories are mixed. Reading the book of soldiers' memories leaves one with the impression that the enclave's isolation affected the soldiers and robbed them as well. What leadership there was, was rigid and rule-bound in situations where rules were not the answer.

Those who read the Dutch collection of eyewitness accounts encounter a different soldier, one I also heard about in my interviews. Some DutchBatters had a favorite child and gave it treats and nice things. Ties were formed, and thoughts about what happened to that child are now painful. One medic used medical supplies sparingly out of fear there would not be enough if soldiers were wounded, while another medic tried to help all of the locals. A soldier tells of a boy and girl whose parents invited him to drink coffee with them. "Those people had nothing, but we were always received warmly. They toasted sunflower seeds for us. Nura and Nourija brought us warm rolls every day. . . . If you are in that kind of situation for a long time, you try to look for something human, to find someone you connect with. I needed that warm human connection."[67] Another soldier said, "I sought out contact with the people who lived there. Bartering, and giving kids candy. There was a girl, about 12 years old. She was learning English at school, and I helped her with the difficult words. In turn she taught me her language. But our 'fearless' leader put an end to that. I thought that was stupid. Why were we really there? Wasn't it to help the people?"[68]

Sabra told me that she and several other women worked for the DutchBatters. "I cleaned their rooms. The area was divided with partitions—there weren't any doors, just partitions—because it was one large space. I washed their clothes; I had to carry them to the river to rinse them." The clothes had to be washed, dried, and returned within a day; they were dried with the help of a generator. "We also had to clean the park around the base. We only got a half-hour break and worked the whole day. In the winter, it was cold. The river was half frozen and we had to rinse the clothes in the icy water. . . . I always had a couple of fingers bandaged. We washed the dirty laundry in large basins. There were 12 of us and each of us washed in a large basin. It was hard, cold work." According to Sabra, the Dutch were different from their Canadian predecessors. They changed the layout of the living quarters and followed a different disciplinary code. Even the women were treated in a military manner, and were kept at a distance from the soldiers. As much as possible, the soldiers tried to live as though they were in Holland.

There was enough to eat while they were working, but Sabra was not allowed to take food home to her starving children. Despite that, the little group of women was responsible for feeding the 250 "protectors" hot meals and taking care of them. It irritated Sabra that she could not feed her own children. She was not paid in money; her salary was a meal. That surprised me, but she accepted it because the soldiers were there to protect her. She also tolerated it when she was promised cigarettes but was tricked as a joke; she accepted the humiliation, because as long as the soldiers were there, she believed, the inhabitants were safe. Her main example of improper behavior was of a soldier throwing eggs at a woman, who tried to catch them. She could not, of course, and the soldiers roared with laughter.

During the interview, Sabra was remarkably calm. Many interviewees tended to focus on all kinds of bad behavior of some of the DutchBatters before 1995, because they are enraged at the behavior of the soldiers during the genocide. There could be a connection between the fact that they were a bad lot before—they stole money, they were involved in the black market—and they were a bad lot later. They were cowardly, or at best untrained for war, and they were inexperienced. Certainly, there is some truth in the accusations; they are not all projection, given the seriousness of the described behavior. The military was a mixed bag; some soldiers were there because of the money, others were there to help people. Because there were good soldiers, some survivors think back with positive feelings toward individual DutchBatters, which can lead to confusing memories.

Stories of Daily Life

During the interviews, an image formed of daily life in the town during the siege. The inhabitants were trapped. They improvised wherever possible to make life bearable and to limit the war damage. Many refugees lived in bitter poverty, as did Vahida. She talked about it at length, because her great misery took place long before 1995. At the time of our interview, she was still living as a refugee; quite possibly, becoming and remaining a refugee was her greatest trauma. Maintaining her dignity continues to be important to her. This was evident in her story about the Serbs (mainly older people) who remained in Srebrenica and also needed food. "We lived. I don't really know how. . . . It was a bad time, there were no food supplies left. At one point, we received some help, but there were days when we had nothing to eat. Children starved to death; the famine was bad in 1993."[69]

There were also wounded people for whom there was no real help. In 2007, I interviewed Sabra Alemić in her house in Srebrenica. She lost her husband in the 1995 slaughter, after having been married more than 30 years. During the siege, she had tried to take care of him after he was seriously wounded.

> His lungs had been damaged by grenade shrapnel. He had gone to the land up there [she gestures], where I kept a cow. He was hit with shrapnel there. He was in bed for six months. I had to fight to keep him alive. He healed. . . . In the beginning, Srebrenica had more doctors, but most of them were killed and some left the town. There were no medications. It was 17 days after my husband was wounded when Bosnian soldiers brought medicine from Tuzla. There was an older man who used to work in the hospital in Bratunac. He lived above the town. He had a job in our hospital then, but more and more wounded went to his house. They didn't dare come to the town.

Because her husband had been wounded in that area, Vahida went to that man's house. The accommodations were terrible for patients and their relatives.

> I stayed there 18 days with my spouse. I had no place to sit, let alone lie down. I took care of him. When the medicines came, and my husband was lucky that they came, the man asked for food in exchange. I had a cow, so I could give him milk. When my husband left that so-called hospital, there was no one in the town to change his bandages. That was horrible. It's difficult to act normal with a deathly ill patient. The wound got infected and began to stink. . . . There were sick people in houses everywhere. And you had nothing to clean the wounds with, except slivovitz [plum brandy]. There simply was nothing. When he got medication, it was the first time medicines were available. But the most important medication was slivovitz. It contains alcohol, so we used it to clean wounds.[70]

The town had to survive and that required a certain discipline. Every day, people were wounded by shrapnel, both on the front and during looting raids. A building was used as a hospital, and it had to be kept clean without soap. The trash had to be picked up; because of the gasoline shortage, it was transported by hand. The foreign soldiers had to be supplied and served, even though the pay for doing that work was nothing more than a meal. Fuel had to be found, new refugees had to be taken in, and, when possible, food had to be planted and harvested. Because so many men were at the front, these chores had to be done by women, even though a number of them entailed heavy physical labor.

The Concerns of Mothers

Caring for the wounded adults was not the only issue. There was also the fear of being wounded oneself or of losing a loved one. Mothers worried constantly about where their children were; a wounded child was a mother's nightmare.

Šefika's son was killed on April 12, 1993, when the school soccer field was shelled. There were 56 dead and more than 100 wounded; the doctors were overwhelmed and did not know how to care for them all. Laurence de Barros-Duchêne, a doctor with MSF, remembered the slaughter and in 1996 wrote:

> The road was covered with blood. The wounded came; they were carried by hand or in wheelbarrows and carts. . . . [Arriving at the hospital, there was] dreadful confusion. There were people everywhere, dead and wounded, neighbors, family, everyone shouted and cried, people moaned and some had vomited. We didn't know where to begin. It was dreadful. Four youths with severe head wounds died almost immediately in our arms, before we could do anything.[71]

Šefika does not know much about all the others, only that her son was killed. She remembers that afternoon in detail but told her story with great difficulty: "A girl stormed down the hall. I asked her, 'Jasmina, what happened?' She said there was a bloodbath on the playground. People were at the school and were wounded on the playground by shell fragments. I cried out, because my daughter Sevda usually went by there. That day, she had gone by there three or four times to fetch water." Šefika was convinced her daughter was one of the dead or wounded. When her husband arrived, he was as white as a sheet; she asked if Sevda were dead.

> He said she had not been killed, then went outside and closed the door behind him. My daughter-in-law asked me to go with her. I didn't think about my son, because he was somewhere down in the house, I thought. . . . [Once we realized he was dead,] we went there; they were laid out on the ground. Blankets were wrapped around them. There were 20 bodies in a row . . . it hurts to talk about it. I kneeled and bent over his body. I could feel it, it was as if he was still alive. Someone threw water on me and I came to.

They took me behind a wall, but I could still see him. I had enough
strength to look at him. As though he was still alive.[72]

The Women Organize

Women have their own tasks and concerns in wartime. Aktiv Zene
Srebrenice was organized on May 15, 1992, to coordinate the tasks that could
only be done collectively. Zene Srebrenice quickly became important to the civil
society. When Srebrenica fell in 1995, 86 women were active; for a population
of 30,000 that does not seem large, but it is relatively large for such a collective.
Their activities were mainly paramedical, as well as practical, such as collecting
herbs that could help the wounded and cleaning the hospital.[73] The scarcity of
contraceptives resulted in pregnancies, which sometimes ended in abortions,
both spontaneous (because of the poor health conditions and lack of medical
care) and induced. There were scabies and lice, which could be controlled, but
that required coordination and ongoing contact with the public. A sports team
was also started in order to give the residents something to do. The women of
the organization quickly acquired all kinds of new knowledge.

The core group of these women later became the basis for the survivors
organizations, but the bonds were formed during the siege. They became known
when they organized the demonstration that stopped General Morillon from
leaving the town. That was an extremely difficult moment, which ended in
what they thought was a glorious victory, namely, the promise of protection.
That promise, and their belief in it, are the source of their current feelings of
betrayal.

Of course, the women's organization was not solely responsible for fighting
to maintain a normal existence. The town's teachers took their responsibilities seriously and worked at the request of the town council. In cooperation
with various NGOs, they organized instruction for the town's children in 1993;
as in all wars, children were regarded as the future. There were morning and
afternoon classes for various groups. One problem was the lack of instruction
materials and writing paper, for which all kinds of solutions were found. But
there was a major curriculum change. With the isolation of the siege, religion—
the factor separating the residents from those who held them under siege—took
on a new importance. Religion was now taught to the children, who up until
then had only known secular education.

The Children

The children had to attend school. The myth of a secular Yugoslavia had
gone up in smoke, and in those perilous times a new and different history was

taught. The town's inhabitants were more Muslim than before. Alma told Lara Broekman:

> All of a sudden, we had another subject, religion, which we never had before the war or anything. I've already explained how I was reared; I didn't even know I was Muslim. Suddenly, I had to learn all about it, including Arabic and reading the Qur'an. Now that gave me problems. And now that subject was required for moving on to the next class. I still remember the first lesson. An imam walked in and asked, "Who doesn't know how to pray?" Many of the kids came from the villages, where belief was more common, so they had learned all that from their parents. My parents still don't know anything about that, so how could I have known? I looked to the right; nobody had raised a hand, that you didn't know how to. I didn't know how, but I didn't dare to admit it, because everybody knew how. As a child, you care about what other people think of you, you know, so you're quick to agree. So I looked behind me and I saw Achmed, another one from Srebrenica who had lived there before the war, with his hand raised. I thought, I'm not the only one. So the imam started ranting at us: "Who are your parents? They haven't taught you anything."

Alma thought for a moment, and then added:

> And there was another time he thought I was being a smart-ass—I had to leave. That wasn't very nice; I didn't like it, that religion. But later on, he got sick. His son replaced him, and he was a cool dude, you know, because he was younger. He would say something like, "Forget that Arabic stuff, let's just rock on in Bosnian," and I thought that was a lot more fun. Sometimes, we didn't have enough tables and chairs, 'cause there were so many kids. Sometimes, you had to write while standing. . . . But it was fun.[74]

Children were the future, and even in this abnormal situation they displayed normal behavior. Alma's conflict with religious education occurred in a war zone, yet her worries about being different or not belonging are perfectly normal for her age. The parents faced a similar conflict. Parents are always concerned about their children, but in Srebrenica they faced decisions that were outside the realm of normal. In 1993, they were offered the opportunity to send their children away in trucks in order to avoid the fate of the children who stayed. There is always a long pause at this point in the interviews. Those who did not send their children away in 1993 often have regrets now. Those who did send them away are haunted by guilt feelings about the premature separation and have uncomfortable flashbacks of that time.

Devleta made the difficult decision to take her children on the convoys. The children did not understand why their father had to remain behind while she went with them.

> Planes were always flying overhead, and bombs and grenades were falling, 33 at a time. It was dreadful. I couldn't take the fear any longer. We could be killed at any moment. And there was nowhere to go. Famine. There were food drops from the air, but we didn't know how to get them. We didn't know where to go or what to do. Then, a second convoy came. . . . The night before, I had made some bread. I took my children and went to the department store and waited. The people already in the truck told me there was no room. I told them to move over some, because, just like them, I was going to save my children. I climbed in the truck and my husband handed me the kids. The kids screamed, "Pappy, come with us; don't let us go to Tuzla alone." We never saw him again.[75]

Vahida's daughters left town in a truck; she stayed behind, because her son could not go. The girls had a lunch packet from a food drop. Later, she learned that had been a good thing. The girls had not eaten the day before, and they were not given anything to eat until after the long trip through the front lines to Tuzla. "The next day, I received a half kilo of flour per person. I sat down and cried my eyes out. I made some unleavened bread. I wished my girls had been there to eat it. I wondered if they would be fed where they were going."[76]

When I interviewed her in 2007, Sabra gave voice to the mothers' grief:

> People left, fled. We sent our daughter away with her child. He was just a baby. We were afraid of everything. We also sent my younger daughter and son away, but we really didn't know where they could go. . . . Our people sent their children away. My oldest daughter, who was married, lived in Skelani. We sent our two younger children there first. Then the Chetniks began murdering; here and there we heard that someone had been killed. So when the last bus left Srebrenica, my husband fetched them and we sent them away. . . . I was a devoted mother. Later, I felt like I would rather be dead. If someone called "Mother," I wanted to die. Everybody sent the children away, so I thought I should send mine away too, that I couldn't let them stay. After I had decided to send them, I just wanted them to go. My youngest daughter was so pretty; I

was afraid she would be raped. When they were about to leave, we cuddled and hugged each other; they kissed me. But all I wanted was for them to get in the bus and leave.[77]

To the End

There is the risk of viewing the stories from 1992–1995 through the lens of the great massacre, which distorts memory and casts a long shadow over the time before. The panic, the immense suffering, and the demise of ordinary life are part of the stories about those years. But if one listens carefully, another side can be heard. There are memories in which the panic and suffering did not yet exist, when there was still a sense of having a future and of working toward it. Not paying heed to those memories reduces the survivors to a gray mass of victims without wishes, dreams, and ideals. It also does not explain how bitter the disappointment was when things went so hideously wrong. Even though everyone knew in the months before July 1995 that things were not going well, there was still the international guarantee and there were the UN soldiers. There was trust, which is why people hastened to Potočari when the message came that they should go there. What happened then was such a tremendous shock that it is almost impossible to remember the earlier positive emotions. But those emotions are there, they are talked about, and they show that, even in the deepest misery, one can remain human.

Srebrenica under siege was a tiny world overflowing with people. It was a world that had shrunk not only geographically, but also emotionally and mentally. Its inhabitants were hardly aware of what was happening elsewhere; they lived every day in mortal fear. That is why the memory of that era is now made up of sharp images of events and places—fear has caused everything else to fade. The resulting vagueness has been enhanced by the grieving over 1995. Before then, the town was brimming with inventiveness; children were born even though children were lost. There was a social and cultural life. The destruction of all that was so traumatic that one can hardly imagine what life was like before—especially if one would rather not remember too much, because it is too painful. If it has become part of the traumatic memory, then often what is left is only a wisp, a feeling that cannot be expressed in words. This is how part of one's personal history is lost.

CHAPTER SIX

VIOLENCE

Srebrenica fell on July 11, 1995. The inhabitants were driven out by the troops and fled to Potočari. Later, the refugees were either deported or murdered. This chapter deals with the memory of that slaughter and the cruelty of those days, and is written from the perspective of those who saw their loved ones perish. The survivors accept no defense or excuse for what happened there; their only aim in talking about it is to give witness. I was puzzled by how to present this material, how to convey what a genocide looks like when seen through the memories of eyewitnesses. There is so much that cannot be put into words, and so much "truth" that has been repeated again and again. At the same time, the interviewees also searched for ways to tell about their shattered lives and struggled to make their stories logical.

There are three categories of eyewitnesses to Potočari. The first is the murderers, who undoubtedly have stories to tell from their own perspective. The second is the people who saw it happen, in this case the Dutch soldiers. There are various legal gag orders and enormous social pressure on former DutchBatters, but it is safe to assume that their psychological focus is on pleading their own case. The third category is the survivors. They are the only ones with no reason to be silent, but it is often difficult for them to be heard. Only they can tell of the enormity of the violence and horror, and of what was done to them individually.[1]

The history of Potočari is one of deliberately staged terror, but *terror* is not something one can prosecute in an international court of law; it is juridically untenable. Yet terror and chaos are the central themes from the interviews; they are crucial for understanding the events and the trauma. A history of those days cannot be written without that panic, and we can only learn about it from those who lived through it. What results is not a historically chronological account, but rather an impression of what has not been psychologically integrated. The terror and chaos of those days in July were a deliberate strategy staged by the

Serbs to reduce the chances of resistance among the victims. Nobody knew who could be trusted, or what the best way out was; everybody wanted to find at least a glimmer of hope. Because the Dutch soldiers had urged the refugees to go there and because they believed the soldiers' promise of protection, part of the survivors' rage is now directed at those soldiers.

Potočari was total bedlam, and the women who survived were part of a sea of people. They could not see everything that was happening, making it difficult to view the history through their eyes. In the NIOD Report, the many pages on Potočari were written from the perspective of examining the role of DutchBat. The report concluded that there were large discrepancies between the accounts of the soldiers and the refugees,[2] which is to be expected. However, rather than just noting the different nature of the refugees' testimony, why were they not allowed to speak for themselves? I feel strongly that those days of horror cannot be fully understood without pondering what it was like to be there, without listening to those who experienced genocide in all its cruelty, violence, bloodlust, terror, and uncertainty.

Historians and Genocide

The necessity of listening to survivors' testimony is no longer doubted. In particular, Holocaust historian Saul Friedländer has demonstrated the importance of firsthand documents and accounts.[3] He feels that what he calls "deep memories"—those which cannot be easily told—must be integrated into the historiography, and not simply out of respect for the victims. He has demonstrated that writing history without them is impossible. The debate over the meaning of memories is mainly waged among historians of Nazism, but I feel it applies to the historiography of all mass violence. In order for psychological integration to take place, the historian should use what we know about empathy, imagination, and connection, which are not usually encountered in "factual" historical accounts. Using such an approach means accepting the survivors' non-neutrality in their testimony. The survivors' stories are no less true because of it.

The term *deep memory* comes from the work of Lawrence Langer. According to Langer, these memories constantly interfere with everyday memory.[4] He and other historians of the Holocaust have pointed out how difficult it is for survivors to confront so much cruelty and humiliation; storing those memories separately, so to speak, is a strategy against this. My findings are the same. Like me, Langer also had the tendency during survivor interviews to guide them back to the safe haven of everyday memory after a traumatic story. The survivors felt the need to talk about what happened, although they also wondered if they could, and their everyday memories were a respite from the grief and anger.

Acknowledging the trauma's significance requires listening to the traumatized. This means that, in describing Potočari, confused emotions are part of the historical picture and inseparable from accounts of the events. It was my task to unscramble and decipher the stories, including memories told in heavily emotional language. Anyone who conducts interviews about those three days in July is confronted with the survivors' rage toward everything and everybody, including the lack of protection, and sometimes also understanding for the impotence of the "protectors," the Dutch soldiers. In particular one encounters grieving in what threatens to become a cluttered labyrinth of memory. This memory was described to me as a series of rapidly flashing images that will not stop.

The survivors of Potočari are victims because they lost so many loved ones, through either the mass slaughter there or the deadly flight through the woods. The real victims, however, are those who lie in mass graves; most of them are men, although there are some women and children. The selective murder of strong young men is characteristic of ethnic cleansing not only in Yugoslavia; other mass murders can be interpreted in this light.[5] Analysis has shown that the Armenian genocide also involved "gendercide,"[6] in which acts against women (rape, abuse, forced conversion to Islam) served to intimidate and create chaos. In almost all other wars or massacres, men who were not in the military but were of a suitable age for service (usually 15–55) were the most vulnerable.[7]

I suspect that my most successful interviews were those in which I told the women about my family background and my experiences interviewing Jewish victims of persecution. That showed I was someone who could understand and would not judge them if their stories were piecemeal. On the other hand, when talking about Potočari, in their eyes I was part of the "guilty" nation and I had to be convinced that DutchBat was guilty. One way was to blame the Dutch in general, and occasionally me as well. I quickly learned not to take offense, and to let them know when the reproaches needed to stop. But usually, by my listening attentively, the "aggression" dissipated on its own.

No oral history interview about trauma can produce a clear historical presentation; after the interview, the historian's complex work begins.[8] There is no single form of not-telling or not being able to tell.[9] How many layers are heard in the story depends on the sensitivity of the listener. Listening enriches our historical knowledge and historical imagination; even fragments of memory about the genocide increase our ability to find new ways to tell and to listen. Listening also opens the inevitable dialogue with the survivor about why these things happened. I was asked many times what I thought had happened, and why. And I too was looking for an ethical explanation in a world overrun with trauma and the inability to listen.[10] Listening gave me, as a historian, the opportunity to bond with the victim and abandon indifference, and through these new connections and facts I have attempted to clarify and understand what is largely incomprehensible.[11]

The Witness and the Accusation

The most common format for most of the survivors' stories was that of making an accusation; however, given the chaos and the widely divergent explanations for what happened, using accusation as a framework can be problematic. Who are you accusing when you accuse the whole world? Šuhra, who now lives in a suburb of Sarajevo, told me:

> I was with my six daughters and my husband. We went to the UNPROFOR, soldiers from the UN. We went to them, to their battalion; we talked to them, they talked to us, but nobody understood anything. We couldn't comprehend each other, but what they said was Potočari. We had to go there. We went there and arrived on July 10. There were an awful lot of people there. We spent the night there, and there were thousands of others. The Chetniks arrived. We were in the last factory in the row, close to the river. There were already a lot of people there the first night. When the Chetniks got to the factories, people began to scream. I stayed two nights in Potočari with my children and husband. The second night, they turned out all the lamps, except for one in the corner. There were screams the whole night. We looked toward where the screams were coming from, but then it was quiet. And then shrieks came from the other side. You really didn't know where they were coming from. Children, women, and men—everybody screamed. On the morning of the second day, I looked around and saw that half the people had disappeared. I didn't know where they were. All of a sudden, I didn't see my husband and my daughter's father-in-law any more.

Šuhra went looking for them and found them. After two nights, the men and the women were separated. Her husband bid her farewell.

> He couldn't say anything more; I'll never forget the look on his face. My daughter's father-in-law gave my daughter-in-law 200 German marks and said to me, "In God's name, take care of my daughter," and then began to cry. My husband said nothing. He looked at the children. We left. . . . In my thoughts and memories

> I especially remember the screaming. I really can't talk about my
> feelings. I don't know what to do with them, or who I can turn to.
> I knew that my six daughters and I were at their mercy.[12]

Accusatory testimony about what the world had let happen in 1995 was
not long in coming. There are two important collections from that early period.
Hatidža Hren's book *Srebrenica: The Story of the Survivors* appeared shortly after
the massacre. Its coverage of Potočari is impressive, with many short sketches
from people who were there.[13] It is a compendium of the atrocities committed
in a few days: slitting the throats of children, carting men away, intimidation,
cold-blooded murder, psychological torture, mocking others' misery. Second,
the Society for Threatened Peoples, originally a German organization, took up
the cause of the surviving women. Over the years, it has published accounts
from them on its website. Fadila Memiševic, who works with STP, was not in
Potočari but became involved with the survivors in the first few days after the
events. One of the most shocking accounts in STP's documentation is from a
man who survived by hiding among the bodies of other men. As one of the rare
eyewitness stories by a male survivor, I am including part of it. I pick up his story
shortly before his escape.

He spent the night in a moving truck. He had noted earlier that something
was in the water the men were given to drink in the morning. He thought it
was poison; in any event, it caused his mouth to dry out. The truck he was in
turned to the left.

> The road was no longer paved. We hadn't been driving long when
> we came to a school. There was shouting, which caused a panic.
> The Chetniks began to shoot at us. When I got out of the truck,
> I saw garages with metal doors on my right. We had to walk past
> the Serb soldiers in a line, and they hit everyone who passed by. We
> were ordered to sing "Srebrenica Belongs to the Serbs," "Long Live
> the Serbian State," and other Serb songs. We had to put our hands
> behind our heads. . . . We had to go upstairs. The classrooms were
> full of men captured in Srebrenica. I went to classroom number
> three on the second floor. All three classrooms were full. When I
> went in, I saw two beaten-up men on the floor. They were covered
> with blood and showed no signs of life.
>
> The windows in the classroom were closed; we sat next to each
> other on the floor. There were no tables or chairs. Only the black-
> board was still standing. We were interrogated and abused there.

After a while, they were ordered to leave the classroom in rows of four. The
men who left did not come back. The narrator passed out. When he regained

consciousness, the classroom was almost empty. His turn came immediately, and he went outside.

> I undressed and laid my papers on a pile. They included my diploma, driver's license, health insurance card, among others. We had to put our clothes on another pile. Our pants pockets had to be turned inside out. We also had to take off our shoes and socks. They bound our hands behind our backs and beat us again. After that, they brought us into another dark area. . . . They kept us there a while, bound fast. Later in the night, we had to climb into the truck, bound, naked, and barefoot. [Before that,] we had to run downstairs and past a floor where I also saw many dead men and blood on the floor. The trucks stood in front of the door to the stairwell. They began to beat us on our backs. They shot at our feet and many were wounded.

In the overcrowded truck the men stood, naked and with their hands tied; when the truck moved, the men fell on each other. The truck came to a lighted area, and they had to get out. They were taken to a field covered with corpses, where they had to lie down. Men with stockings over their faces began to shoot. "I can still remember that it began to buzz; I didn't know where the shots were coming from. I fell among the dead while others fell on top of me. . . . Fully aware of what was happening, I burrowed in deeper among the dead." People around him moaned and rattled, but after a while the shooting stopped. He lost consciousness. After he regained consciousness, he realized that the Serbs had left him for dead. "I don't know how long I was there; I passed out once more and then woke up. The first thing I felt was pain in my arms. My hands were tied and the rope had cut the skin; there were wounds. I thought immediately about my family and tried to stand up." Another survivor warned him to wait a while longer. The two of them succeeded in escaping, naked and barefoot.[14]

This kind of testimony has shown the world the atrocities committed not only in 1995 but also in the preceding years. These documents must be regarded as truthful and as following sufficiently the juridical model for argumentation. The same applies to the book by former DutchBat interpreter Hasan Nuhanović,[15] who filed a lawsuit against the Dutch government. He was placed on a list of Bosnian men who were to be evacuated with the soldiers, and hence removed from danger. However, he did not succeed in saving his brother. His case is based on DutchBat's broken promise of protection.[16]

Other forms of accusation include the statements at the Yugoslav Tribunal during the trials against various Serb leaders and their henchmen. Reading the transcript of the trial against the Serb military leader Gojko Janković, for example, leads one to ask why the fate of the women did not receive more attention. The answer lies in the opinion that such knowledge would not contribute to the legal argumentation, and hence it was not actively pursued.

One witness was a housewife, who was testifying about the division of labor within the family; at that time (just as in the rest of the village) the big decisions were made by men and the administration was controlled by men. She remembered, "I think it was about 37 or 38 degrees [Celsius] and we looked for shelter under some carts. We searched for some shade and water, but there wasn't any water." Asked about the time she stayed there, it seems to have been two nights; but then she wanted to tell about "black Thursday." Actually, she wanted to tell her entire story, but the judge had already heard enough of such stories—and there was already enough evidence about Potočari, so it was not needed. Her story was part of a judicial proceeding, so she was expected to limit herself to the questions asked. She continued:

> Black Thursday came. It was early in the morning and my child was still asleep, the child that would be taken from me. I woke him and told him we had to leave, that we had to go to the trucks. He got up. He wanted to eat. I asked him what he wanted, knowing he wasn't going to eat. He complained he was dirty. He had on a white shirt. I took it off and cleaned him up a bit. I still had some clothes in my bag and I dressed him. I tried to calm him. I told him that we would be taken away shortly to a place where there was a shower and we could wash up. We approached the fence. . . . I knew that he didn't feel well and might faint. I looked around for water, but there was none.

A man she knew fetched water for her; he was shocked at what he had seen. He cried and told her there were lopped-off heads and unattached body parts. Her child still looked as though he might faint. "Finally, I came to the front of the line and we could leave. I thought to myself, 'Thank you, God.' After everything I had seen, after I had seen how people were separated, I thanked God, because it seemed that we had come through."

But her son was noticed, even though he had only just turned 14. He had to put his backpack on a pile and walk away: "But I grabbed his hand and repeated, 'He was born in 1981, what do you want with him? What are you going to do with him?' I begged, I pleaded his case. I asked them why they were taking him; he had been born in 1981. But they repeated the command. I held him tightly, but they took him." Her son was dragged away. His backpack was still on that pile. He asked his mother to take care of it. "My other child wouldn't stop screaming. He yelled and screamed, 'Mommy, they took my brother away. They have my brother.'" That child was inconsolable.[17]

Murder and Confusion

In their book about trauma, *The Haunted Self,* Onno van der Hart, Ellert Nijenhuis, and Kathy Steele[18] note that the inability to give meaning to what has happened is characteristic of those who have suffered trauma. In order to get a grip on their lives again, victims need to attach meaning in various ways to what happened and to find a tentative explanation of why it happened. The events that led to the trauma must become a reality, specifically a reality in the past and not one in which the events happened to another self, or were dream-like or far removed. What happened must be accorded a place in one's life story and be available for conscious reflection. But it is extremely difficult to accept that something is part of you if it is draped over your consciousness like an inexplicable, black layer of fear. In the course of that process, new psychological bonds between the person and the surrounding world must be made, and this is precisely what most survivors cannot do. It is not their fault. How can they understand what happened when there are still so many secrets surrounding the events? Why was Srebrenica left unprotected, and how could they have believed they were safe there, despite the constant shelling?

Nermina has stored those events in her memory as a dream. Everything is overshadowed by her husband's farewell.

> My husband kissed the children. He took the oldest in his arms, crying, and said, "My son, you might not see your father ever again." He wept, then he took his youngest, Omer, in his arms and said, "My son, you might not see your father ever again." The whole war, everything we went through, was not as dreadful as that farewell, that goodbye. He went to the youngest and then went to the back. He stood at the fence, crying. He left.[19]

Immediately after recounting that, Nermina said they did not seem to be her own memories, but rather they were like a film that was being played repeatedly. The trauma is not part of her life story; it has never been integrated.

The confusion, of course, is not the fault of the survivors, and it is compounded by the lack of clarity surrounding the enclave's fall. That lack of clarity feeds the ongoing stream of new explanations about what happened. The fact that Mladić still has not been captured, and seems to enjoy international protection, exacerbates the confusion and makes it difficult to see clearly what happened and what one's own place was in it all. An employee of the Yugoslav Tribunal and a former journalist, Florence Hartmann, has been at the center of a heated debate and a lawsuit regarding document confidentiality. Her unlawful indictment, which is contested by government officials, writers, and activists from all over Europe, seems to confirm the suspicion that there is a worldwide conspiracy. Although the book she wrote which led to this uproar is not widely read, people are aware of it.[20]

Talking about Potočari was possible, but it was a difficult task because the interviewees had to allow both the images of the slaughter and their feelings of confusion and terror at that time to surface. By setting boundaries and not allowing oneself to feel too much, it is possible to create a fantasy about where one was and what one saw. A few times, interviewees added fictitious atrocities to their accounts in order to convince me of how terrible things were. Sometimes, people believed that they had experienced something that in fact they had heard about from others. To them, it seemed real, and it allowed them to fill in what was forgotten with fantasy; this is normal. Stories that are repeated gradually drift further from what once was their original truth.

Every time something is recounted, there is an opportunity for the teller to add new facts and new meanings to what happened. That does not make the story less true, but it showed me how difficult it is for a traumatized narrator to place herself within the story. Gradually I realized that it was better to have one very long interview rather than to come back and begin again with the same story of trauma. If the interview went well, the interviewees gained their individual places in the history. Up until then, many had felt alienated and knew their stories did not add up as they retold them again and again. Now, with interest from outside, their perspective on what happened was being taken seriously. There were also interviews marked by long periods of silence and great bouts of grief.

If things went well, the interviewee regained a part of her identity through the rediscovery of her personal history; this explains why some of them felt lighter, even cheerful at the end. This was not the obvious outcome of talking about Potočari, but it happened often enough for me to realize that retelling pieces of one's history helps to integrate them into one's psyche. *Self-realization* is the term for this in trauma psychology. I have no other explanation for the intensity and friendliness of those sessions.[21]

The women I interviewed survived a world in which a moral vacuum had become normal and all normal ties were disrupted. In such a situation, the survivor can find herself confronted during an interview with parts of her story which are deeply painful. Many survivors had to look on helplessly while atrocities were committed. They did not have one last opportunity to show their relatives how deeply they were loved, and they did not succeed in giving their lives to save their children. The Serbs rejected the mothers' appeals to kill them instead of their sons.

Potočari was a well-directed show in the foreground to distract attention from the well-planned slaughter being carried out secretly in the background. Chaos and intimidation were part of the strategy. The refugees did not know what to do or whom to believe; they were terrified and confused. The shame a normal person feels in normal circumstances disappeared,[22] and was better forgotten. There was physical and sexual violence against women, and girls were taken. Women and girls were raped during the evacuation, women were undressed violently, babies both born and unborn were killed, and there were threats of sexual mutilation. Many of the women are still humiliated by the foul language used by the soldiers as they threatened to cut off their breasts and enlarge their vaginal openings with knives. I will not give literal translations of the soldiers' words.

A woman testified for the Research and Documentation Center (RDC), a new archive for Bosnian war memories located in Sarajevo:

> The first evening, nothing happened. The second evening, they dragged me outside. They carried me into a corner and began to beat me. With nightsticks, guns—they hit me all over. There were a lot of them. I screamed for help, but no one dared to help me; they were scared themselves. It lasted 10 or 15 minutes. They forced me to lie down on a filthy black floor. My face was down. They were all Chetniks I didn't know. I think they would have raped me if a man from UNPROFOR hadn't stopped them. He pulled me up out of the mud. I lost consciousness, but I came to. The next day, there were blue bruises all over my body. My whole body was sore.
>
> They took a lot of girls to that place, especially girls wearing headscarves. They were raped. Later, they told us that. They stuffed filth into the vaginas of some women. I'm still scared. I dream, I have fears, I tremble. I can't forget what was done to me.[23]

Watching in Shame

The women watched as their men were taken away; some were murdered before their eyes. They looked on as their daughters were raped and cowered at the violence. They could do nothing, and that impotence complicates things; doing nothing leads to feelings of guilt, which also applies to the women who were victims themselves. There are a number of analogous histories of witnessing murder. Judith Zur, in her article on the war widows of Guatemala,[24] wrote about how the government forbade the women who had witnessed the murders of the men of their village by the army to talk about what happened. They could do nothing to stop the murders, which led to painful and shameful emotions, as is always the case when a loved one is killed before one's eyes. When that happened in 1981, the women had already lived through a long history of violence against them and their families. In contrast to Potočari, the women in Guatemala were forced to watch the murders. Afterward, there was no talk of what had happened; that was officially forbidden, and the slaughter was erased from public memory. Despite the public silence, however, an unofficial history came into existence as the women told each other what happened, keeping the memories of their husbands and the events alive. Yet the women complained that they could barely recall their own memories because of the enforced silence. According to Zur, "Their guilt is more than 'survivor guilt'; it stems from the paralysis which prevented parents who witnessed the murder of their children from acting to protect them."[25] Those women also live in a psychologically desolate place where the dead have not been buried.

Zumra said something similar in an interview with Velma Sarić in Sarajevo. "I couldn't say anything more. I had the feeling that I was paralyzed and I cried rivers of tears. I didn't shriek or scream. I didn't say that they must not take him. I didn't ask, 'Why him?' Nothing, nothing. I'm not saying now that, if I had said something, it might have saved him. But I couldn't help."[26]

Chaos and Terror

The choreographed chaos was meant to terrorize people. Because they were too panic-stricken to offer resistance, the sea of people remained controllable. Šida, one of the oldest interviewees, who remembered World War II well, was hesitant in her narrative. It was difficult for her to talk, and in truth she did not want to. She would have preferred to just drink coffee.

> People were screaming. They were killing them off, taking people away, they were destroying everywhere. Women and small children were screaming. Some women gave birth to their babies there. All those things at the same time. What could you do? We didn't know where to go. We were stranded, so to speak. It surprises me that anyone who lived through that hasn't gone crazy. And they [the Serbs] were also screaming and singing.

She was afraid, but for her the real misery was the lack of water in such heat. She could stand up to the rest of the trauma better than the others, because she had already been through so much.[27]

The bedlam was also the result of the huge number of people there; dealing with them was an almost impossible task. On one hand, the men had to be taken away and murdered without attracting the attention of the news media covering the situation and without inciting the women to a stampede. On the other hand, the women and children had to be transported, but the soldiers were often drunk or under the influence of drugs. Ajša managed to express her terror in words:

> Early in the evening, they were drunk and walking around with their weapons. We were all sitting on the ground. . . . We had no idea what they might do. They were drunk and had bloodshot eyes. We sat there helplessly, waiting to see what would happen. We sat with our hands in our laps, and they did what they wanted to. So sometimes they let us through, then again stopped us and sealed off everything with a rope. . . . I wound up in a bus. They separated us from my father; they separated me from my husband. They said they had to go in the other direction and they would come later. There's a house in Potočari; if you're coming from Srebrenica, it's on the left. There were bags in front of that house, there were so many bags. God knows what they had done with those people. My father, husband, neighbors were taken to that house. Now, they say that they disappeared. No, they didn't disappear, they were living when they were taken from us.[28]

In addition to the murders, she complains that she was terrified, that she suffered during those days and did not know what was happening to her.

On the Road to the Compound

The early chaos was a tactic to keep the people herded together in and around the compound and ready for a quick evacuation. It struck me that the flight to the compound was also chaotic and violent. The DutchBat soldiers urged people to go to Potočari and gave the impression they would be taken care of there. Even then, the Dutch soldiers were cooperating with something they did not grasp and probably could not fully understand. From a number of villages, the way to the compound is not straightforward; it is easier to find an escape route in the direction of Žepa. Yet an endless stream of people walked to Potočari. Nobody really knew why they were fleeing there, except that they thought the UN base would be safe. But even that was not certain. They were being shot at and were mortally afraid. Their fears were justified. There was carnage among the refugees; some died in the crush of people on the road to Potočari, while others were killed. Another witness from the RDC reported:

> I was taken prisoner by the Chetniks. My village is about 20 minutes from Srebrenica. The Chetniks took me prisoner there and

took me to the hospital in Srebrenica. When we reached the hospital, they took off all my clothes. It's difficult for me to talk about this; it would have been better if I had died. I was completely naked. There were other women in the hospital, but they were old and invalids. I was the youngest. When they tore my clothes off, they wanted to rape me. There were two of them. One was younger, about 30 years old, and the other was 50–60 years old. They were from my village, but I didn't know their names. Another neighbor from the same village recognized me and told them to leave me alone. Later, the Chetniks gave me a blanket to cover myself with, and I set out for Potočari. On the road from the hospital to Potočari, the Chetniks chased me with knives. One of them kicked me in the back and I fell on the pavement.[29]

Thousands of people were on the road; those familiar with that road know it is quite narrow. People were pushed, shoved, and run over. When more villages were taken over, the stream of refugees increased. People tried to climb on anything that could be ridden. The Dutch soldiers shut off part of the compound and let people know that only those within could be cared for, which gave the impression that those inside would be protected. Ultimately, however, they gave no protection, even though it had been promised. The same reproach applies to the United Nations, which did not live up to its promises. Outside the enclosure, an estimated 20,000–30,000 people gathered, many with nothing more than the clothes on their backs. It was a hell in which normal human functioning was impossible. Terror and confusion dominated, and escalated further when the Serbs ordered the supposed UN protectors, the DutchBat soldiers, to take off their bulletproof vests and to swap clothing with them, which they did. Mladić entered the compound on July 12, after it had been handed over to the Serbs. The situation seemed hopeless.

What was it like to be in the midst of that massive procession—that long ribbon of humanity—moving slowly and ominously toward the compound? No one knew what would happen.[30] How fearful does a person have to be to expose him- or herself to such danger? How scared does one have to be to shove a stretcher in front of a truck in order to stop it, or to take other risks that could cost your life? All the interviewees told of how fast it went, how chaotic it was, and that they still cannot understand it. How could the Serbs kill frail, elderly people? What purpose did that serve?

Vahida was with her sick, elderly father, who had trouble walking. She cannot understand why he was not allowed to live; he was too old to be an active soldier. When the deportations began, she and her father reached the place where men and women were being separated.

They only let as many people through as a bus could carry. There were Serbs on every side. When a bus came, one stood at the front door and the other at the back door. They took all the men out. There was a large walnut tree. Every man had a small bag containing a bit of bread or something. But then I saw how many men were culled out and how their things were tossed aside carelessly. . . . People vanished, they simply vanished. . . . My father turned around and called out that we would never see him again. My mother still had his jacket in her hand. He turned around a couple of times while he was walking away. A Serb walked behind him, so that he wouldn't come back. I asked my mother to give him that jacket, because he might need it.[31]

Her mother succeeded in giving him the jacket, and her father disappeared into one of the waiting buses.

The chaos was so great that it makes remembering difficult. People were led to believe that moving quickly would help them to survive, but nobody knew why they had to hurry, why the villagers had to walk quickly to Potočari. The journey to Potočari was orchestrated, and people were not given time to think about what was happening. The haste contributed to the feeling that it was a dream playing out. In the confusion, "normal" disappeared. How survivors remember those days in Potočari and being loaded in buses and trucks for transport to a "safe area" depends on where and how long they stayed. In turn, that affects whether the memory has been integrated, or if what they saw still seems unreal. The greater the individual suffering, the greater the risk of not having integrated the experiences, and of feeling as though they are not part of one's personal history.

I interviewed Mejra in an old school, where she, her mother, and her three daughters were living; it was temporary housing in a refugee camp. She told me how she had sent word to her husband on the front that the surrounding villages had fallen. She wanted to warn him, but "we hadn't walked 100 meters before my husband appeared." He had heard from a fellow fighter about the situation and wanted to see for himself how his family was doing. There were Serbs nearby who yelled and cursed at them.

When my husband appeared, he took my little girl in his arms and we went to a place higher up in the hills, Pašonjin Dol. We sat down; we weren't alone. There were others who had left the village, refugees who had left in 1992, and also people who had lived in the surrounding villages; some of those villages had not yet been taken. We got to Pašonjin Dol and sat down. It was three in the afternoon. Planes flew over to bomb their [the Serbs'] positions. They dropped two or three bombs and we saw fire; the earth and heaven were burning. Then, the Serbs started attacking the spot where we were, making it impossible to get to Potočari. But my father went with me in the direction of Potočari. My four brothers and my husband stayed on the hill. They cried and kissed us. . . . My brothers remained on the hill. After the farewell and after my father and mother had hugged each other, one of my brothers fainted. . . . [When he came to], he put his hands in front of his face and cried like a baby. They waved at us as we walked away.

Later, a man came along who said that Srebrenica had fallen. Women and children had to go to Potočari, and soldiers had to gather that evening in Jaglići. . . . So we left.

They joined a group that had formed around an armored personnel carrier (APC) and waited for daybreak and the chance to go to Potočari.

We couldn't all hide behind the APC. It was such a throng that I lost sight of two of my girls. I heard my Sabina crying. She had a little red fur coat on her arm. She was in the second grade. . . . There were a number of older men from the villages, along with their wives and children. They said we shouldn't listen to the men in the APC, but we should go to Potočari immediately. "Otherwise, they'll kill us here tonight," they said.

The evening I arrived there, I had no clean clothes for the children. They were sweaty and had no extra clothes. I had a black petticoat that could pass for a skirt. I took off my *shalwar* [large shawl] to cover them—they were so hot—so they could undress. I carried my little girl in my arms; Sadeta was on one side, and Sabina on the other—she was still so little. Three children. My mother couldn't help me; she was carrying a sack of flour she had brought so we would have something to eat while we were there. My father had a watch; when we arrived, he said it was 12 o'clock. That night, more and more people came from the surrounding villages, all through the night. We were outside the compound; we weren't allowed in because there were already too many people— women and children, tiny babies and little children. We were outside and UNPROFOR was right across from us. There was a stack of wood, and my father said we should sit next to it, to protect ourselves from the wind and the cold. There was morning dew and our teeth chattered because we had cooled off as we rested. At seven in the morning, the Serbs from Srebrenica came to the base. We could see seven or eight men. Our people cried and realized that it was all over. They tried talking with the Serbs to convince them, [but then] we saw them [the DutchBatters] taking off their clothes. They took off their bulletproof vests. I was close and I saw everything.[32]

Mejra is referring to the fact that the Serbs forced the DutchBatters to shed their UN uniforms. The Serbs put them on and pretended to be UN soldiers. According to Mejra, that led to even more confusion, because it seemed as though UN soldiers were involved in the murders. Those soldiers, along with the heavily armed, black-clad Serbian soldiers, asked about specific persons by name, trying to find out where people from the surrounding area were. They asked what had happened to friends from school. They also ridiculed the women who were trying to prepare flatbreads over a small fire, asking them what they thought UNPROFOR was for.

In our interview, Mejra could only describe what she saw during those days in Potočari. She tried to bring order to her chaotic impressions. The confusion at the time concerned her. Should people from the villages have gone to Potočari, or not? Soldiers in the Bosnian army advised against it, but they went anyway. She described the turmoil and the cruelty somewhat clumsily. Who could still be trusted? People she knew asked about friends and classmates from their childhood, with one goal—terror and murder.

Fear and confusion dominated every interview. They were women with children and sickly old men against armed young men. In the interviews, two kinds of chaos flowed together: chaotic memories of a chaotic event.

Accusing DutchBat?

What remains is the feeling of being abandoned. That can lead to a heavy accusation, and that is the truth of most of the women. Abandonment is what they saw and experienced. There are also interviewees who realize that the real decisions were made elsewhere, and that the soldiers were afraid and not well prepared, thus making conclusions less obvious. But no matter which position the women take, everyone knows that life goes on and that hate is a dead end.

Fazila had this to say about DutchBat:

I'd never say something I didn't mean. I won't hide anything, even if it's about my brother. Those people were just doing their jobs, in the way they thought things should be done. They are human beings, just like all soldiers. If they could have done something but didn't, that depends on the individual. Besides, they weren't safe either. They were also scared when the Serb soldiers came to Potočari. Everyone was afraid for his own skin. If a man's life is in danger, he's not going to think about his father or his child. They feared for their own lives and probably didn't dare to help us. I don't blame them for not being able to help us. I do blame them for dancing and singing, that they celebrated on the occasion of our tragedy. They weren't on our side, they partied with the Serbs. As human beings, they shouldn't have done that. I accept that they didn't help us because they were afraid for themselves. The important people from the United Nations should be reproached for that. . . .

Put yourself in their position. What could 50 people do against an entire battalion of Užice and against all of Serbia that attacked Srebrenica? They could have been killed, nothing less. But if someone had sent help from Tuzla or had ordered them to help, then maybe something could have been done. Why should I blame those people? I can't hold it against them personally. They were stuck here and apparently had to act the way they did. But they didn't save my child, and I really wish they had. But what can I do about that now?[33]

No one knows what really happened, nor who made the decisions. Everyone knows they were abandoned, but not why. And that is why Hatidža, who now lives in Srebrenica, cannot hate the Dutch soldiers. She does not blame anyone; she also knew Serbs who were at Potočari, and some of them assured her that as an older woman nothing would happen to her. She was more shocked than afraid there. Like so many others, Hatidža had closed the door to her house behind her and never returned. She had planned to milk the goat, and to take things for making coffee with her. "The flowers were beautiful. They'll never be like that again. I wanted to water the flowers in the hall. Some plants were laden with velvety blossoms, so I wanted to give them a drink. I closed the front door and asked Fedo to wait a moment. But some neighbors were screaming at me, 'You have to go, Tidža. Go now!'" She asked the son of one of her friends to look after the house and her things; she expected to be back in two or three days. Suddenly, someone yelled that everybody had to go to Potočari.

Shell fragments were falling everywhere; nobody knew anything. The men left. My sister said goodbye. We were crying; everybody was crying. I told her I couldn't watch her leave, that I couldn't take it. My mother and I took my brother's children with us and we left. Some cookies that were in the pantry were divided among us. But everything I had brought with me was left behind. We couldn't carry everything. We were afraid, we were crying, we didn't know where we were going. There were so many people all the way from the bus station to Potočari. All we heard was crying and shouting. Bullets followed us on the road.[34]

According to Hatidža, DutchBat soldiers brought some water; that was her first contact with them. Some of the Serbs she encountered were old acquaintances, and she assumed they would not bother her. She was right. Her story is not ambivalent; she was not at the site of the greatest terror, and she is well aware that she was gone when the worst happened.

Munira did rage against the Dutch; she has turned her mourning into both anger and a search for the truth. As one of the core members of the Mothers of Žepa and Srebrenica, she is now well known as a fierce complainant and an excellent strategist, but at that time she was, like many others, first and foremost a mother. She was in the compound and witnessed the Dutch soldiers giving up their UN uniforms to the Serbs, which created even more confusion.[35] She and her son arrived together.

> He was 18, going on 19. When we got there, we understood the situation. The Dutch kept saying we had to go in the compound. They kept saying that being inside they could guarantee our safety, but not for the people outside. Some realized they were being duped and tried to get out, but the Dutch didn't allow that. Five or six men who left the compound are still alive. . . . I'm most angry that they didn't notify their government and minister of defense immediately.

According to Munira (and I have heard this from others), people's appearances were changed in a heartbeat by the terror. Some people's hair turned gray; others felt as though they were already dead.

> It was incredibly hot, everything stank of blood, of something offensive. Probably, the smell came from the men they had slaughtered. The abuse began in earnest when the people were separated. Rape was the order of the day. Doing away with people had begun. Everything happened in those hours, minutes, and seconds. . . . A baby was crying. A Chetnik told its mother to quiet the baby, but she couldn't. The baby was about three months old. Suddenly, he cut off the baby's head. We were totally stunned. A girl was raped right in front of us.

She told bitterly of how her son was taken from her: "They took my child. I asked them to let him go. I begged, I kissed their hands and feet and asked them to let him go. My boy expected my help. He looked at me and wept. They took him. I never found him. I fainted and regained consciousness in the hospital."[36] She was soon evacuated from the compound hospital.

The complaint against DutchBat is one of broken trust in a place where everything that was good vanished. It is about trust not just in the United Nations, but also in old friendships. A number of women asked their Serb friends and acquaintances for help, assuming that the old ties would prevail over the bloodlust. That was understandable, and there were remarkable incidents in which old neighbors really did help. Although a number of Serbs walked around with lists of known persons and others with lists of prominent people targeted for revenge, it was still assumed that old friends and acquaintances could not suddenly become murderers. For some reason, that inspired some Serbs to do their best to be cruel. The last glimmers of trust and friendship were erased at Potočari, thus heightening the trauma.

DutchBat could see what was happening and should have done everything possible to prevent the genocide. Those who listen to the survivors hear about how many Dutch soldiers they saw and especially how much the DutchBatters saw. Vahida told me:

> There was panic. People were being hit, they walked among the people. They took women and little girls with them. They came under the cover of darkness. Some came back, but not everybody. The Dutch should have said openly how many people were taken away on stretchers, how many corpses were carried out, how many people tried to commit suicide out of fear, and how many simply died of fright. DutchBat took them away in the mornings, two at a time on a stretcher, to their compound. That was their work in the morning. I don't know exactly where they took them, but they were aware of what was happening.

In the lawsuit of June 2007, not reporting misdeeds and not giving help to the victims of genocide were the reasons given for demanding compensation. Accounts such as these were the basis.

Severing Ties

Cutting the last ties with the past—and that is what this is about—is a major historical fact for the survivors. That is also true for the historian who is trying to understand what happened there and how it felt to be completely alone in a throng of people. The last shred of hope was gone, and all that remained was a world of violence. Rapes were committed in full sight of everyone. Men and women were stripped of their dignity along with their clothes, and their genitals were targets of aggression and torture. A world of decency had been replaced by one that no one wants to acknowledge. Sharp slivers of memories dominate the stories. The testimony of Šuhreta, whom I interviewed in Sase in 2004, is a good example.

> There was so much going on—mothers were crying, they couldn't say goodbye to their children, their sons. If you heard a man crying, . . . I'll never forget that. We went there, and when we were halfway there, my daughter said my oldest son was there. . . . I saw my son with a kind of backpack. He was married and had come to Potočari with his wife and mother-in-law. They didn't have children. When I was with them, I asked him where he was going. He said he didn't know. We came to a halt, there in Potočari above the factory, on the road from the village. I saw a group of soldiers coming down the road, along the woods.

Then came the moment of farewell:

> I stroked his hair one last time, something in me knew. . . . His eyes were wet with tears. . . . I was really afraid the Serbs would grab him in front of my eyes. I said, "Go, my boy, your mother will kiss you once more." I hugged and kissed him. [She turned around once while walking away. He looked at her.] Then I said, "Oh, God, take care of him; let me see him again." But that didn't happen.

At that point, she knew that none of the men would survive.[37]

Into Desolation

The reverse of cutting ties with the past is hoping that something good may still happen. The murdered children and men still live in the minds of many women; as long as their bodies are not found and identified, they continue to exist. Suada (a pseudonym) told me:

> Many people have tried to comfort us with words. That is the conclusion of what happened. I live alone now, but I don't know how much longer, or how. I find it difficult to live here now, because I see the war criminals every morning as they walk past my house, if I may put it that way. And every morning I wish them a good morning. . . . Something keeps me going, because of my children. My life is not more valuable than the lives of those three [her husband and two sons]. . . . I hope all mothers have the patience and

strength to fight for their existence, and that God makes it easier for us all. I know I can never forget my children, I can't forget my husband, my brother, his only son.[38]

When I visited her in 2004, she was still waiting, despite knowing it was unreasonable to hope. Their deaths are still not a part of her present life, although she can talk rationally about the situation.

It is unreal now; the events are unintegrated and dreamlike. I wrote earlier that few women were able to tell a chronologically clear story about Potočari. It was surreal to the end. They knew that nothing good awaited them, but such murders are always incomprehensible. The traumatic memories in the minds of those women seem to stand apart from their everyday memories, and whoever allows the traumatic memories in must also remember everything.

Zumra told the researchers from Sarajevo[39] that she felt she had plenty of time to leave her house. She could not imagine that this was the end. The enclave had been promised protection. She landed among the tens of thousands who had already assembled around the compound, which was not large enough to hold them all. The first day was bearable, but during the next two days there was too little to eat and drink, and there were no sanitary facilities. The great suffering had begun.

> Those three days were like the worst in an overcrowded hell. It was hell on earth. But I survived. [There were] 35 [or] 36,000 people in one place, old people, women, children, and a couple of men. . . . But we didn't think it was the end. We thought we could defend ourselves there, that afterward we would return to our homes. When we left, we still had food in the cellar, hidden under firewood. I put it there so we would have something to eat when we returned; if someone came for us, they might find it and eat it. We never thought for a moment that we wouldn't return. We didn't even lock the door when we left. My husband said, "We won't lock the door, because if someone comes, they'll break it down and we can't afford to spend money on nails to fix it. Leave the door open, and we'll just take the key with us. If anyone wants in, then let them. They can take what they want." . . . From the moment we walked out the door, it was a dreadful sight. We were the last on our street; no one left after us. There were people who were returning from the woods. They came out of the woods screaming, shooting, and screeching.

The woods had been stripped bare and no longer offered protection. "People had used the wood to build fires to warm themselves. Talking about this, I'm getting that same feeling I had when I saw them coming down from the hills."

Religion as Support

Religion can be a way to find meaning in what happened and to integrate it psychologically. Religion can reduce feelings of shame and make questions less thorny. If everything is in the hands of the Almighty and everything is predestined, then "why" becomes less important, and there is no answer to be given anyway. Although religion makes integration of the trauma possible, I am not suggesting that this is an easy journey. But it is a path that has been offered to the women from the beginning by the Bosnian religious authority, who has always done his best for the survivors.

In Bosnia, religion is paired with the collectively felt need to work toward making certain that such things never happen again. This feeling of "never again" is shared widely and well beyond the religious survivors; it is directly related to the former Yugoslav ideology of tolerance. This Yugoslav Islam preaches tolerance of other religions and equality. The ideal is a society in which people live peacefully with others—despite differing opinions and religions—and resist alternatives not based on acceptance of those differences. It is based on dialogue, diversity, and tolerance. The women survivors are painfully aware of the necessity for this fundamentally open attitude. They know from bitter experience what its opposite—nationalism—can lead to, even in the future. Although one might expect the survivors to be rancorous and defensive, they have every reason to avoid the dangers of nationalism.

Religious feelings were woven throughout Fazila's story and are part of her perspective on what happened. They do not make her story any less true, nor obscure its emotional tenor.

> I hate nobody. Why should I hate? Why? I could hate, if I knew who took him [her son] from me. I could wish him a dreadful fate. But I couldn't kill him. I can't kill, never. Let God judge. I could never kill a child, no matter whose child. Whoever he is, he is a child and has a soul. And I love people, I love animals. I have a cat, a chicken, and two lambs. I returned here to Potočari so I could keep animals. I love nature, I live with nature. I know when it is spring, autumn, and winter.[40]

Her story is filled with little moments in which she thanks God for the chance to be a good person, even in extreme circumstances. Her religiosity comes from her strict mother, who married a worldly man, her father. Her mother taught her many things that helped her later in the war. She was so talented at handwork that later she made things from scraps to sell. By her own admission, Fazila came from a mixed marriage, but the war caused her to turn more to her mother's religion. This deeply religious woman has worked through what she witnessed in her own way.

> There was a great deal of shooting at the beginning of the day. I slept in one room and my husband in the other. We slept apart because of the shooting. We thought, if one of us is killed, then the other would survive. But I was really scared and went to his room. I said, "What is this? Is this . . . ?" He said something was going on, because there had never been so much shooting. Our children were in Srebrenica that day [she was in Potočari]. I was terribly upset about my children. My husband told me that I shouldn't be so concerned because our children were smart.

Finally, both her children were safely in her home.

> I was happy to see them, but I was so anxious. I didn't know what to do with them, or where we should go. You know, I can talk a lot, I can tell about everything, but when I remember that moment when I left my home, when I left everything behind . . . My spouse sat in the room and didn't want me to do anything. He repeated that I shouldn't panic, that Srebrenica wouldn't fall. That evening, one of the neighbors came by and said that everybody was leaving or had already left. He asked why I was still waiting. I took a bag and put some underwear in it, nothing else. And I stuffed a jacket in it—stupid me, I couldn't imagine I would need anything else. Panic makes it impossible to think straight. I made a kind of backpack. My son warned me not to make it too large. I used a curtain from the window for it. I left the house and told everybody goodbye. I walked to the road below and saw a long line of people that stretched from Srebrenica to the compound. I turned around; I wanted to see my son one last time. He walked with me to the bridge over the river. His chin trembled and he said, "Mother, don't cry—the more you cry, the harder it is for me." No matter how strong I was, that was too much for me; that wounded me. I can't stand it, I can't stand it. He was guilty of nothing; he owed nobody anything. And I don't even know where his bones are.

Fazila sighed and called on God. After a while, she was able to continue the story of her journey to the compound.

> I was with my daughter. They were letting us inside, four by four. When they closed it all up, I couldn't go anywhere. I laid and sat on concrete. I had a towel, that was my blanket, my pillow, my

mattress, everything. There was no food. At a certain moment, an interpreter brought us three candies, one for breakfast, one for lunch, and one for supper. That's how it was for two days and two nights. But I wasn't hungry at all. I was scared and cold. It was July and really hot, but it felt really cold to me. I had shivers up and down my spine. I was in the factory, and an interpreter told me my husband and son were there. But I couldn't go to them. My husband tried to bring me food and water, but he wasn't allowed in.[41]

She had explained to me earlier what these events meant in her life. Naturally, she mourned the husband and son she lost there. But there was more; a process that had started earlier was strengthened. She became religious. The core of her story resembles that of many other women, but what makes hers unique is religion, and continuing her mother's skills.

During my marriage, I thought I should pray to God and fast during Ramadan. Nobody expected me to do that. It happened and it got stronger during the war. I read books, educated myself, learned new things, especially around the time of my mother's death. Before she died, I told her about what I had learned. Even though she was ill, she smiled, happy that I had accepted her ideas. . . . I'm not as active with my faith as I should be. But I am grateful to God; if I hadn't had my faith, if I hadn't turned to God, then everything would have been much more difficult. It gives me comfort. Before the war, I believed in people, I believed more in them than in God or myself. Now, I believe more in God than in people, because people can change. . . . Sometimes you think someone is your friend and a good person, but if all controls are lost and nobody has control, then a human can become an animal. . . . If the same should ever happen again—may God prevent that—then I would choose to go through it again. I've become wiser and I've learned things you can't get from a book and that aren't told about in stories. If I hadn't been in Srebrenica, that wouldn't be the case. And I wasn't murdered, I'm alive. There was starvation, there was so much [that was terrible]. War is not only murder and death— it is immorality, prostitution, hunger. Everything that is bad and even worse comes to the surface. Especially lies, lies, lies. Lies from journalists, lies in the media.

Fazila is well aware of the propaganda war still being fought by both sides. "I prayed to God to let me live, so that I can tell small children about what happened in the war." Fazila is not an activist. To pass on the memory of the war, she collaborates with others at the memorial center in Potočari. She runs a small flower kiosk where she also sells other items, including CDs of Djelo Jusić's beautiful music from *Srebrenica Inferno*, which is performed every year at the memorial. At the beginning of the performance, the crying begins—thousands of weeping men and women with pained faces. In the middle of the requiem, a little boy sings, calling to the mothers not to become complacent. Everyone who listens and knows what happened realizes that just such a little boy could have been murdered there.

Religion was a bulwark against human avarice and dishonesty in many stories. Munira, president of the Mothers of the Enclaves of Žepa and Srebrenica, is just as religious as Fazila, even though she does not wear a headscarf. She comes from a religious family; her interview cannot be understood without its religious dimension. To her, religion and honesty are on the same plane:

> There is a God, I am certain of that. There is a power that we cannot know. I don't know how to explain that to you. My faith was deeper before the war than after it. I don't use my faith for a purpose. I believe because I have faith in people. I've always said that real communists before the war and real believers are cut from the same cloth. I'm not talking about the imitations. A good person is a good believer, because every good person must have the same traits: no lying, no murdering, no cheating, and that's what religion teaches. Not a single religion in the world teaches people to murder, steal, cheat, kill, or grab. But here in Bosnia everything, including religion, is manipulated. People hid behind their faith, but they really didn't believe. For them, religion is a mask in order to do certain things.[42]

Chaos Also Dominates Positive Identity

Even if a woman is proud of her past, the results of the chaos still dominate. Occasionally, things seem to be going well for a survivor, but her life has still been damaged. Such is the case with Nezira, who was a soldier at the front above Srebrenica. She has a positive self-identity and does not seem to be a victim, especially when she talks about her military role, but that appearance is deceptive. When I interviewed her in 2004, she lived in Ilijas, a suburb of Sarajevo. She had yet to find permanent housing, and (like many of her fellow survivors) she was having trouble holding her own. She did not give the impression of being a soldier, but rather seemed like a downtrodden woman who hardly knew why she was alive. She lived in desolation and saw no way out. Unlike some of the other interviewees, religion was not a solution for her.

I still believe, but I'm not really a believer, and also not a nonbe-
liever. I pray when I feel I should, but if I don't feel like it, I don't.
Sometimes I'm angry with God; that feels like a sin and then I ask
him to forgive me. Sometimes I say that I don't have anybody to
pray for, because he took everyone from me, and why didn't he take
me? I don't believe in God or the government. Nothing interests
me any more. I'll never vote again; there's nothing more to be in
favor of. Living doesn't interest me. I've lost everything I had. I have
nothing more, nothing. But death doesn't come. Sometimes I think
I'll die if I don't have a cigarette. But suicide? I'm normal enough
not to do that. Sometimes I'm happy to be alive, sometimes not. I
have a child, but that's not really important to me.

I asked if there were many women on the front lines; that was something I knew
nothing about. Suddenly, the character of the interview changed. Her answer
took me by surprise—there had been many women there. She was there with
her sons.

I was a cook, a nurse, I was all kinds of things. I did whatever and
went everywhere to protect my children. They were still rather
young, innocent. I wanted to actively protect them; that's why I
took part in the war. I saw the intestines coming out of people,
people without heads, people with only hair and no eyes. Broken
arms or arms that had been cut off. I saw all of that and I wasn't
afraid. I got rid of my fear and now I can stand the sight of blood.
It does nothing to me now. I was busy with the last line at the
front, because I had a baby. [But] if I got an order, I was a normal
soldier.

Her daughter was staying with Nezira's parents; they were hiding in a cellar.
That cellar was also a radio station and a kind of headquarters. Soldiers from the
UN came there, and the commander of the Bosnian troops stayed there often.
He knew the radio codes that she did not.

Nezira was happy to take in young women who approached her about
joining the army, because she wanted her children to be treated that way if it
came down to it. It was a difficult time.

The fear was always there. I didn't take my boots off, and for two
months I never wore pajamas. When I did take off my boots, my
feet looked like they had been boiled in a washtub; they didn't look
normal. We slept in the woods, because we didn't dare to spend the
night in the house. You could never just relax. We always thought

they'd come during the night, and then they'd come during the day. They'd attack in any event, and that's what we told ourselves. That's how it was—peaceful one day and an attack the next. I was especially scared when they called my name on the front. They saw me.

Neighbors always recognized each other. It seems that Nezira, besides her soldiering, also tried to plant grain on land that was behind the front lines. Her neighbor, who was on the Serb side, told her when it was safe to plant and when there was a change of guards, making the border between the fronts dangerous. When he was on duty, there was no shooting.

This proud soldier is still suffering defeats: she was almost evicted from her house, and she has failed to pick up the thread of her life again. The last time Nezira saw her sons, they were walking down the hill with other soldiers. She was not yet aware that Srebrenica had fallen. The army was going to reposition and try to force a breakthrough. Her older son waved to her, and the younger one hugged her one last time. She also cared for her 75-year-old father.[43] In the interview, the caregiver and the soldier were constantly changing back and forth, but in the end only the desolate mother remained.

Violence against Women

I wondered if women could really talk about rape. It is well known that there were all kinds of violence against women in Srebrenica and Potočari, but it always seemed to happen to someone else. It was difficult to find women willing to talk about it in the first person. Talking about such things in the third person is a good defense, both against shame and against an environment that often reacts aggressively. A number of women did manage to talk about it, especially in Sarajevo, where things were more anonymous. Occasionally, the women had not been raped, but rather "toyed with" sexually, because the Serb men were too drunk to actually rape them. Gang rape, in which men think they are proving their manhood, is part of ethnic cleansing.[44] Unfortunately, as Amnesty International has pointed out, the juridical difficulties surrounding such crimes make prosecution almost impossible.[45]

I have the impression that often men who tried to commit rape were inebriated and under pressure. They did not always succeed, became enraged, and often turned to other forms of violence. Sometimes it was just too much, even for the thugs and bullies. They too suffered from the summer heat and had little to eat, but far too much to drink. But what difference does it make? It was still aggression.

Below are the stories of two women who were physically attacked. They are not "average" or "normal" rape victims, because ultimately there is no such thing.

Told in Confidence

I know S quite well. She is a tiny woman. In the past, she was a rascal, a cheerful braggart, but now she has sad eyes and falls silent at a moment's notice. We have an appointment with an interpreter; she wants to talk. The last time was not a success. In her hotel apartment, we create a space that shuts out the world outside. It is intense. Zlata interprets, and we are all three doing our best.

> I was in Potočari two days. I left the third day, maybe about one o'clock at night. Of course, it is difficult for me to talk about this. It was—how to put it—an unconditional separation. I didn't know if I would ever see them again. That's the most painful part of war, being separated from my children, my husband, my father. How can you survive that and remain normal? And you still didn't know what was going to happen. I call it an unconditional separation, because it is too painful to explain. . . .
>
> I found my father the second day in Potočari. They wouldn't take him in the APC [armored personnel carrier] and he couldn't walk, so he crept a kilometer. A whole night and a whole day, I tried to get to the fence's boundary. I don't really know any more how I got to Potočari. I tried to find out through asking around where my father was. I was told he was inside the compound enclosure, but the people I talked to weren't soldiers. I don't know what they were. I didn't know. I found him and took him to my mother, so we were all together. My sister's father-in-law, his brother, and [the] brother's wife were there too. We were all together, six old people in one spot.
>
> While I was outside the compound—I was never inside— things got worse from hour to hour and minute to minute. Mladić came—I was standing only two meters away from him—and there were Serb soldiers in all kinds of uniforms. They mingled among the people. I begged the Dutch soldiers for help, but they said nothing or something terrible. Nothing, no help. They couldn't or wouldn't help. Maybe they were also helpless.

A cameraman from a Serb television crew encouraged S to smile because, he said, she was going to her own territory.

An old man was sitting nearby. A Chetnik waved his knife and cut off his genitals. The blood . . . He stood briefly, swaying, until he collapsed. People panicked and ran away. They were shoving, pushing, and all landed on one side. So he was completely alone on the spot where he fell. There was a Dutch soldier there. The fear made me act; I went to him and asked, "What's happening? What are you doing?" As best I could understand and could translate, he said that what was happening was good for us. But it was not good for us. What he said was true for him, not for us.

They took away some men farther up and I asked the soldier again why the men were singled out. He used the same words. At a certain moment, I realized he had a weapon. Why didn't he shoot it in the air? I asked him why he had that weapon. Something in me was boiling. "Do something," I said. But there were tears in his eyes. I think he was also scared. I don't know. There was so much carrying on. People screamed, children were taken from their mothers; they dragged them away and said all kinds of things to us. They hit us and took girls with them. I looked around me, but there was no place to hide. "The earth was hard, the heaven high, and you weren't a bird who could fly" [a Bosnian proverb].

It was summer and hot, but I was wearing a wool jacket. I don't know why I had brought it. No idea. I took the jacket and noticed that it felt best if I pulled it over my head. And I tried to find a solution. When I looked around me, all I saw was suffering and I heard shrieks that gave me the shivers. I tried to stay in control and not sink into depression, lethargy. I tried not to forget who I was.

She thought of her sons, and that gave her strength.

My father fainted. He was sick and exhausted and lost consciousness, so I used that jacket; and the quiet and the darkness helped me to stay in control, to remember where I was and in what condition, to be aware of who was around me and how things were developing. I knew I had to fight. . . . I could have gone crazy at that moment—many women did, so many ended their lives.

I wrapped my arms around myself under that jacket. I hugged myself and said to myself that I was worth it, that I was most important to myself, and that I had to endure all this for my children. . . . And one way or another, that helped me to win out over all that horror. I was hungry, thirsty, and exhausted. And then there was the terror. As I turned around, I saw more frightful things. . . .

I tried to fetch some water for my father. It was perhaps 40 degrees [Celsius] and we were sitting close together. One of my neighbors had a jerry can. There was a faucet by the road, but the Chetniks were there; Dutch soldiers were walking in between. It was about five meters away, and I asked one of the Chetniks to let me by. He said, "Do you still dare to speak to me? I could rip you to shreds with my teeth." One of my neighbors, an older woman my mother had known, walked with me a bit, so I wasn't alone.

I had to walk 300 meters farther up a path; there were houses and I found water in a stream. I could not imagine what I would see and experience there. There were five or six Chetniks sitting under a tree. There was a tree stump used for cutting wood, and there were murdered people. They indicated I could get some water. Pity I didn't know them, [I knew] nobody. . . . I don't know who they were, if they were from around there or strangers. All I know is they had long beards and big knives on both sides. They had cartridge belts—I can still see the bullets. They let me pass and I went in the house. The Chetniks had made a shambles of the house and they let me go inside. The glass door was broken and I went in through the broken glass. They had damaged the water line; there was a water spout that almost reached the ceiling. Because of the water pressure, I couldn't fill the jerry can, only half of it. I got to the steps leading outside and they were at the door. One of them ordered me to give him some water to wash himself. And there was another woman who had lost her way. She didn't know where to go and had hidden herself in the house. She asked me why I was there. While I got the water, she warned me that they would kill both of us. But I summoned my courage and found the strength to leave the house. She walked along with me. Three men came downstairs and murdered her—maybe five meters from me. Then I thought I would be murdered like that.

One of them asked me to pour water from the can so he could wash. He cupped his hands together. I tried to keep the can from shaking, but I spilled water. He looked up and hit me, saying, "Why are you shaking so, filthy *balinkura* [a pejorative for a Muslim woman]?" the soldier asked. "Just look at you, you don't even weigh 20 kilos." I weighed 42 kilos. I was thin; indeed, I was 20 kilos thinner than now. I couldn't say anything. I had no voice, nothing. I didn't scream. I couldn't do anything. I was terrified. At one point, I didn't know who I was any more. He hit me again and took his gun and began to hit me with it and he kicked me with his foot. I fell down. Then he took his knife, and I looked at the air above me. I stared at the air. I didn't want to see anything else. I knew he was going to kill me, but I wanted to look to heaven. I don't know what happened; I lost consciousness.

When I came to, I didn't know who I was, where I was, or that there was war. I knew nothing, absolutely nothing. Suddenly, I remembered. I knew I was in Potočari and that I had gone to fetch water. I knew there was war, I knew it. Suddenly, I knew it all again and tried to stand up. I couldn't. I tried to get on my hands and knees, but fell over several times. I began to hurt. I tried to stand up. There was a little stream, about 10 meters from the house. I let myself fall in that. I don't know how long I was there. A tiny stream with muddy water. I don't know how long I laid there with my head halfway in the water. I am crazy about water, I love it. I think the water helped me clear my head. It refreshed me, and I recovered myself. I regained some strength and energy, I got stronger. I tried to stand up, but still couldn't. I sat in the middle of the stream and splashed water on myself with my hands; then I waded through it on my hands and knees.

S returned, covered with bruises.

Hamra's Rape

Through discussions regarding Hamra (a pseudonym), I learned about the Dutch obsession with making sure that no DutchBatter was involved in the violence. Hamra was raped, and according to her the man responsible was a Dutch soldier. For her, it is another reason to feel betrayed.

She had said she would never talk to Dutch people, and it took a great deal of convincing from my go-between to get her to agree to speak with me. At the end of our interview, she sighed and said she didn't know there were also Dutch like me. It was hours—and many cigarettes for her and the interpreter—later. We embraced. It was no longer a question of nationalities; now, there was space for friendliness and kindness. She felt well, she said, relieved that she could tell her story meticulously. As I left, I felt that the memories were beginning to be accorded a place in her present life.

I know there are people who will not believe her story, but I also know how difficult it was for Hamra to tell it. I know how many tears fell during her interview with a Dutchwoman, and how we and the interpreter (who played a major role in all this) decided there was no enmity between us.

Hamra had given birth 40 days before arriving in Srebrenica.

The shooting began. It was really bad. We ran, but we had nowhere to go. Planes circled above our heads. I ran with the children. I'm usually very afraid if things aren't going well. I get fearful, anxious. I was carrying the baby. I carried my son in one arm, my daughter in the other. I carried them. We were ordered to go to Potočari. Everybody from the town had to go to the industrial zone at Potočari. Not the men, only women and children. Men went to the woods, over the hills, and we went to the industrial zone in Potočari. There was a lot of shooting; there were planes, shell strikes, bullets, flashes on the asphalt and both sides of the road. We heard grenades somewhere. I didn't know where to hide and I had my children in my arms. I don't know, I can't describe how it was. I don't know. We arrived in Potočari, at the factory. The Serbs came also. They and the Dutch soldiers were on the land where we were. The Serbs approached us and told us not to be afraid, that they wouldn't hurt us, that we didn't need to be afraid, that we would go on to Tuzla, that they would take us. There was no water in the factory. I sat on a concrete floor; after all, it was a factory. I sat there with my little ones, and since I had no water I asked a woman to look after them for a few minutes, so I could get some water. I saw that the terrain above the factory was full of soldiers, thousands of Serbs. I can't describe it; they looked like ants coming toward us. I saw a horse walking in circles, running, because it was on fire. . . .

General Mladić went to the front of the factory. He said we should prepare to go to Tuzla. There would be buses. He said all women and children would leave without problems, only men older than 15 would not. He was escorted by Dutch soldiers. I was afraid; I saw them by the door. I hid myself behind a machine; it was a battery factory and there were machines. I hid myself with my children behind the machines. They couldn't have seen me. People began to scream and yell. It got dark. I stayed in the factory. I couldn't go anywhere else. . . . I was helpless with such little children. I couldn't go anywhere, I had no other place to hide, they were everywhere. Everybody screamed. I tried to rest. I still remember that screaming, when women and children began to scream. . . . They screamed they were going to murder us. All of them at the same time. I jumped up and felt like I lost consciousness, as though the baby had just been born. The yelling and screaming lessened. People went to their places. When the women and children began to cry and scream, they all stood up. I don't know how that went, I don't remember everything any more. Then it got quieter . . . and it was daybreak. Everyone was glad it was getting light. That gave us strength. Mladić came again the next morning at about 10 o'clock, again accompanied by those soldiers. He told us not to worry and not to be upset. At 12 o'clock, buses would come to pick us up.

I couldn't get there [to the buses]. The stronger ones with no small children made their way to the buses and trucks. So I stayed behind in the factory. Another night in the factory. And that night, the same thing happened. The noise, the screaming. I begged God to let the day come, to let me make [it to] a new day. In daylight, you could see what was happening; at night, you couldn't, you couldn't see where your child was, nothing. I sat the whole time with my kids, I stayed with them.

The third morning came. The worst morning. Four soldiers approached me. They yelled and pointed a finger at me and barked, "You, with the little baby, go there and get something to eat." Two Dutchmen and two Serbs. One was an interpreter. The interpreter laughed; he had a helmet, a bulletproof vest, and a weapon. A Dutch soldier. I wasn't expecting anything; I couldn't imagine something might happen. All I thought about was getting something to eat. My children and I hadn't eaten in three days. I went with them and took my children, and went with them behind the factory. There was a white tent. They told me to wait there. They closed the tent from the outside with a zipper and told me to wait for the food. Yeah, I waited—it was hot, maybe 40 degrees [Celsius]. It was stuffy and hot. My children and I were sweating. There wasn't enough air in the tent, but I couldn't open it from the inside and there wasn't another opening. You could only open the tent from outside.

I could tell from the light in the tent that the sun set, and it got dark. You couldn't see any more, but I saw a light through the tent canvas. I saw someone coming from the direction of the factory. The tent opened and a hand appeared; I saw a hand. The tent was opened from the outside and they came in. I thought they had brought me something to eat, so I stood up to take the food. They were the same men as those [I saw] in the factory. The man who laughed was blond, very light, very blond; I remember the hair, the eyes, the hands. I remember everything. They were drunk. If the interpreter spoke close to me, I could smell the alcohol; his breath was loaded with alcohol. One of them came to me and hit me in the face. Really hard. I think he hit me from the left. When he hit me, it felt like something broke. Then my nose began to bleed. I saw blood coming out of my nose, and after that I know and remember nothing. My children were close to me, but I remember nothing, absolutely nothing.

I do remember things as in a dream, and in that dream I was fighting. I shoved something in front of me away, I don't know. I don't know, but in the dream, I was in pain here [she points to her lower abdomen]. Here. I opened my eyes and it was day. It was morning. I tried to turn over, but I couldn't move my head at all. I didn't know what was wrong with me. I couldn't see where my children were. I couldn't move my hands, legs, nothing moved, and I heard my little boy crying. He called, "Mama!" He called me. I saw him and then lost consciousness again. Later, I came to a bit. When I came to the second time, I saw that I was bloody and covered with bruises. My arms were black and blue. My legs . . . blood everywhere.

Her clothes were ruined. She tried to leave the tent. She wound up in Kladanj; she had been evacuated, although she does not know how. She had been in a bus, but she only became fully conscious on an examination table in a medical center. She came to because she was cold; she was covered only with a sheet. The medical assistant brought her children to her. She had been raped in front of them, and that is a humiliation she can never forget.

When I told Hamra's story at a gathering in the Netherlands, I was immediately challenged. Dutch soldiers would never do such a thing. My answer is that every "peace" operation is marked by excesses, so why not this one? I have been back to ask Hamra if the perpetrator might have been one of the mercenaries hired by the Serbs, who were from many nations, including Greece, Russia, Ukraine, and Bulgaria. But she knew how the Dutch language sounded through contacts with DutchBatters. I have also been asked if I can prove her story, but rape under such conditions is almost impossible to prove.

Dražen Erdemović, the war criminal convicted of dozens of murders at Srebrenica, became agitated at the question of rape during his trial in The Hague: "It means that if a woman just says, 'you raped me,' then nobody, not even God himself, can deny it." Erdemović then called into doubt the existence of justice. The judge, however, refused to accept that line of reasoning.[46]

Truth and Silence

There is much that has not been told or cannot be told. There is a lot of shame about things, shame that I gradually began to understand. Sometimes,

I already knew a great deal in advance about an interviewee, and that was a help. One woman seemed to tell me everything, except what I already knew. Everyone around her knew that her daughter had been raped and her husband had hanged himself, but those events did not cross her lips. It was a strange experience to interview someone about her life and to be aware of the secrets she did not talk about. What is not said is as much a part of an interview as what is said. The time may not be right to talk about some events, or perhaps it is not the right place,[47] or perhaps there is not enough time to get to that part of her story, although she bravely attempts to convey it all. This interviewee wanted to support my work; she wanted to help bring the truth to light. But there were things she could not say to me. Searching for the truth and wanting to know what happened form the framework of many women's stories. This is understandable; finding answers can help in finding some peace. The women know all too well that, increasingly, one version of the events is being manufactured, but it does not match their truth or their perspective on the past.[48] They do not, however, have the political power to change this.

There are taboos about what can and cannot be said. Whoever breaks through the silence is both vulnerable and courageous. Attempted suicide was one taboo most women were able to discuss, and mental illness was another. Occasionally, a family member was accused of atrocities, and the interviewee knew more about what had happened. With regard to the looting raids for food, some of the women committed acts they would have considered impossible in times of peace, and many of them would not repeat them again, even in wartime. They are well aware of what is right and moral, hence they remain silent. There is also shame involved in talking about what happened within the family itself in dire circumstances. Family relationships, like all relationships, are affected by stress, and living in cramped quarters can make life unbearable. Sometimes, I could hear these things clearly, although they were not put into words.

Learning from the Survivors' Interviews

At first read, the interviews about Potočari may seem disjointed, but they do tell a story. The interview I had with Ćamila Omanović is a classic example. She was chosen by her fellow townswomen to negotiate with Mladić. As a key figure in the trial that investigated Mladić's role at Srebrenica, she has told her story often. Usually, she is portrayed as the negotiator. She was powerless, but her attempt to call on the old ties of friendship was remarkable (see chapter 3). Her self-image, however, is not that of a negotiator, but of a mother who seemed capable of the task. She had fled to the compound after years in a happy marriage, about which she digressed at length. That happiness has never returned.

Her fear was primarily for her children, and that was the main theme of the long interview we had in her house in Srebrenica. The following fragment, which emerged after hours of interviewing, begins with the fall of Srebrenica. She was concerned about her daughter's baby. It would need diapers if they decided to leave. The diapers were drying on a clothesline on the balcony; retrieving them was risky because of bullets whistling across the balcony, but Ćamila succeeded. As the Serbs approached Srebrenica, she was in her brother's house on the edge of the town, about 10 minutes' walk from the town center. "There was shooting from all sides and we were herded in one direction. . . . We stayed close to walls for protection, and we saw how people ran out of their houses in the direction of the town. We reached the center. The shooting stopped about the time that we got there."[49]

They spent the night in the town center, but the next morning she decided to go back and cook the chickens she had slaughtered, so they would have food to take with them.

> They were half-cooked when the shooting began all around; it was a hell. I packed all the chickens, even though they weren't done; I really didn't know what to do. There was shooting and fire everywhere. I put them in a plastic bag; I got some things for the baby and put them in the stroller. Everybody was heading in the same direction, so we followed them. I pushed the stroller while they were shooting at us from all sides. We heard the bullets and grenades whistling. When someone was hit, he was left on the side of the road—nobody did anything; he was left there. We walked the five kilometers to Potočari under fire. When we got there, they told us that babies and young women with babies were being put in the battery factory. But by the time I reached the yellow enclosure, it was closed; they had taken in enough people. I didn't know whether the Serbs had ordered it closed, or if they had decided on a specific number to let in. So we couldn't enter the factory. I really wanted my daughter and her baby in that battery factory, and then we would stay on the grounds in front of the factory. . . . I wanted to protect the child; what happened to the rest of us was not that important.

Ćamila and her husband found a spot and covered it with grass, so that sitting there was more comfortable. During the interview, Ćamila was first and foremost a woman caring for a child. When she negotiated with Mladić, she did so as a mother who was trying to reduce the chaos. She wanted to convince him of the need to restore order. During the talks, she told Mladić that she was there as a grandmother, a mother, and a wife. She wanted to know what could be done about the things that were happening. "We were driven here like cattle; we have nothing to sit or lie on; we have nothing to eat, nothing to cover ourselves—nothing—and there are many babies."

Later, she felt she had put her children at risk by trying to negotiate; in addition, the responsibility was too heavy for her. Ćamila is usually interviewed as the town's negotiator who was brushed off by Mladić, in other words as a well-known person. Naturally, she brought charges against the aggressors and testified against them. When I interviewed her, however, what she told me was not suitable for a formal court case. She wanted me to know that she is an average woman, not a politician. And because she is an average woman, she was not prepared for the visibility of her position; it was too much for her. This kind of interview—with a mother who had been in a situation so dangerous that at one point she wanted to die—shows how overwhelming the fear and panic were. For the historian, the relevant information about emotions comes packed within other stories. In this interview, the happy times of brief vacations and hope for a future that could only get better contrast starkly with the total terror and desolation of July 1995. Of course, the account of the negotiations is important, but the other knowledge is crucial in order to understand who she was and how deeply wounded she is.

The image of the mothers in Potočari looms over Ćamila's story and adds to the scenes of horror described in all the other uncomfortable stories. As the women tell what they felt and experienced during those days, they contribute to our knowledge. It is about more than losing all that was dear to them, although that was dreadful enough. It requires calling up that which is most painful— memory—which threatens to unravel their psyches. It requires pulling back a veil, often forcefully, that shrouds both psyche and memory. I chose to listen closely to these women, while cordoning off our work. Terror and fear can only be understood within a context, and here I have chosen the challenges of memory. Describing Potočari is describing trauma, which by definition is always unfinished.

Hadžira Ibrahimović lives on the edge of Sarajevo. She is old and did not succeed in telling much. She has lived through two major wars. I wanted to know if one had been worse for her than the other. The hunger was more severe during World War II, she said, but the last war's devastation was far greater.

She is not really angry with the Serbs; she realizes that people must live together again, although she does not know how that can be done. She is also not angry with DutchBat, except that she thinks they should have warned the residents of Srebrenica.

They should have told us earlier. They should have explained when they came. They should have said, "Go away, run to somewhere," or something. But they waited, and when the Serbs came to Srebrenica they didn't do anything. They should have warned us earlier, but they didn't. . . . When it happened, they all said, "See to it that you leave; there are Chetniks. See to it that you leave; run away, run away!" So we went to Potočari. But they should have told us. And that's why we regard them as guilty. They were in contact with our people on the front lines. They should have told us what was going to happen. They were in Srebrenica, just like us. They lived among us. And when the Chetniks came, they were also afraid of them, afraid they'd be murdered.[50]

CHAPTER SEVEN

DEPARTURE WITHOUT ARRIVAL

Reaching the buses seemed to be the end of the nightmare. There was a rumor that the women and children were going to be evacuated to Tuzla, and it seemed best to leave Potočari as quickly as possible. But was that true? Was it a trip to Tuzla or to a concentration camp? How much risk would there be for the women during the trip? Today, we know the answers to these questions, which evacuees asked themselves during those days in July. We know that men were taken off the buses, usually to be murdered, and that many young women were also taken off, abused, and raped. In a number of cases, women were beaten up. The buses did not go directly to the "safe area," as had been promised. Groups of unruly Serbs stopped buses, searching for plunder. Food (but not alcohol) had been scarce for them. They wanted cigarettes and sex. They were tired of shooting at Muslims. It no longer made sense to them either.

Before there could be a departure, the women had to reach the buses. Memories of those moments often bring up rage against the Dutch soldiers who looked on and did nothing. Once again, a soldier one knew (or perhaps not) was asked for help, and again there was that gesture of refusal. A number of soldiers say they were powerless, but the women only saw their refusal. In the women's stories and memories, the soldiers watched and did nothing. Some people excuse the soldiers because they were nothing more than "bystanders," a word often used in the debate over Srebrenica. In particular, it is used to point out that the soldiers could not do anything. Being a bystander, however, is not an explanation.

A major debate has been waged in the historiography of World War II over the role of the bystander. The term was originally used for the average German, who stood by and watched the slaughter of Jews and others.[1] Could they have done something? Did they in fact want to do something? The discussion surrounding the bystander's role also includes whether nations could have done something, and how much responsibility belongs to those who instigated the crimes.[2] It is generally accepted that watching violence and not intervening is a form of complicity. The world looked away while the slaughter took place, thus making the debate about more than simply an excuse.[3]

Grünfeld wrote that the role of the bystander is crucial at the point when the victim can no longer offer resistance.[4] The aggressor's behavior may escalate as a result of the lack of reaction from onlookers. He compared the behavior of NorBat (Nordic Battalion) in Tuzla in 1994 with that of DutchBat in Srebrenica in 1995. In 1994, heavily armed Danish peacekeepers fired on Serbs who attacked them, thus stopping the Serb attack. Of course, they had heavy weapons and tanks, and DutchBat did not; it was a mistake to send the Dutch soldiers equipped with only light weapons. According to Grünfeld, many of the Dutch soldiers knew what was going to happen, and those who did not intervene are blameworthy. The lawyers who represented the survivors in their lawsuit against the Dutch state went even further and stated that the lack of air support was deliberate. The Dutch government did not want an air strike out of concern for its troops.

To the victim, the bystander who did not respond to the call for help and looked away is difficult to separate from the threat and actions of the aggressor. The women in Potočari observed that DutchBatters did not stop the violence in the compound and on the grounds around it. The separation of the men and women took place under the noses of the Dutch soldiers; indeed, they helped to keep the situation "orderly."

The traumatic stories of going to the buses, which included the separation of the men and women, and of the journey through enemy territory in the Serb Republic are all jumbled together. It is impossible to tease them apart, because everything happened as if in a dream. Violence and terror were everywhere; gradually, the victims became exhausted. What happened during the journey has only been recorded in the reports of the Yugoslav Tribunal and told to me in my research. There is not a single account in the international reports, which are concerned mainly with the fall and with the statistics detailing the victims.

The buses only drove to the front line, which was 5–10 kilometers from the actual border. The territory between the warring parties had to be crossed on foot, a dangerous undertaking. At the end, the survivors had to go through a tunnel that was dark and uneven; by the time they reached the tunnel entrance, they were already in quite a state. Once the evacuations were in full swing, there were Bosnian soldiers to guide them and to help those who had difficulty walking. Despite that, the survivors only felt safe once they reached the other side.

Departure

Departing meant a release of the enormous tension that had built up in the compound and its surroundings, which had increased along with the violence and cruelty. Sevda talked about how unbearable it was.

All I wanted to do was to go to the buses, no matter what happened. I told myself, whether they murder us or not, I can't stay here any longer. There was that great mass of people; my child was hungry and crying. I left my child with my sister-in-law and went looking for my mother. I found her nearby in a garden, digging up potatoes. I told her we had to go, that the buses were there. She said, "I'm afraid to go with the first buses; they're going to finish us off." I said, "Well then, let them, but let's go. Let's just go to Tuzla. I can't stay here any longer." I was worn out with the fear, the hunger, everything, and had been since I left my home. [My mother] followed me through the crowd; everybody wanted to leave. The Chetniks were lined up there. If you were lucky that day, you could get to the buses in about an hour. I don't know how it happened, but I was one of the first to leave. We sat in the first or the second bus. My mother, my sister-in-law, and my child were with me. My husband's sister said I should go with my mother. She remained behind and I lost sight of her. I don't know who went with whom, I don't know any more. We went in the direction of the barracks; we grabbed our children and our bags and made our way through the crowd. People were shoving and there wasn't enough air. I put my child on my shoulders. I held her tightly out of fear that she might be separated from me and trampled underfoot by the crowd. It was horrible, that throng of people. I got to the fence and they stopped us. . . .

When we arrived in Bratunac, a Chetnik got on the bus, counted the seats and the number of people, then left. He didn't say anything. He got off the bus and shut the door. There was no water. I had a half a bottle, but the heat was unbearable. I was afraid my child was going to faint.

The five buses made their way to the border between the two armies.

They stopped the bus and said we had to go farther on foot. They didn't say we had reached our area. It still wasn't our land. Chetniks were lined up along the road. We got off the bus. . . . I had a bag and I was wearing a long dress; it got in my way as I walked. There were Chetniks everywhere. We were going in the direction of a small roadside restaurant. As we were walking, they yelled at some of the girls, "What a cutie!" I asked them to walk slower—we were walking in a row, like soldiers. I told the girls not to react to their remarks and to look straight ahead and keep walking, like we had been told. There was a stream and my daughter wanted a drink.

I told her not to go anywhere. "You've made it this far; just keep on a bit longer. We'll come to a place with water." We didn't know where their territory ended and ours began.

I don't know how long we walked, but we came to a tunnel. Our people from Tuzla came out of the tunnel. They called out, "Don't be afraid; we are your people."

At the end of the tunnel, they were welcomed and given tea. That was the experience of the first refugees, when there were still supplies and the aid workers still had energy. Later, there was such a crush of people that the warm reception Sevda experienced was no longer possible. The enormous influx was a major logistical problem.

Sevda and most of the others were driven to Dubrave, where a tent camp had been set up. When they arrived, there were no sanitary facilities and the living conditions were poor, but they felt welcome. The fear of being murdered was in the past, and they found some peace as they waited for news of their men. Sevda was there for a month and talked about the waiting. "While we were there, we expected to find those who had gone through the woods. Occasionally, a group did come." It was still assumed that the men would come, but with the passage of time that changed.

A cousin appeared and took her and her child to his house. That move to another location created a bureaucratic problem later. When Sevda tried to register as a refugee, she was told that she was not one, because she did not live in a refugee center. She was turned down repeatedly. She had nothing, not even a mattress to sleep on. "I worked during that time. I did digging, I helped with haymaking, I picked plums. I knew how to do all sorts of things, so I did chores to earn some money."[5]

Muška told Anna, a student who interviewed her, about the dreadful time after Potočari.

> And then the time comes when you have to leave as well. We were the last. The last day, Thursday evening, or maybe it was afternoon. We were told, "Make sure you don't have anything sharp with you, not even manicure scissors. Sharp objects are not allowed. They are regarded as dangerous." . . . We were also instructed that they took young women and girls, so we rubbed ourselves with ashes. You wore the ugliest clothes you had and made yourself as unattractive and inconspicuous as possible. We were put in a truck, and you know the way there; on one side are the Dutch soldiers and on the other the Serbs. The Dutch soldiers just stood there looking at us

and let us go by. They said nothing; they were also scared. I still remember that one soldier from the military cried when we had to leave. He said he would never forget the faces, that he saw the people taken away and he was part of what happened. . . . I saw he was deeply disappointed with the whole operation. At one point, he began to curse—"Karremans' cancer pit" [Karremans was the DutchBat commander] and "they're useless, they have no guts"—as a kind of apology. And they started to cry, the men really began to cry loudly. They were bawling, not just sniffling. When we had to leave, they tried to put us at ease by saying that maybe we would come out okay. You also saw women whose children were taken away, even though they were only 12 or 13 years old.

A woman who walked behind me had a little boy, a son. He was skinny and tall for his age, but had a child's face. Good Lord, you could see he was a child. They told him, "You have to go over there and your mother over here." She went up to the Serb soldier . . . and latched onto him with her whole body. "Then you take me as well; if you take him, then you take me too! He's 12 years old!" She was screaming and yelling. . . . He couldn't get her off himself. So he said, "No, they're being taken another way." She said, "No . . . you're going to murder them, you're murdering them. I know it, I know it! So just say it!" So many traumatic happenings right before your eyes—some said they wanted to die, that they didn't want to know what happened to their children. That's how it was. They screamed, they were pulled off and taken to the truck. That woman was thrown in the truck, and the others were told it was their job to make sure she didn't get out of the truck. Otherwise, she really wouldn't come back. So what do you do to prevent something worse? You grab hold of the woman and put her down—and we sat on her. . . . From the bus, we saw a large field full of men. The first thing I noticed was how many men there were. I didn't know so many men had gone to the base. You saw that the life had already gone out of them. Their eyes were empty. They knew they were looking at death, and you could see it in their eyes.

On the road to Bratunac, the people of the town threw stones at the bus. Along the way, they also saw large groups of men with their hands above their heads. They had been captured. She saw shooting on the mountain where the men from Srebrenica had probably gone. She hoped that she would see a number of the men in Bratunac.[6] "Then we went in the direction of Tuzla, then past Kravica . . . and you saw the same thing. A lot of men, you saw really a lot of men who had been captured. They stood with their hands above their heads."

After her family recovered from the first round of hardships, then the waiting began. "You knew nothing, and it wasn't clear if anybody had survived. There was so much uncertainty and you asked yourself who had survived. It was difficult for us, especially when we heard that people had died. I still had hope, but that vanished and I feared the worst. We sat in the camp in Dubrave and had to wait. . . . I didn't know where to go, I just didn't know any more."

Muška currently lives in the Netherlands.

Violence and Terror

Šuhra, president of Women of the Podrinje, told me how scared she had been in Potočari when the Serbs set dogs on the men. In the moonlight, everyone could see what happened. She went with her children to the truck; a ladder leaned against it so that the women and children could climb in.

> I had on a backpack and a shawl over my head. I looked down so as not to draw attention. I let my father-in-law, who was 71, climb up first. He was already in the truck and only had one leg on the ladder when the man who had placed the ladder grabbed him and told him to climb down. He was taken behind the truck and we never heard from him again. I was in the truck with my children and we went to Tišča, and from there to Kladanj. When we got out of the truck, there were Serbs in uniform standing every 10 [or] 20 meters on both sides of the road. In a kind of zigzag pattern. They ordered us to walk faster in the middle of the road, and not to leave the road because of land mines. They predicted that our own soldiers, in other words Muslims, would kill us. . . . We had to climb over barricades and in some places we had to crawl under. Finally, my children and I came to the tunnel. I sat down to rest and suddenly saw our soldiers. While I was sitting there, a man came up to me. I recognized him; he was one of my cousins.[7]

The journey itself was not the only danger. The trucks were crowded and girls were culled out to satisfy the sexual needs of the Serbs. The entire enterprise had a sexual undertone. There were almost no men in the buses, leaving the women at the mercy of the Serbs. During the journey, women were raped and murdered. On the other hand, there are stories of some bus drivers who were not drunk; they had had enough of the madness, and simply wanted to deliver their cargo.

Sabra was driven by a resident of Srebrenica who stopped for every patrol. Through the window, she could see murdered men "like fallen trees," she told me in her little house in the spring of 2007. She was angry with me, a Dutchwoman, when I interviewed her in Srebrenica. I understood. That spring was a time of serious doubts about the feasibility of continuing to live in the town; an evacuation had been threatened, and a couple of weeks later it became a reality. The town's reconstruction was a failure, but the thought of leaving made Sabra nervous and aggressive. She did not know where else to go.

Her bus had also been stopped, by Chetniks wearing black gloves. Different groups of Serbs had different dress codes. These gloves had no fingers; their clothing was black and they wore either ponytails or bands on their foreheads. Blatant manliness was part of the intimidation, and often resulted in mass rape and cruelty toward exhausted people who were deathly afraid and crying. These men would never experience so much power again in their lives. Sabra was told that she had to give them her money or her throat would be slit. She had been afraid the whole time she was in Potočari. She was older than most of the women I interviewed, and the same was true when she was in Potočari. The bus driver kept stopping the bus, and the women continued to be threatened. "He let them mistreat us. It just kept on; you didn't know whether you would live or die."[8] That insecurity continued even when they reached the front, even though things changed drastically there. No one in the bus knew that the soldiers they now saw were not their enemies, but had come to help. Some people could not go farther without help, so stretchers were brought. Then, the women realized they had reached friendly territory.

There are horror stories about the Serbs plundering for money and jewelry, including intimate body searches. Those who could look outside saw groups of male prisoners, some of them half naked. After the women arrived at the airfield in Dubrave, it was unclear what would happen next. There were so many women and children, but no diapers and clean clothing; there was not even enough drinking water in the beginning. The situation seemed impossible. The main question for the survivors was: How do we find our men in this crowd? An enormous rumor mill developed; every time a few men appeared from the woods, they were bombarded with questions about what they had seen.

Some women were able to leave the emergency shelter fairly quickly, while others had no place to go. The shelter was chaotic because everyone had been so affected by what they had experienced. Even the foreign soldiers who volunteered to help could not maintain order. There was screaming, and those without stole from those who had. Timka told me that at least she had been given a blanket to wrap her children in. Her brother-in-law, who lived in Tuzla, found her and took her to his home so she could wash, eat, and recover. She found a temporary place to stay in Živinice, but it was the beginning of an odyssey from interim shelters to provisional housing. The spaces were too small for a family with children. Some places had no laundry facilities, which meant washing clothes outdoors in the winter.

Mejra also had a long journey through temporary shelters. She had no shoes and had walked the last miles barefoot. She told me how little it mattered to her when she was given food and drink, because she had lost the will to live. In the beginning, there were no tents, and the refugees (again) had to sleep in the open air. It became clear to her early on that almost nobody had gotten through the woods, and the fact that so many were missing could only mean one thing. They were bused to camps and schools farther up, in order to ease the overcrowding in Tuzla. The bus trip itself was an ordeal during which some died. The passengers reported that there were celebrations in Bratunac after the capture of Srebrenica.[9]

Hanifa talked about being fearful during the bus trip when I interviewed her on a somber afternoon in her small house in Grab Potok. She was quite surprised that her husband had disappeared so suddenly. "We cried. Everyone cried. And the driver asked us why we were crying. Why hadn't we fled when it was still possible?" The driver felt that his passengers deserved their fate; that was Serb territory and they should have left long ago.

> I didn't know where we were any more, although I knew that area well. I knew all the areas around Srebrenica, because I used to frequent them. I knew the direction we were heading in, but I didn't know where I was. That was because of the fear. My child in my lap began to cry. She was afraid of where we were being taken. A man stopped the bus. The driver saw that the man wanted [to get] on the bus, because he knocked on the window. The bus stopped and the door opened; the man came in the bus with a knife—not a little knife, but a big one. [He threatened to kill them all and demanded money.] What else could we do but cry? A woman sitting in the back handed over some money. I saw it was German marks, but I couldn't tell how much. He left and we went farther.[10]

The Serbs were looking for money, cigarettes, and food because they had none. They said they had been forced to fight. They understood that there was no money, but threatened a penetrating search later. If they found money then, the women's throats would be slit. After a while, the bus reached a village on the other side of Vlasenica. The driver was hot; he stopped and wanted to get a cold beer but was refused because he was supposed to keep on driving and not leave the women in the hot bus.

The women and children in the buses were afraid because the Serbs were grabbing at anything of value. Šefika told me that the women knew even then what was happening to the young women. Despite that, she was still optimistic that things would turn out well for most people. When she saw a large group of men undressing near Tišća, she thought it was a Serb army drill. It never occurred to her that those men would be murdered; she only realized that later. "I was so stupid, but you lose your bearings because of the fear. You get lost in it, you lose your wits."[11]

The fear remained. Alma Mustafić told Lara Broekman how afraid she was of the many older Serb men. "They were fat, dirty Serb men who were drunk." Alma and her mother acted as though they were crazy, thus driving everyone away. "They let us go. A bit farther up, they had two girls—they weren't yet 18 or 19—they raped them. They had gone mad. It was horrible to see." Alma was determined to make it through unharmed. She had a small knife and decided to commit suicide if something went wrong.

> At Tišća, we had to get off the bus and walk to the free territory. I held my mother tight on one side and my brother on the other. They told us to walk in that direction, toward the Muslim fighters. They said they were letting us go, but those fighters were going to shoot us dead. . . . Serb soldiers were standing alongside the road, but the farther we walked, the fewer there were; it was a wonderful feeling. At one point, we didn't see anybody; we were walking on the road, but there was nobody. I saw a soldier in the woods; he nodded to me. I sensed and knew he was a Muslim. You could also tell from his uniform; he was in the Bosnian army.

The quest to find out what happened to the men began almost immediately. Her uncle had made it through the woods; he said that all the men who remained behind in Potočari had been murdered. The family was taken to the airfield, where they were given bread and a blanket to sit on. Alma's mother was distraught. Shortly thereafter, her mother began to look for a place to live. "She was still looking for my father. Occasionally, we heard that he had arrived somewhere, and we went to see. But the rumors were never true; it was someone else with his given name. Every time, she came back very disappointed."[12]

Waiting and Not Finding

Zejna, who was interviewed by Arieke Duizer, now lives in the Netherlands. She also talked about the fear.

You expect them to be there and waiting for you, and so you are waiting for them. But on the road, you saw that our men were taken. There were two meadows full [of men] on either side of the bus. You saw how they were gathered. I could see that from the bus. There we were in a bus full of women and children, and nobody said anything. Fortunately, the driver was a good person. When we left Potočari, we were stopped by the Serbs; they yelled at us and wanted to get in the bus. He told them, "There are only women and children here, no men. Let me drive on." He just kept on driving to the place where we were let out. Others who were in trucks went through a lot. They were badly mistreated, even by Serb civilians. . . . I went through a lot too, but others had it much worse. They were abused by the Serbs, really abused.

When we got to the end of the Serb territory, we had to get out of the bus. There were still Serbs guarding the border, but then we had to walk a couple of kilometers to the federation. That's where our people picked us up. We got out of the bus and my mother-in-law said, "Hurry up. Soon we'll see . . . our sons, with our husbands and brothers." I said, "No." I began to scream and cry. I said, "We have no one any more." "How's that?" I said, "We have no one now, because I saw everything." . . . I had seen how they had been taken away on the asphalt and on the road and herded together. I said, "We have nobody!" How many men had been gathered on the soccer field and another group in a meadow? I said, "We have nobody left!"

In Tuzla, an acquaintance took Zejna and the baby to her home. She called Zejna's sister in Sarajevo to let her know she was still alive and staying in a crowded school. "You were given a blanket and you could stay there. You got something to eat. People came with clothing, food, all kinds of things. But the men didn't show. Every day someone came, then someone else—but not everybody. About 3,000 men arrived during those days. They had gone through the woods and over the hills." I asked the obvious question, "Did you hear stories about what happened then?"

Yeah, but you heard what you wanted to hear. The answer to all questions was, "I don't know any more, I just don't know. I didn't see anything else, and there was such panic in the woods when we were attacked with grenades. I really don't know what happened." A few said, "Yeah, that's where I saw so-and-so for the last time," whom you or your brother knew, and he didn't dare to go farther, or he was caught and taken away, or he came back and died. They had been shelled with grenades in the woods. It was like it was sleeting.

Zejna remained in Tuzla, waiting and wondering when the men would return. On the 20th day, her youngest brother-in-law arrived; he had gone to Srebrenica first and then through Žepa, via the detour, to Tuzla. Most of his group had been caught. She asked him where his brothers were, and he did not know.[13]

Magbula told me that the waiting drove her mad.

> Every day, I went to the student hostel in Tuzla, where the men were being lodged. We sat there and waited. If someone had made it there, we got the information around 10 [or] 11 o'clock in front of the hostel. So every morning around 10 [or] 11, I took my children there. . . . It was difficult, waiting there—it made me crazy. We listened to the news, watched TV, and if someone we knew arrived, we pounced on him and asked if he had seen so-and-so, or if someone we knew had made it. Or you went straight up to him and asked if he had seen your husband or brother. Those were difficult days.[14]

She was living in a shed next to her husband's cousin's place. She managed to get an apartment because the former tenant had died.

Through the Woods

Although this is a book about women, it would be incomplete without the trek through the woods. There were some women who went through the woods; some who were physically strong did survive. Only men have told me about their experiences, but the women faced the same dangers as the men. Muriz, a soldier interviewed by Mark de Vries, told how difficult it was. He tried to reach safe territory by taking the detour via Žepa, which many took. They passed by villages taken by the Serbs years earlier that had since been abandoned. There was no food except for unripe fruit, which they ate. The group endured heavy attacks, and many of them were killed, but hunger was the greater enemy. He knew the area and searched for food in houses he knew. The terrain was rough and difficult; when he reached Tuzla on August 6, he had lost 20 kilos (44 pounds). He wondered if his family would be there; he had worried about them during his trek.[15] He did find his wife and children.

The men had to struggle and persevere to get through. Ramo, who was interviewed by Esther van Zeijden, described how difficult the journey was and how they were attacked almost every day. "You didn't feel the hunger as much as the lack of strength, and the fear also took the edge off the hunger." He felt that the water had been poisoned because some people suddenly exhibited strange behavior. "A neighbor's younger brother started babbling. He took off his socks and began to wash them. He said, 'I'm home, too, and I have to wash my socks. The other one said, 'Are you crazy? You're not at home,' and began to laugh at him." After a while, the man returned to normal.

Whether the Serbs used poison gas on the fleeing men remains another open question. "I myself had a really difficult evening. We had to walk in a row and all I wanted to do was sleep. I couldn't go any farther—that was after five days or so. I couldn't go on, my eyes kept closing, and I began to hit my head against the trees." He told Esther that he had so many images in his head, and that he wanted to tell everything, and yet he could not.

> I can tell you what happened every day and every evening, which rivers we crossed, what I saw, but that takes too much energy. . . . I get emotional and then really tense, especially if I haven't talked about it at length. I just can't do it at one time. I survived and I reached a safe place in the area around Tuzla. I can't describe that moment. I didn't know yet that I had lost a brother and [his] family. You thought everybody would make it through, and you knew what you had survived; you just couldn't imagine how much luck you'd had and that you had made it. You heard about the others only later.[16]

Hidajet was still young and wondered what he should do when he heard that Srebrenica had fallen. He, like all the young men, was a soldier, and he talked about his journey at length.

I interviewed him and his mother in a suburb of Sarajevo. He was impatient during his mother's interview, because she stressed different things than he would as a soldier. She talked about grief, the children, and her concerns. He wanted her to talk about what he considered the hard facts—military strategy, guilt, and surviving as a man after Srebrenica's fall. I understood his impatience and tried to let him know through the interpreter (who was having difficulty with the situation) that my work dealt with what the women had experienced. I pointed out that their stories, and not only those of the military, were of interest.

In the beginning, he had walked with his mother part of the way to Potočari, but he was suspicious. "I was afraid of walking into the arms of the Serbs." He asked people in the army if there was another possibility. People had already begun to flee; clearly, what awaited them at the compound was not good. He was ordered to join the men who were retreating to Tuzla; as a soldier, he had no choice but to obey. The Chetniks were coming from Jadar; because Srebrenica was a long, narrow town, they decided to leave from the other side.

> Two columns were formed; each was two men wide. Some columns were more than 10 kilometers long. We realized that not everyone had reached the column by a long shot, but we couldn't wait any longer. There were only men. You wonder why we moved so slowly. I know that sometimes we only took two steps, then stopped for two hours, then took two more steps. It was worse than having to run. It was exhausting—psychologically and everything else.

The group arrived in Buljin the next morning; they had made little progress. Hidajet talked further about the slow tempo.

> I felt like I had been in transit for centuries. And we had just begun—actually, we hadn't even really begun. I was already tired and we still had to cross the border into our own territory. So we began to wait again. . . . We were continually under fire from shells and cannons. I recognized my neighbor, a Muslim, who had a head wound. But you couldn't help anybody. If you picked someone up, you had to carry him, and to carry a man you needed a group of four men rotating. It was more than 100 kilometers to Tuzla. It would have been difficult to carry someone that far; we had only just begun.[17]

The wounded neighbor told his son to walk on, and not to wait for him. He remained behind and was never seen again.

> The column did not hold up. Everyone got lost, nobody helped those who were wounded—nobody could help, even if they wanted to. Brothers ignored brothers. People's faces changed completely. In Kamenica, we paused briefly. Those who had food with them ate something and drank some water. We all were thirsty for water. I had none with me; I hadn't brought anything. At the tail of the column, we were ordered to wait for the last man. We didn't have many weapons—one rifle per 10 men. And the weapons we had were old and didn't work well. When we started up again, we were under fire. It was already dark, but it seemed like the land was ablaze. That lasted for a half hour. You really didn't know who was shooting at whom. We were walking over dead and wounded men.

It was chaotic, uncoordinated; the men worked only in small groups. Suddenly, there was a large bang and Hidajet smelled some kind of gas, probably one used as a weapon. It smelled horrible. From that moment on, many began to surrender, encouraged by Serbs who had insinuated themselves into the column. They had volunteered as guides, because they knew the way, but instead they led them to the enemy. "I never considered surrendering, not even for a minute. All I could think about was getting through, I wanted to go farther and never back. There were wounded people, wounded and dead all around; they were lying there and you couldn't do anything. . . . Quite a few committed suicide; they blew themselves up, taking those around them with them." Hidajet thinks the gas affected people's rationality.

He met a man who knew the way. They took a detour and avoided being ambushed. They came to a road and found a man who was moaning. "The man was in the middle of the road, bound to a chair. He was tied in the chair and was covered with cuts. He couldn't talk and his ears had been cut off. His eyes had been gouged out. . . . In particular, I saw that his ears were gone. He was bound up, his face was mutilated, his nose had been cut off, and his tongue had been removed." He was there to attract people because there was a land mine under him. Later, one of the soldiers put him out of his misery. The column continued to advance slowly and was ambushed; again, many were killed. The fifth day it rained; it began to hail. Hidajet was cold and became ill. Again, men blew themselves up out of desperation. Their tempo increased, but none of them had slept in six days and there was too little to eat. On July 18, he and 3,000 others crossed the lines.

This was yet another type of violence, although parallel to the other kinds. There is an international discussion about the use of poison gas, but what purpose does it serve? Clearly, the people fleeing had been viciously assaulted. How can one discuss this without letting the survivors tell about their desperation and how they succeeded in reaching safety? The point is always made that civilians were murdered; however, this is complicated by the fact that some of the men in transit were going to fight. But the majority of them were not capable of doing so, because they were unarmed and also because their exhaustion made them easy prey for the larger Serb forces and their psychological and physical violence.

Fadil told Ragna Louman in an interview that he left to fight in defense of the free territory. According to him, the men became hard and embittered. They suffered from hunger, and during the day they rested. On July 12, his group of soldiers was attacked in the mountains. "More than a thousand people died there." He and his brother were stretched out on the ground. He woke up, covered with blood; his brother was gone. Fear gripped him. He covered 10 kilometers by himself; periodically, he was shot at. He traveled alone at times, then with a small group; he saw people fleeing who were scared to death and those who had already died. He knew the roads, the woods, and the villages, even in Serb territory, and he and a small group ultimately broke off in an attempt to escape. The thousand or so people they left behind were murdered shortly after their departure. They succeeded in hiding themselves and made progress through the Serb territory; after six days, they arrived in Tuzla.

"I couldn't find anybody," he reported. During that time, he slept underground near Tuzla; all he was capable of doing was resting and eating. He was completely exhausted, and the world seemed like a bad dream to him. Again, dreaming was used as a metaphor for a confused state of mind. He had expected to find his wife and children in good circumstances, but was shocked at their living conditions when he found them a month later. The war experience "was completely different for us" than for them, according to him. His family was happy to see him, but "I felt nothing, absolutely nothing. I was numb, soulless, and indifferent, but my return was cause for a great celebration for them."[18] He slept that night among the people in the school where his family had found shelter. He had become accustomed to sleeping wherever necessary; as long as it was dry, the place did not matter.

There are many women's stories about difficulties with husbands who had been in the military and had lived among men for a long time. Such men were no longer used to normal family life. In addition, the men and the women had different experiences; often, they felt guilt regarding their partners. The women were well aware that the men had been in greater danger, and that they had endured atrocities during their journeys. However, the men had left their wives and children unprotected and defenseless against the Serbs. Many women wanted to return to a family lifestyle, but that was not possible in temporary shelters. Those women whose spouses did not return had to take over the chores and responsibilities normally handled by men. This is a problem for many women in postwar societies.[19] In Bosnia, a number of survivors organizations continue to offer support to the women during this transformation of their responsibilities.

From Aktiv Zene Srebrenice to Plaintiff

The women had already begun to organize themselves during the siege of Srebrenica.[20] We have seen how they helped in the hospitals, learned first aid, and tried to help people. They also organized sports and other activities in order to keep people busy. They were active in many areas and also supported the "protectors." When the French general Morillon visited Srebrenica, they stopped him from leaving the town. The core members of the group looked for each other in Tuzla, but finding their loved ones was their main concern. Their nerves had already been strained to the breaking point; now, waiting for news was unbearable. More than anything, the women wanted to know what had happened. Their demands and desires were legitimate, but Tuzla was overflowing with refugees in those days, and acknowledgment that something tragic had happened in Srebrenica was slow in coming. It would take months before the enormity of the slaughter became apparent to the world, and the local authorities did not know what to do with the refugees.

The women reorganized themselves and regrouped as a real NGO that could act more effectively. Ultimately, there would be three organizations of women survivors from areas outside Srebrenica. Those from Srebrenica could only regroup once return to the town was a real possibility. The Women of the Podrinje was composed of women from the area around Bratunac, and in Sarajevo the Mothers of the Enclaves Žepa and Srebrenica included women survivors from Žepa, the other "safe area." The members, who came from nine communities, had been in Srebrenica during the war, including women from Višegrad and Zvornik. The Women of Srebrenica, based in Tuzla, was concerned mainly with refugees from the canton. With increasing numbers of survivors returning to Srebrenica, a new organization was formed. Whoever speaks with the women in these organizations discovers quickly that they deny any differences between them. Everyone is looking for the missing, and everyone wants to know why this happened.

In 1995, when the Dayton Accords were signed and the land was divided, many Serbs left the part of the Sarajevo canton which had been granted to Muslims. In turn, a group of Muslim women moved there, because return to Srebrenica was not yet possible. According to the Dayton Accords, Srebrenica was in the Serb Republic, and the territory was too dangerous. It was assumed that those who fled had abandoned their property. Many women were convinced that their men were in prison and that it was their task to find them. If their men returned, they would need a place to live.[21] They asked the cantonal government of Tuzla for information and help, and houses were repaired there. But there were administrative problems for the refugees. Not everyone could register as a "displaced person." The canton defended the rights of its inhabitants, many of whom had no houses, and tried to designate as few houses as possible for the others, the "displaced persons." The thousands of refugees were not welcomed with open arms. They received no help, and had no rights.

The first street protests in Tuzla took place in 1996, and led to confrontations with the police. The women were driven away, but they marched on the cantonal government offices, where they threw stones and demanded to speak to the local authorities. Two months earlier, there had been a women's demonstration in Vozuća, near Zavidoviči; the demands were for better living conditions, more food, and more care. Vozuća was a village that had been destroyed and had no electricity, yet 1,800 refugees lived there. There was no school for the children. The refugees felt they had been deserted. They blocked the main road between Tuzla and Zenica and demanded improvements.

These were first and foremost demands for better living conditions, but from the beginning the women also wanted to know what had happened to their men. Because of their agitation, efforts were made to improve the worst conditions, but things did not get better. At the end of January, mass demonstrations began in Tuzla, at first in front of the International Red Cross building. The women demanded clarification about where their men were. There were also accusations even at that time regarding the allocation of funds designated for the survivors. Not all women participated, but a number of discharged soldiers in uniform who had survived the flight joined the protesters. No arrangements had been made for the veterans either. Bosnia was one enormous refugee camp of destitute people, yet no one seemed to understand why this group was so bewildered and insistent in demanding to know what had happened. That they were different was obvious—they were survivors—but no one understood what that meant.

There were angry protests in the national media against the international community, but anger at local authorities was barely mentioned. A delegation was given permission to meet the president of the Federation of Bosnia-Herzegovina in Sarajevo. Originally, seven buses were planned, but only one appeared. More buses were demanded, but they did not come, so they demonstrated in Tuzla. The meeting with the president led to vague promises about looking into the situation of the exiles.

Return became the central problem in Bosnian politics. In 2003, the UNHCR observed that there were still 67,785 displaced persons in the canton of Tuzla.[22] The majority of those could not return because either their houses had been destroyed or they could not prove ownership. As a result of certain regulations, a number of women lost their property to their in-laws. A depressing 76 percent of the people did not have steady work, a sad statistic even for Bosnia. During the war, 2 million Bosnians had been displaced, and the refugees exerted enormous pressure on local economies, even though relatives who had moved abroad did provide substantial financial aid. One would expect that all the funds from international aid, plus the funds and resources sent by family members abroad, would have stimulated the economy, but that was not the case. The surviving women I met were—and remain—poor. I saw a great deal of hunger and too many stoves without fuel. Many houses have dirt floors. This is true not only for the survivors of Srebrenica, but for the thousands of poor in Bosnia. Among those who ask for help, the survivors stand out as a distinct group that has organized mass protests. The protests seem to be about money, which was and still is a problem. The real complaints, however, are about the silence, the lack of truth, and the lack of acknowledgment of their suffering and betrayal.

The women organize demonstrations in the streets of Sarajevo; every July 11, they march as a memorial to the murders. The German Society for Threatened Peoples was quick to come to their assistance; their Bosnian representative, Fadila Memišević, has been a real anchor for the survivors. She was in Germany when Srebrenica fell; as soon as she heard what was happening, she began stirring up public opinion. She has continued to work to bring attention to the plight of the survivors of Srebrenica's genocide. In 1997, there were plans to commemorate the second anniversary of the slaughter, including a visit to a number of the mass graves. (At that time, the idea of a busload of women visiting Srebrenica was unthinkable.) Bosnia was governed then (as now) by the Office of the High Representative (OHR), which is appointed by the international community; the woman responsible for helping the survivors almost immediately wanted to lower the number of women to be bused to the gravesites. She was of the opinion that the women were too traumatized and would give vent to their emotions rather than behaving diplomatically. In the end, 70 women were allowed to go with the buses, but flowers and placards were forbidden.

The women had planned to place flowers on the graves as memorials, so they objected to the OHR's restrictions. The bus was stopped by IFOR military (Implementation Force, a multinational NATO-led group). The women were warned that 300 armed Serbs were waiting for them farther up. The situation was dangerous; helicopters were circling overhead. Fadila encouraged the women to follow her with their flowers and signs. The bus could go no farther; the road was blocked. The women walked five kilometers. They reached Đulići in the republic, not far from Zvornik. Fadila remembers:

> We came to another checkpoint—barbed wire—[staffed with] American and Russian soldiers. They separate[d] the men from the women; the men were not allowed to go farther. It seemed as though Potočari was being repeated. Every one of us was frisked, just like back then . . . dreadful. On the second anniversary of the fall, women went through this again. We were not allowed to enter Đulići, but we did go to the cemetery in Masuča, where a speech was given and the women could pray. The helicopters were really noisy. I realized then how important it was for the women to organize themselves.

The situation in 1997 was critical. A large number of women lived in Vogošča, a suburb of Sarajevo, in apartments abandoned by Serbs. Suddenly, a group of Serbs returned. Those Serbs had a meeting with the mayor of Vogošča, and the women wanted to be heard as well. The police prevented that. All of a sudden the atmosphere was tense and unpleasant. The women surrounded the building and the town hall. They wanted to know if they were being evicted. It happened spontaneously. They had heard about the meeting because they lived there, and they wanted to be included. Instead of including the women, the mayor sent the police, who beat them. At that time, the high representative wrote that a horde of wild women had attacked the police. . . . I wrote him a letter in which I questioned whether he could execute the responsibilities of his office, given his attitude toward the survivors. I reminded him of what the mothers had experienced and that they had the right to scream, that nobody should call them a wild horde, and that they had not behaved (as the media suggested) in an uncivilized manner. Was their separation from their children, for whom they were searching, civilized? Or the fact that they wanted the truth? . . . They had been traumatized. They had been manipulated and abandoned. Terrible. It is terrible when someone loses her loved ones, but not knowing how and what happened compounds the misery further.[23]

Kada told about what happened in Vogošča. She felt that she and a number of women had been deeply humiliated by the mayor. He told them to their faces that they were horrible people, and "working with you is impossible." The women tried to explain that their lack of legal status had created an abnormal situation. The end result of all the actions and protests were some basic services. But, Kada added, "He hurt me. He did that when I asked the government where the missing were. He cursed that we simply had to accept their deaths. That really wounded me, because we still thought that our people would come back alive. We didn't think they were dead."[24]

The women's needs were both material and psychological. Fadila knew that: "I understood that the women had been left to their fate, and yet at the same time their thoughts were extremely conflicted. They faced a dilemma. They didn't want to admit that their loved ones were [permanently] missing; during that phase, they still had hope." Fadila did not want to disillusion them, even though she was convinced that the men were dead. One of the primary goals of all of the organizations was to search for the missing. Knowing what happened was also important for legal reasons. A pension could only be granted if the man was declared legally dead, which was usually not the case at that time. The women lived on the edge economically as well as psychologically, and were stigmatized by the citizens of Sarajevo who did not approve of the influx of impoverished refugees from the provinces.[25]

Widows Want to Know

The idea to gather on the 11th of every month and visit the OHR and foreign embassies was inspired by the Mothers of the Plaza de Mayo in Buenos Aires, Argentina. The women wanted to draw attention to the fact that all the aid given to Bosnia was not getting beyond the embassies, and to demand answers regarding the missing men. The monthly demonstrations ended at the Red Cross, which at that time was the organization responsible for discovering the whereabouts of the men. Yugoslavia had been an authoritarian communist nation, hence there was no tradition of peaceful demonstrations. There was friction with the police. Fadila was advised against continuing to associate with the "riffraff," and was threatened with prison and with being held personally responsible for any damages.

> We were escorted by the police. It rained; it had never rained so hard. The streets were rivers. I had never seen it like that, and I thought that no women would come. Everything depends on the weather here. But the first time, a thousand women came. They walked, even the older women and women who had difficulty walking. The distance to the Red Cross building was five kilometers.

From that time on, the women demonstrated on the 11th of every month, and the same happened in Tuzla. By October 1998, it had become a regular event, and 5,000 women took part.

Things did not always go peacefully. In July 2000, the women blockaded the road from the coast of Sarajevo and demanded protection for their return to Srebrenica and better housing.[26] They demanded to return to their former homes and the land they had owned. There were more protests after that regarding the fact that the women still did not have permanent residences. They protested that their displacement was a violation of their rights. Over the years, they had accepted that their men were dead; now, they wanted to bury their dead and to find peace. The burial demands resulted in the establishment of the cemetery in Potočari, where there was a suitable site across from the compound. Potočari was chosen based on a survey that drew an enormous response.[27] Every year, a reburial of some of the victims is held there; I was present when the cemetery was officially opened.

Burying the dead proved to be easier than returning to Srebrenica. The first attempt took place in 2000; the women sized up the situation and visited their old homes. When a group of them passed through Bratunac on May 11 of that year, they were pelted with rocks.[28] No protection was available for the returning women.[29] Gradually, their organization became a full-fledged NGO. When I visited for the first time, the offices were shabby and the first interviews were held on folding chairs in a bare space frequented by birds. In 2007, the women in Sarajevo moved into a lovely office with suitable facilities, although the organization was growing rapidly and would soon need even more room. In Tuzla, they have a small but pleasant office that is filled with photographs. They are sponsored by IKV, a Dutch NGO.

Things have not gone as well for the two other organizations. The Women of the Podrinje, an organization of approximately 1,500 women, is based in the Sarajevan suburb of Ilijas. In the spring of 2007, it was still short on funds, although its offices had improved over the years. It is run by a tightly knit group that supports the women in combating loneliness and financial need[30] and that organizes those who are searching for their loved ones in the region around Bratunac, including those murdered in 1992. Many who survived in 1992 went through the eye of the needle again in 1995. Composed of mothers and victims, these survivors organizations have become a voice in Bosnian politics, which traditionally had little room for women.[31] Elisa Helms wrote about how difficult it is for women to combine politics with respect in the former Yugoslavia. Respectability forces women into the roles of victim and wife in search of husband and sons, and it is difficult to break out of these roles. Their communal identity as an organization is based too much on the past, which in turn is a hindrance to looking forward and to replacing the role of victim with a more active one.[32]

Those who are familiar with the warmth and conviviality of the organizations are aware of how much support and structure they give to days that are otherwise empty. The women are active and involved, and the companionship is healthy. The organizations have almost become surrogate families, where the women can discuss their new, nontraditional responsibilities. This is comparable to AVEGA (Association des Veuves du Genocide), the organization of women survivors of the Rwandan genocide. The Bosnian and Rwandan groups are remarkably similar; both were stigmatized in the beginning but gradually developed into NGOs. In her lovely autobiography, *Survivantes: Rwanda dix ans après le genocide* (*Survivors: Rwanda Ten Years after the Genocide*), Esther Mujawayo discusses how difficult it is to be alone and powerless when facing new tasks, compounding the confusion and the unresolved grief.[33]

Apparently, the world does not want to hear widows' voices; neither does it want to be confronted with their overwhelming grief. This seems to be a pattern. Oral historian Alessandro Portelli also noted the disturbing nature of widows' complaints in his book *The Order Has Been Carried Out,* about the mass murders by the German occupiers in Rome during the Second World War. It was not long after the murders that the widows confronted the bureaucracy regarding pensions and jobs; they organized themselves to support each other.[34] The women marched everywhere and openly showed their grief, and that was not acceptable. Portelli noted that excessive mention of death in daily life is apparently not allowed. The all-too-obvious pain and the women's ongoing bad fortune are abominations that make it impossible for others to forget the past. He described how the Italian widows were always given priority in shops, which they thought was out of respect. In fact, the other shoppers wanted them to leave as quickly as possible.[35] The confrontation with grieving widows in search of answers was too intense, and that is also the case in Srebrenica.

After the Waiting: Closure and Depression

At a certain point, there is news; it is expected, but its arrival also means the end of hope. The news of a loved one's death usually marks the beginning of a period of passivity and reflection. Then, one prepares to bring the obituary to the annual reburial in Potočari on July 11. One works toward that emotional milestone through alternating periods of deep grief, confusion, and reliving the past.

Often, I did not dare ask about that painful moment when the news came. Nermina had attended a July 11 memorial in Srebrenica. Red Cross workers told her that someone had been found, but they were not yet certain. She told me that she had given her phone number to the Red Cross.

> They called on the 12th. My sister answered; my brother was at work. When my sister said the call was from Tuzla, I was scared. I was afraid that the neighbors had left the faucet on and my apartment was flooded. I was 100 percent convinced the call was about a leak; I said I had to go home. My sister told me to take the phone. It was Enver from the Red Cross. He asked where I was and if I was still in Mihatovići. I told him I still lived there, but at the moment I was in Srebrenica. He said he didn't have much to tell me, except that my husband had been found. . . . I managed to control myself. The children were also there and I didn't want to make a scene. . . . I began to cry and my eldest son asked me what was wrong. I said they had found their father. I was crying and so was my sister.

The family returned immediately to Tuzla. Nermina's son told her brother, who "never wanted to admit my husband was dead. He asked me why I was crying and [her son] told him. [Her brother] said then, 'They are lying, my child, your father is alive.' Meanwhile, he looked at me and his chin was quivering."

The initial identification was based mainly on clothing. Then came the DNA test, which is often complicated because it is a sensitive technique and the remains in mass graves are often contaminated by other remains and earth.[36] In the early years, the recovered bodies in Tuzla were kept in a salt mine; the tunnels were not suitable for that purpose, however, and stank. In 2000, a large new morgue was opened.[37] It was obvious that there were still thousands of bodies in the mass graves. Everything was done to help the survivors identify the bodies and bury their loved ones. The process was complicated; for example, there was the question of safety when digging up graves in the Serb Republic, where forensic experts were regarded as prosecutors. The new morgue turned out to be inadequate. Although it had seemed that the tunnels in Tuzla would soon be emptied and the remains properly stored until their reinterment, there are still remains in the tunnels.

During the G7 conference in 1996, the International Commission on Missing Persons (ICMP) was established, which began work immediately on a better facility. The ICMP's scope is broader than simply matching victims with their families through DNA testing. The victims' families are closely involved in the commission's work, the idea being that the survivors are contributing to rebuilding a civil society in Bosnia. I have admired the ICMP's work for years. Bosnia was the first place where DNA testing was used on a large scale to identify victims in mass graves.[38] It is also a classic postwar situation involving identification problems with bodies that have been moved. There are projects and training courses to ensure that people are qualified to look for their loved ones. The ICMP looks for ways to encourage recognition and understanding of the families' needs and problems. As a result, there are close ties between the organization and the survivors, which may well help the reconciliation process.

The survivors demand that the world join in their mourning. A visitor to Tuzla is shown the morgue, and tours visit one or more of the mass graves. In her book *The Stone Fields,* anthropologist Courtney Angela Brkić describes how she worked alongside the excavators.[39] One can get used to anything, including digging up corpses and washing them. The recovered bodies then need to be reburied. Potočari was chosen as the site of a collective cemetery, but the last gravesite available was used in 2003. Since then, the cemetery has been the site of the July 11 memorials. Tens of thousands come every year, but this media-dominated event gives more attention to the people on the VIP platform than to the thousands on the hills who are mourning, praying, and trying to remain upright. Standing among them, one can physically feel their grief. For thousands, the journey there is a hardship, given the traffic jams lasting for hours and especially the emotional intensity. Many interviewees doubted if they would attend the next year. But, if people they knew are being buried, then they go, even if they did not know them well. Depending on the speakers, the scenario changes every year, but standing among the grieving remains the same. It moves me deeply when I see people I know, who are grieving and looking for comfort. One year, I felt helpless and embarrassed because the Dutch government had not sent a representative, except for the ambassador to Bosnia, who frankly acknowledged that things went amiss in Srebrenica.

Burying the fallen is the desire of widows from all eras and all wars. The Red Cross and sometimes the ICMP bring the news that ends the waiting. It can come when one least expects it, even during a party, although those delivering the news try to find an appropriate time for the visits with the help of the neighbors. Haša told about how she heard the news. That day had not begun well; she wanted to go back to bed. Her downstairs neighbor said a man was looking for her. Her mother-in-law lived a bit farther up; the man had gone there. Haša went there as well. The man asked her to join him for coffee, but she refused; she suspected the reason for his visit. He asked if she had taken any tranquilizers; she told him yes. He told her he would return the following day, and asked her not to fast. It was Ramadan.

> Then I asked him, "Tell me now why you are here. Of course, you can come tomorrow as well." He looked at me earnestly. He was sitting on the sofa in the corner. I was sitting next to him. He wanted to tell me something that he really didn't want to say. The downstairs neighbor came in and said, "They found your youngest son." I didn't cry. I wanted them found so their bones could be buried. I said, "I thank God that he's been found. Now I know where to go to pray. I'll bury him at Potočari."[40]

Return or In Transit

After living as refugees for over 10 years, they have had enough. A real resettlement began after 2004. It is mainly the stronger families who have succeeded in returning to Srebrenica and building a new existence. The other group that is returning consists of older widows; some are alone because their children live elsewhere, others because they no longer have children. According to the journalist and authority on Bosnia Leen Vervaeke, 3,000 refugees still lived in "collective centers" in 2009.[41] Rukija, an older woman who lives on the edge of Srebrenica in a sparsely populated neighborhood, had enough of living elsewhere.

> Serbs were living in my house, and I asked the authorities to evict them, just like I was evicted from where I lived in Sarajevo. . . . Mladić had promised them our possessions, but they should have

known better; they were so stupid to fall for that. They should have known you can't just help yourself to others' property. I wouldn't have believed it if someone tried to sell me that nonsense. I know that's only possible if the owner gives you his property.

I was ordered to clear out, and they were too. It took them long enough, but I moved out immediately. It took them a long time, and it caused me problems when they didn't leave. . . . When my house was finally empty, I decided to come here. My children didn't like the idea of my living alone here, but I wanted to be in my own home; that's my preference. This has been my home for 75 years. I gave birth to my children and raised them here, made men out of them and taught them to be good workers. I wanted to come home and nowhere else. I was able to fix the house up with a gift, and I returned.[42]

Some of her neighbors live in houses that have not been finished because there is not enough money. Many houses remain unoccupied. The town's desolation, especially in the surrounding villages where life is hard, is dramatic. Often, the houses are in such a state that making them livable again is questionable. The rebuilding has been slow and spotty.

During the first few years after the genocide, people in many places lived in wretched conditions; some still do, because they feel attached to the area and have nowhere else to go. Hatidža returned because she simply could not go on as a refugee. She lives alone, but hopes that the rest of her family will follow her. After she returned and rebuilt her home, it burned again. "I went to look at it for the first time. I asked the authorities to repair my house, because I wanted to return. I showed that I had to move out of the house where I was living, but they didn't want to do anything, because it had burned a second time. But I wanted to live there. There was no electricity, no water, but I wanted to live there." She lived for a while in the house; it had a roof, but the floor was dirt. I have seen that a number of times; it has to do with the manner in which help is given. The first time Hatidža returned was in 2000, to visit her husband's grave.

I passed my house. I saw the front, but no roof. The fence, the door, the stoves—everything was destroyed. I wanted to go inside, but a policeman wouldn't allow it and kept me at a distance. . . . We were allowed to go to the cemetery, but not to the center of the town. When I first saw it, it was awful. When I wanted to get closer to my house, a policeman called out, "Don't go there, Grandmother." I asked again if I could go in my house.

She was assured that she would be allowed in soon. The work began quickly; it was one of the first houses to be renovated. Then it burned again, but despite the heavy damage she still moved in. In that early period, there were arguments on a regular basis; Serbs were being evicted from houses belonging to Bosniaks who wanted to return. This led to suspicion and fear. When I began interviewing in 2002, a number of women were hostile toward all outsiders. Hatidža Habibović and I talked about the fear. "Sometimes people cursed us out and wondered what it was that we wanted. I didn't let that bother me. I just kept going. Other women cursed back, but I didn't listen. . . . In the beginning, it was really difficult. We didn't expect anything any more. No electricity, no toilet, no water, nothing. . . . There was a leak by the front door and in the winter it iced over."[43]

She lived for a year without electricity and water; whether there would be money to renovate was uncertain for a long time, especially since the last fire did extensive damage.

Those who returned thought at first they were better off than the people in the collective centers and in the houses of Serbs who had been driven out of the suburbs of Sarajevo. Hatidža Mehmedović, who tries to organize the women, told me:

> The support here is very inadequate; everything concerning Srebrenica is poor. There is no Srebrenica. . . . No one can live here normally, nobody has a normal existence. Everybody talks about there being help for Srebrenica. People have good intentions, but the help goes from Sarajevo to Banja Luka [the capital of the Serb Republic] and from there to Srebrenica. And if it reaches Srebrenica, not much is left; it has simply vanished. . . . I came here when it was possible. I had a police escort. There were meetings, but I went immediately to my house. And that's when the process of returning property started.[44]

I asked what it was like to return, and she answered, "Don't ask. I wouldn't wish on anybody the life I had to endure. Nobody—not even those who did this to me."

Is There Something Unique about Srebrenica?

Living so long in turmoil has major consequences for the surviving women. Over time, they become physically worn down by the tension and the difficult living conditions.[45] Everything takes too long, and there is an excess of uncertainty. To my mind, the trauma of Srebrenica lies in that uncertainty.

In a society in which so many suffered because of the war, the survivors organizations have claimed a special place for those who experienced Srebrenica. In a discussion with survivors of the mass rapes at Foča, I found myself faced with their incomprehension. Many women had come out of Potočari "untouched," but the same could not be said for their town. This raises the question of what is unique about the trauma of Srebrenica. That question also played a role in the proceedings against Kristić at the Yugoslav Tribunal.

The judge questioned a psychologist, Teufika Ibrahimefendić, about the degree of trauma involved. She testified:

> In my contact with the victims from Srebrenica, women and children, we used various questionnaires in order to assess their psychological condition. We had a number of conversations with them, and on the basis of such conversations, it was possible for us to come up with an assessment as regards the level of trauma. . . . That level was exceptionally high, and the symptoms that they presented were at a very, very high level of trauma, because the events relating to the month of July 1995 were, globally speaking, events that involved a very large group of women and children and also other survivors, such as elderly people, for example, who all happened to be at one place together, and they experienced that suffering together.
>
> For all of them, it was a sudden event, unforeseeable, of course, and it is true that they may have felt a certain safety, security, at one point, but trauma occurs in a sudden manner and it has vast consequences. This all took place in an atmosphere which was beyond their control; there was nothing that they could have done. They were completely helpless.
>
> So in such a situation, in Potočari, when people arrived in Tuzla, the stories that they told were very painful, hard, human stories and very touching. Many women at that point in time simply lost control over their feelings, over their behavior. The children as well were beyond themselves. Everybody kept asking themselves what was happening and why it was happening.
>
> However, the most serious problem was the fact that women and men had been separated. Part of the menfolk had parted with the women and had gone through the woods. One part of the male population stayed with them in Potočari; however, they were separated again in Potočari. Even boys were separated from women in Potočari, and they were wondering what would happen with young boys over the age of ten, for example. . . .
>
> Among the women we worked with, and we use the sample of women with more serious psychological problems, their memories

are still vivid. They still have images of what happened. These are so-called flashbacks. Suddenly, these pictures appear, excerpts from the experience they lived through. In the course of their normal activities, walking around town or somewhere else, they come across something that reminds them and this provokes the flashback.

Many of those women still suffer from terrible nightmares, feelings of fear, and other symptoms: irritation, nervousness, aggressiveness, a loss of concentration, irritability. Many avoid talking about those events because they are so painful. These are also symptoms of avoidance. In contact with the victim, we can easily recognize the dominant symptoms depending on the personality, its structure, its mental functions, the way the personality reacts.

But if this symptom of avoiding remembering dominates, they become depressed, apathetic, passive.

Regarding the differences from other victims, the psychologist stated:

I have noticed certain differences and within our team we discussed them. We all agreed that the victims of Srebrenica have something that we have described as the Srebrenica syndrome. They suffer in a special way. They have problems that make them different, especially as of July 1995, because this is a vast number of persons who were in the same place at the same time, and they went through common suffering and they have common shared experiences.

They only remember the moment they bade farewell, the moment when they had agreed to meet in a spot that would be safe. And this is still something that still guides them in their thoughts.

This is exhausting, discouraging. They think that life has no value.[46]

The Dutch Debt of Honor

In the spring of 2005, a group of students interviewed survivors of Srebrenica who now live in the Netherlands. Almost all of them reported that their memories are at odds with the Dutch debate. That is understandable; a victim's memory is different. But the problem goes deeper. They are bothered by the Dutch fixation on DutchBat and the manner in which the story of Srebrenica is interwoven with politics. Also, they had expected more tolerance for the fact that their trauma makes it difficult for them to handle certain situations.

Zejna told Arieke Duizer that she had been preoccupied on a daily basis for years with the men who had not returned.

If they were murdered, then it doesn't matter if I live, if I exist. I couldn't focus on the future here, on getting a residence permit. Mainly I cried, and that really hurt my little boy. We both could have gone crazy. We were sick with fear. For example, I had to have a lawyer to get a residence permit, but why did I need a lawyer? Hasn't everybody seen what happened in Srebrenica? We came here as survivors, but still I have to repeat what I went through again and again.

Zejna found the waiting unsettling. "You're handled, like all the other refugees, like a sort of criminal. What you did is not allowed. Meanwhile, your heart is shattered, broken. You have no strength left and no future. You have no idea of how things should be in the future. I needed help, warmth, and peace. I didn't get them."

Zejna was no match for the intricacies of the Dutch bureaucracy. She also resisted the idea that the Dutch military were forced by the Serbs to do what they did.

Srebrenica also fell because the Dutch battalion promised protection. What it all came down to in the end is that they handed us over to the Serbs. I don't know if they could or couldn't have done something, but we expected it—we thought we were being protected. They're accused now because they were there. But they had promised us protection and safety. We couldn't know that they weren't prepared for real action to give real protection.

Zejna feels that the guilt is being deflected. "Nobody wants to know how things really were. Nobody says, 'Okay, we didn't react in time.' Nobody is looking for the real culprits."[47] Another woman said: "No one can ever ease my pain and my loss. But a different attitude might give some peace. We're beginning to understand how things stand now; when it comes to Srebrenica, the feeling is that we are the guilty party. We're the victims, but we're being handed the guilt."[48]

Conclusion: The Mothers and the Search for Closure

Finding their place in the world again, peace, and a home—these are the survivors' needs. They are not always attainable. Even if they are achieved, the situation remains precarious and vulnerable as long as there is no clarity regarding what happened to their loved ones and who the guilty parties are. That is the history which is important to them, and this book acknowledges that history.

The victims' core desire is for recognition, which goes far beyond juridical or material compensation. Recognition has been defined as a "reciprocal relation between subjects, in which each sees the other both as its equal and also as separate from it. This relation is constitutive for subjectivity: one becomes an individual subject only by virtue of recognizing, and being recognized by, another subject. Recognition from others is thus essential to the development of a sense of self."[49] To be denied recognition—or to be misrecognized—is to suffer both a distortion of one's relation to oneself and an injury to one's identity, because survivors need to reconnect to a society and a world that seem to have been lost.

We must remind ourselves that lost social and cultural capital is extremely hard to restore. One's right to exist as a human being must be acknowledged; this is a crucial factor in being able to go on living. One desperately wants to return to a normal daily life and to escape the maze of legal and bureaucratic regulations. To know and to remember are two sides of the same ongoing process of mourning. They both reflect the need to give these horrendous events their rightful place in history, which is almost impossible.

Identity and memory presuppose clarity about one's place in the world. These survivors live in a chaotic nightmare in which context and connections have been blurred and their place in society has dissolved. It feels as though nothing is left. What remains is a story of grief and loss—a story that others do not want to hear. I was privileged to give these women the opportunity to talk about what bothered them the most and what they had experienced. It was a first step, both for them and for the historiography of Srebrenica.

The end result is this book, which is about the confusion that was deliberately created in this war—confusion over who the enemy was, who could be trusted, and ultimately confusion about one's own perception of the past. If all those images run together, if no one tells the truth, and if what happened increasingly vanishes in a black hole, then where is the history? First, one searches for the missing, to see if they are alive or dead. Then, the question of the truth and the question of guilt arise. The women can regain their own history only through filling in these lacunae. Not allowing them to speak denies them the reality of their experiences, and hence silences them for a second time. "The victim's cry has to overcome not just the silence of the dead but the indelible coercive power of the oppressor's terrifying, brutal silencing of the surviving, and the inherent, speechless silence of the living in the face of an unthinkable, unknowable, ungraspable event," wrote the literary scholar Shoshana Felman.[50]

I emphasize my responsibility as a citizen of the Netherlands, the nation of the "protectors," which has had great difficulty in acknowledging its responsibility.

The subject of Srebrenica is contentious and stirs up fear in Dutch society. The political climate is still against admitting that DutchBat, albeit inadequately armed and unprepared, did a really lousy job. Politicians seem to work overtime to keep such questions out of the public arena. When I looked for funds to conduct this research, I met with resistance. The Dutch government at that time stated flatly that individual life stories do not contribute to the integration of the trauma, despite extensive evidence to the contrary from research on the Holocaust. The government was also fearful of what the women might say; this was stated in a letter signed by former ministers. (All this is chronicled in the Dutch edition.) Years later, a senior public official was surprised to learn that being ostracized had not stopped my research.

I was able to listen to the survivors because of the incredible courage and loyalty of the mothers. They have become dear to me. I witnessed how alone they were when they pressed charges against the Dutch government and the United Nations, and I sat in court with them. It would have been better if things had not been allowed to progress that far. A gesture of reconciliation should have been made toward the women much earlier.

Despite repression, some stories always come out. Although the women told their stories in fragments, they were determined to make their perspective on what happened public. At the same time, they wondered why everything seemed to remain so chaotic. During interviews, accounts of catastrophes are not immediately understandable; rather, they are what Cathy Caruth calls expressions of "a crisis of witnessing."[51] She considers such eyewitness accounts to be rooted in the dislocations of history.[52] Talking about trauma often means reliving it in all of its pain, difficulty, fear, confusion, and shame. According to Dori Laub, an American psychiatrist and one of the founders of the Fortunoff Collection at Yale,[53] "There is a need for tremendous libidinal investment in those interview situations: There is so much destruction recounted, so much death, so much loss, so much hopelessness, that there has to be an abundance of holding and of emotional investment in the encounter."[54] There is an emotional dynamic between the two who sit together, having committed themselves to the story. In this difficult process of remembering, the use of existing narrative genres is a way to escape personal memories. This complicates any understanding of what is being told. The interviewer has to continually question if the story is indeed personal, or if the narratives of others are being used.

Laub was referring to the testimonies he recorded about the Holocaust, and I share that experience. I began my career as an oral historian interviewing Holocaust survivors. The comparison with the Srebrenica interviews is striking, and the similarities are numerous. Holocaust survivors also were ignored in the years immediately after the war. The enormous challenge in both cases is to understand the impact of genocide on all those individual lives. Surviving requires a complex set of skills; the world after the slaughter is not one of gas chambers or mass murder in the villages of Bosnia but should be one of respect and coping with the past that still lingers. It is our task as historians to show all of history's dimensions.

I favor comparative research on the experience of genocide. By taking such a broad approach, we should be able to understand what Srebrenica now means to the survivors. I have indicated a number of elements that should be more closely examined, for example the forced unity under Yugoslav communism, the shock of neighbors becoming murderers, and the pervasive influence of a long history together.

Srebrenica was the destruction of a familiar world that was considered good and of a sense of home that inspired love and trust, despite the tensions among the different groups living there and the misery of the post-communist era.[55] The Bosnian war tore apart a pluralistic culture that perhaps had been taken for granted for too long. Even today, there is no better example of a harmonious society where cultures, religions, and national identities mix the way they did in eastern Bosnia. The genocide resulted not only in death, but also in desolation, endless waiting and hoping, and bewilderment at the dramatic and far-reaching social changes for the women. More and more, they have begun to realize that living in a temporary shelter is unbearable. They are returning to destroyed houses in Srebrenica and the surrounding villages, despite the specters of devastation that hover over the area. The women are forced to rebuild without much help and to raise their children in poverty, but they survive.

In December 2006, the Dutch soldiers received medals for their mission in Bosnia. Almost no one has access to the records of that mission, and many documents are still confidential. The soldiers who served there are under a gag order not to discuss what happened during the fall of Srebrenica; their frustrations and traumatized stories have been kept confidential. The medals were a slap in the face of the women who have spoken out in this book—not because they have no compassion for the trauma of others, but because their trauma has not been acknowledged. (I have emphatically and publicly protested their treatment.) Despite this, the women and some of the soldiers have stayed in contact; they realize that the others are also victims. The medals were also a slap in the face of those Dutch citizens who acknowledge a moral debt and want a dialogue.

The women survivors search for a relatively safe world that once existed and then collapsed, leaving them displaced and in a state of confusion. Apparently, that is still not understood in the Netherlands. In the summer of 2007, police were used to keep these middle-aged women far away from government offices in The Hague. The women had traveled hundreds of miles by bus, and should have been received in a dignified manner.

Srebrenica remains a small town full of women surrounded by the hostile environment of the Serb Republic. The Dayton Accords saw to that. According to the current mayor, the donations given to help the refugees do not reach them, and nothing is done for women who live outside the town. So far, the Netherlands has been the largest donor, giving large amounts because of a guilty conscience. It was called a "debt of honor," but the government is also nervous about future lawsuits and their outcomes.

It is an alienating experience for me to live in a nation where these women have long met with hostility. The Dutch edition of this book was received in 2008 by the minister of development cooperation, Bert Koenders. He and a number of others in parliament had supported my work. During those years, I sometimes thought that public opinion was beginning to shift, mainly because of a growing body of academics and artists who felt that the world should pay heed to the reports of betrayal by, for example, survivor Emir Suljagić and others cited in this book,[56] as well as the work of a number of NGOs. However, my optimism always seems to vanish. The judicial case against the Netherlands and the United Nations was declared inadmissible, and there is no place else where the women can register a complaint. Their case seems to be about financial compensation, but for the survivors it is primarily about discovering the truth. The women's questions are: Why did things turn out the way they did, and why were we betrayed? Why did we trust in the protection of the Dutch soldiers? And, most important of all, who is responsible? The women are apprehensive that their stories of what happened will be buried under the excuses of people with more power, who exonerate themselves. The women want what they experienced to be remembered and their suffering to be acknowledged.

For years, the women were dismissed as hysterical, but that image has changed. No one dares to call them that now, and they are justifiably compared more and more with the "crazy mothers" of Argentina. Like all war widows and mothers who have lost children, they tell about the loss of those they loved. They are disturbed and angry, and they have worked passionately on this seemingly impossible undertaking. Telling what happened can be physically dangerous in some areas of the region. It is also psychologically dangerous to allow all the memories to surface, yet the women who spoke with me did that. They wanted to be named, and they named those who struck, tortured, murdered, raped, and watched.

At the beginning of 2009, the European Union declared July 11 to be a day of remembrance. Several Dutch members of the European Parliament were active in making this happen. I was in close contact with some of them during this process, and I could see it was not easy, not in the parliament nor with the Dutch public. And in July 2009, the Dutch government still refused to send representatives to the commemoration in The Hague. Formal reasons were given—for example, that the real commemoration is held in Potočari—but at that event there was, as always, only the ambassador, although other nations sent much more important dignitaries. Sometimes, members of the Dutch government have attended, but they are nearly invisible. The Dutch do not want to remember what happened. This is embarrassing to me, and I denounce it. The very least we can do is to remember.

Sabaheta worked with me on this book. She wanted all the names of those she misses so much included and said:

> Somewhere it will be written that a Sabaheta Fejić existed, and that her husband was Šaban Fejić and her son was Rijad Fejić. Even after I die, I think I will still love my husband and my child. Nothing can replace them. Believe me, the only and last love that I feel is for my husband and my child. But they are different kinds of love. What I want most in this life is to live long enough to find out what happened, no matter how painful it is. And if they are dead, I want their bodies to be found and identified. Then, I can bury them as they deserve. Then, I will no longer be alone.

I was there when Sabaheta finally buried her child, and in the future some of the other women speaking in this book will be able to do the same. I hope that they will find some peace.

Notes

Preface

1. NIOD, *Srebrenica, een "veilig gebied": Reconstructie, achtergronden, gevolgen en analysen van de val van een Safe Area* [*Srebrenica, a "Safe Area": Reconstruction, Background, Consequences, and Analyses of the Fall of a Safe Area*] (Amsterdam: Boom, 2002) (usually referred to as the NIOD Report); *Rapport d'information de MM. René André et François Lamy, no. 3413, depose le 22 novembre 2001, en application de l'article 145 du réglement* (Paris: National Assembly, 2002); *Conclusions of the Government of the Republic of Serbia in Relation to the Report of Its Commission for Investigation of Events in and around Srebrenica between 10 and 19 July 1995*, No. 02/1-020-1301/04 (October 28, 2004); S. Čekić et al., *Genocide in Srebrenica, United Nations' "Safe Area," in July 1995* (Sarajevo: Research Institute on Crimes against Humanity, 2001); J. W. Honig and N. Both, *Srebrenica: Record of a War Crime* (New York: Penguin, 1997); H. Nuhanović, *The Role of International Factors in Srebrenica: Chronology, Comments and Analysis of Events* (unpublished manuscript, 2002); D. Rohde, *Endgame: The Betrayal and Fall of Srebrenica: Europe's Worst Massacre since World War II* (Boulder, Colo.: Westview, 1997).

2. There is a great deal of debate about the statistics, including the number of victims from the entire Bosnian war. I cannot and will not join this debate. It is estimated that between 2,000 and 3,000 people (mainly men) survived the flight through the woods (International Commission on Missing Persons, Civil Society Initiatives). See Mirna Skrbić, "Counting the Dead: New Research into the Number of War Dead Proves Divisive," *Transitions Online* (April 4, 2006), http://www.tol.org, which describes the debate between Smail Čekić, director of the Research Institute on Crimes against Humanity, and Mirsad Tokaca, who started his own research institute in 2004. The debate can be followed in *Oslobođenje,* an important Bosnian newspaper. The Serb side is also busy with statistics, and tends to soft-pedal the number of incidents. Natasha Kandic in Belgrade is a dissident Serb who tries to expose such distortions. *Transitions Online* also pointed out in an editorial comment of the same date that the nature of the crimes rather than the number is what is important, especially in the case of genocide.

3. Mustafa Salihović, *Pokdani Pupoljci Podrinja* (Sarajevo: Istraživačko Documentation Center, 2005).

4. The Research and Documentation Center (RDC) in Sarajevo estimates 7,711 victims, of which 100 were below the age of 15; they included 20 babies, 222 children from 5 to 10 years old, and 58 children from 10 to 15 years old.

5. See R. v. d. Boogaard, *Zilverstad: De Haagse verduistering van het drama Srebrenica* (Amsterdam: Prometheus, 2005); D. van den Berg, *Zwarte Spiegel: Nederland-Srebrenica 1995–2005* (The Hague: IKV, 2005).

6. F. Grünfeld, "The Role of the Bystander in Rwanda and Srebrenica: Lessons Learned," in R. Haveman and A. Smeulders (eds.), *Supranational Criminology: Towards a Criminology of International Crimes* (Antwerp: Intersentia, 2008), 457–486.

7. Writ of summons for Van Diepen Van der Kroef Attorneys to appear before The Hague Tribunal, June 4, 2007, in the name of a number of victims. The translations are of a juridical nature and have been redacted; one does not hear the victims' voices.

8. S. Power, *A Problem from Hell: America and the Age of Genocide* (New York: Perennial, 2002).

9. David Rieff, *At the Point of a Gun: Democratic Dreams and Armed Intervention* (New York: Simon and Schuster, 2005).

10. See, e.g., C. W. Ingrao and T. A. Emmert (eds.), *Confronting the Yugoslav Controversies: A Scholars' Initiative* (West Lafayette, Ind.: Purdue University Press, 2009); and Silvie Matton, *Srebrenica: Un Génocide annoncé* (Paris: Flammarion, 2005). Mark Danner is known for his inspiring articles in the *New York Times Review of Books*: "Great Betrayal" (March 26, 1998), "Bosnia: Breaking the Machine" (February 19, 1998), "Bosnia: The Turning Point" (February 5, 1998). Chuck Sudetić, who knows the region, wrote an excellent novel, *Blood and Vengeance: One Family's Story of the War in Bosnia* (Harmondsworth, England: Penguin, 1998). E. Suljagić's *Postcards from the Grave* (London: Saqi, 2005) is a remarkable memoir of the war.

11. *Conclusions of the Government of the Republic of Serbia; Report of the Commission for Investigation of Events in and around Srebrenica between 10 and 19 July 1995* (Banja Luka: June 2004); *Addendum to the Report of the 11th of June 2004 on the Events in and around Srebrenica between 10 and 19 July 1995* (Banja Luka: October 15, 2004).

12. The accords, which ended the Bosnian war in 1995, divided the area of Bosnia-Herzegovina into two states, a Muslim-Croatian federation, and the Republika Srpska (Serb Republic). Both states have a degree of autonomy, but are bound by a shared presidency and governing apparatus.

13. An exception is the work of Janja Beć, who voiced her horror in a series of miniatures. See, for example, *The Shattering of the Soul* (Lubljana: Helsinki Committee for Human Rights in Serbia, 2007), http://onlinebooks.library.upenn.edu/webbin/book/lookupid?key=olbp11774.

14. NIOD Report, 3173ff.

15. There are many excellent parts of the report, including the work of Ger Duijzings on the history of Bosnia and the sections on life in the enclave and the relations between the military and the local population.

16. See the special issue "Het drama Srebrenica: Geschiedtheoretische beschouwingen over het NIOD-rapport," *Tijdschrift voor Geschiedenis* 116:2 (2003), 190–327; *Bijdragen en Mededelingen betreffende de Geschiedenis der Nederlanden* 118:3 (2003), 293–356.

17. J. Wieten, *Srebrenica en de Journalistiek: Achtergronden en invloed van de78 berichtgeving over het conflict in voormalig Joegoslavië in de periode 1991–1995: Een onderzoek naar opvattingen en werkwijze van Nederlandse journalisten* (Amsterdam: Amsterdam School of Communications Research/NIOD, Boom, 2003) (CD-ROM); J. Wieten, *Background and Influence of Media Reporting of the Conflict in the Former Yugoslavia during the Period 1991–1995: A Study of the Views and Methods of Dutch Journalists* (Amsterdam: NIOD, 2002).

18. G. Snell, "Het nationalism van DutchBat," *Vrij Nederland* (July 2, 2005).

19. H. Hren (ed.), *Srebrenica, het verhaal van de overlevenden* (Amsterdam: Van Gennep, 1999). Rabbi Awraham Soetendorp wrote the introduction, and he compared the lot of the Jewish victims of World War II with the lot of the survivors of Srebrenica.

Sabaheta's Story

1. Interview with Sabaheta Fejić, May 2004.

1. Farewell

1. Interview with Safija Kabilović.

2. H. White, *Tropics of Discourse: Essays in Cultural Criticism* (Baltimore, Md.: Johns Hopkins University Press, 1978).

3. Dominique LaCapra, *Writing History, Writing Trauma* (Baltimore, Md.: Johns Hopkins University Press, 2001), 91f.

4. Psychoanalysts work from the assumption that a narrated account or memory is meant to tell something; they do not judge it on the basis of historical "truth." See S. Felman and D. Laub, *Testimony: Crises of Witnessing in Literature, Psychoanalysis, and History* (London: Routledge, 1992). I referred to this debate in my previous book, *De Mensen en de Woorden: Geschiedenis op basis van verhalen* (Amsterdam: Meulenhoff, 2004). See especially 102–139 for a discussion of trauma.

5. LaCapra, *Writing History,* 91.

6. G. Benezer, "Trauma Signals in Life Stories," in K. Lacy Rogers, S. Leydesdorff, and G. Dawson (eds.), *Trauma: The Life Stories of Survivors* (New Brunswick, N.J.: Transaction, 2004), 29–45.

7. D. E. Miller and L. T. Miller, *Survivors: An Oral History of the Armenian Genocide* (Berkeley: University of California Press, 1993); N. Adler, *Beyond the Soviet System: The Gulag Survivor* (New Brunswick, N.J.: Transaction, 2002); A. Applebaum, *Gulag: A History* (New York: Allen Lane, Penguin, 2003); D. Bertaux, P. Thompson, and A. Rotkirch, *On Living through Soviet Russia* (New Brunswick, N.J.: Transaction, 2004).

8. Benezer, "Trauma Signals"; D. LaCapra, "Trauma, Absence, Loss," *Critical Inquiry* 25:4 (1999), 696–727; D. Laub and N. C. Auerhahn, "Knowing and Not Knowing: Massive Psychic Trauma: Forms of Traumatic Memory," *International Journal of Psychoanalysis* 74 (1993), 287–302; O. van der Hart and D. Brom, "When the Victim Forgets: Trauma-Induced Amnesia and Its Assessment in Holocaust Survivors," in A. Y. Shalev, R. Yehuda, and A. C. McFarlane (eds.), *International Handbook of Human Response to Trauma* (New York: Plenum, 2002), 233–248.

9. S. Totten, W. S. Parsons, and I. W. Charney (eds.), *Century of Genocide: Eyewitness Accounts and Critical Views* (New York: Routledge, 1997); R. Crownshaw and S. Leydesdorff, "On Silence and the Words of the Victims," introduction to the reprint of L. Passerini, *Memory of Totalitarianism* (New Brunswick, N.J.: Transaction, 2005), vii–xiii; A. Dirk Moses, "Conceptual Blockages and Definitional Dilemmas in the 'Racial Century': Genocides of Indigenous Peoples and the Holocaust," *Patterns of Prejudice* 36:4 (2002), 7–36.

10. N. Wood, *Vectors of Memory: Legacies of Trauma in Postwar Europe* (Oxford: Berg, 1999), esp. ch. 3, "The Victim's Resentment."

11. Ibid., 8.

12. O. Bartov, "Seeking the Roots of Modern Genocide: On the Macro- and Microhistory of Mass Murder," in R. Gellately and B. Kiernan (eds.), *The Specter of Genocide: Mass Murder in Historical Perspective* (Cambridge: Cambridge University Press, 2003), 87.

13. Ibid., 96.

14. J. Waller, *Becoming Evil: How Ordinary People Commit Genocide and Mass Killing* (New York: Oxford University Press, 2002); E. Staub, *The Roots of Evil: The Origins of Genocide and Other Group Violence* (Cambridge: Cambridge University Press, 1989).

15. Svetlana Broz, *Good People in an Evil Time* (New York: Other Press, 2005). Originally written in Bosnian, this book is devoted to examples of individual courage.

16. Interview with Ramiza Zukanović, 2006.

17. S. Leydesdorff, "Nederland moet Srebrenica niet in de steek laten," *De Volkskrant* (March 28, 2007).

18. Interview with Timka Mujić.

19. There is a body of literature on Bosnian Muslims' satisfaction with their place in the former Yugoslavia. In Bosnia, the region is now referred to as the land of the wars of Milosević (predictably, Serbian and Croatian literature have different takes on this). The region's historiography has been strongly colored by the wars. I found the more anthropological studies of Bosnian social structure to be helpful, e.g., the work of Tone Bringa, "Averted Gaze: Genocide in Bosnia-Herzegovina, 1992–1995," in A. L. Hinton (ed.), *Annihilating Difference: The Anthropology of Genocide* (Berkeley: University of California Press, 2002), 194–229. This article continues the work in her *Being Muslim in the Bosnian Way: Identity and Community in a Central Bosnian Village* (Princeton, N.J.: Princeton University Press, 1995). See also M. A. Sells, *The Bridge Betrayed: Religion and Genocide in Bosnia* (Berkeley: University of California Press, 1996).

20. Bringa, "Averted Gaze."

21. For the relation between criminality and a postwar economy, see P. Andreas, "The Clandestine Political Economy of War and Peace in Bosnia," *International Studies Quarterly* 48 (2004), 29–51.

22. Interview with Nermina Smajlović, Mihatovići, 2004.

23. J. B. Young, *Writing and Rewriting the Holocaust: Narrative and the Consequences of Interpretation* (Bloomington: Indiana University Press, 1990).

24. R. Culbertson, "Embodied Memory, Transcendence, and Telling: Recounting Trauma, Re-establishing the Self," *New Literary History* 26:1 (1995), 169–195.

25. *Srebrenica* (September 12, 2006) can be found at http://video.google.nl/videoplay ?docid=5126512112668960041. Leslie Woodhead, *Srebrenica: A Cry from the Grave* (1999), can be found at http://www.pbs.org/wnet/cryfromthegrave/eyewitnesses/eyewitness .html.

26. This was analyzed by R. A. Wilson in "Judging History: The Historical Record of the International Criminal Tribunal for the Former Yugoslavia," *Human Rights Quarterly* 27 (2005), 908–942.

27. To name a few: Leslie Woodhead, *Never Again* (2005); Srebrenica Zemlja Zlocinara, *Srebrenica 2005* (May 17, 2006); *Srebrenica* (September 12, 2006); IKON, *De Vrouwen van Srebrenica* (July 11, 2006); Mustafa Ibrahimović, *Land der Vermisten* (2008).

28. Interview with Haša Selimović.

29. Interview with Bida Smajlović, Potočari.

30. Interview with Ajkuna Kremić.

31. See, for example, G. Duijzings, *Geschiedenis en herinnering in Oost-Bosnië: De achtergronden van de val van Srebrenica* (Amsterdam: Boom, 2002), ch. 5.

32. Danner has written extensively about the procedural aspects in the *New York Times Review of Books*: "America and the Bosnian Genocide" (December 4, 1997),

"Clinton, the UN, and the Bosnian Disaster" (December 18, 1997), "The Killing Fields of Bosnia" (September 24, 1998), "Endgame in Kosovo" (May 6, 1999).

33. Irfan Ajanović (ed.), *I Begged Them to Kill Me: Crimes against the Women of Bosnia-Herzegovina* (Sarajevo: CID, 2000). See also S. Hunt, *This Was Not Our War: Bosnian Women Reclaiming Peace* (Durham, N.C.: Duke University Press, 2004), ch. 1, "Hell Breaks Loose."

34. D. A. Nuruddin, "Poruka silovanim zenama" [Message to the Raped Women], *Islamska misao* 155 (May 1993), 25–27.

35. See R. C. Carpenter, *Born of War: Protecting Children of Sexual Violence Survivors in Conflict Zones* (Sterling, Va.: Stylus, 2007).

36. Zumra Šehomerović in the film by Woodhead, *Srebrenica: A Cry from the Grave.*

2. An Orphaned World

1. S. Leydesdorff, "Nederland moet Srebrenica niet in de steek laten," *De Volkskrant* (March 28, 2007).

2. According to a report by Arjan Uilenreef from the Ministry of Foreign Affairs in January 2006, during the years 2003–2005 the Netherlands gave Bosnia €47.5 million, 22.9 million of which went to Srebrenica. The amount for 2006 seems to have been higher.

3. *Documents on Crimes Committed in Srebrenica: Dokumenti o Zločinima u Srebrenici* (Sarajevo: July 1997).

4. *Statističi, Podaci Popisa Stanovništa 1991: Godine po opštinama* (Sarajevo: 1992), a map published by the Bank of Sarajevo with the exact land divisions.

5. L. Silber and A. Little, *The Death of Yugoslavia* (London: Penguin, 1996); A. Paković, *The Fragmentation of Yugoslavia: Nationalism in a Multinational State* (Basingstoke, England: Macmillan, 1992); C. Rogel, *The Breakup of Yugoslavia and the War in Bosnia* (Westport, Conn.: Greenwood, 1998); M. Thompson, *A Paper House: The Ending of Yugoslavia* (London: Vintage, 1992).

6. S. P. Ramet, "The Dissolution of Yugoslavia: Competing Narratives of Resentment and Blame," in C. Ingrao (ed.), *The Scholars' Initiative: Confronting the Yugoslav Controversies,* available at http://www.cla.purdue.edu/academic/history/facstaff/Ingrao/si/scholars.htm.

7. See also T. Bringa, "The Peaceful Death of Tito and the Violent End of Yugoslavia," in J. Borneman (ed.), *The Death of the Father: An Anthropology of the End in Political Authority* (Oxford: Berghahn, 2004), 148–201.

8. E. Redžic, *Bosnia and Herzegovina in the Second World War* (New York: Frank Cass, 2005); R. J. Donia and J. V. A. Fine Jr., *Bosnia and Herzegovina: A Tradition Betrayed* (London: Hurst, 1994); M. Velikonja, *Religious Separation and Political Intolerance in Bosnia Herzegovina* (College Station: Texas A&M University Press, 2003), 148–201 and ch. 9, "A War over Differences: The Religious Dimensions of the Conflict in Bosnia Herzegovina."

9. Donia and Fine, *Bosnia and Herzegovina;* Velikonja, *Religious Separation and Political Intolerance,* 235–287.

10. F. Ajami, "Under Western Eyes: The Fate of Bosnia," *Survival* 41:2 (1999), 32–52, argued for preserving this multiethnic tradition, while acknowledging the difficulty of

doing so. He considers the secular tradition in Bosnia, which is conditional on the multiethnic tradition, as the best hope for survival.

11. D. Sekulić, G. Massey, and R. Hodson, "Who Were the Yugoslavs? Failed Sources of Common Identity in the Former Yugoslavia," *American Sociological Review* 59:1 (1994), 83–97.

12. According to the 1990 Census, the percentages of mixed marriages were changing. In some rural areas, it was less than 10 percent, while in the center of Sarajevo it was 36 percent. According to a study of nationalistic orientation financed by the Democratic Party and carried out by Miklos Biro and Nenad Lozović in March 1990, only 30 percent of the Serb population was nationalistically oriented at that time. See the discussion of Report 11, "Living Together," in Ingrao, *Scholars' Initiative*.

13. T. Bringa, *Being Muslim in the Bosnian Way: Identity and Community in a Central Bosnian Village* (Princeton, N.J.: Princeton University Press, 1995), 9f., 149ff.

14. N. Botlev, "Where East Meets West: Ethnic Intermarriage in the Former Yugoslavia," *American Sociological Review* 59 (June 1994), 461–480; N. Botlev and R. A. Wagner, "Seeing Past the Barricades: Ethnic Intermarriage in Yugoslavia during the Last Three Decades," *Anthropology of East Europe Review* 11:1–2 (1993), 29–38; R. M. Sommerville, "The Family in Yugoslavia," *Journal of Marriage and the Family* 27:3 (1965), 350–362.

15. C. Sudetić, *Blood and Vengeance: One Family's Story of the War in Bosnia* (Harmondsworth, England: Penguin, 1998), 69.

16. Donia and Fine, *Bosnia and Herzegovina*.

17. Statistics are from *Zemljišna karta sa Nacionalnom Strukturom Republike Bosne i Hercgovine* [*Map of the Republic of Bosnia Herzegovina and the Structure of Nationalities*] (Sarajevo: Bank of Sarajevo, 1992), which was given to me by Professor Smail Čekić, Institute for Human Rights, University of Sarajevo.

18. Emir Suljagić targets this elite in *Postcards from the Grave* (London: Saqi, 2005). He shows convincingly how the conflict for power during 1992–1995 divided the town, allowing room for various factions and gangs.

19. These interviews were in part carried out by the NIOD research team, in which Duijzings had a position while he worked on his own book. This interview is one of his.

20. C. Bennett, *Yugoslavia's Bloody Collapse: Causes, Course, and Consequences* (New York: New York University Press, 1997).

21. C. J. Russo, "Religion and Education in Bosnia: Integration Not Segregation?" *European Journal for Education Law and Policy* 4:2 (2000), 121–129.

22. Interview with Behara Hasanović.

23. Interview with Ramiza Zukanović, April 2006, Tuzla.

24. She is also one of the main characters in David Rohde's *Endgame: The Betrayal and Fall of Srebrenica: Europe's Worst Massacre since World War II* (Boulder, Colo.: Westview, 1997).

25. Interview with Ćamila Omanović.

26. Interview with Bida Smajlović, December 2005.

27. See P. Miller, "Contested Memories: The Bosnian Genocide in Serb and Muslim Minds," *Journal of Genocide Research* 8:3 (2006), 311–324.

28. Interview with Hatidža Mehmedović.

29. Interview with Fikreta Hotić (conducted by Camilia Bruil).

30. In order to understand what I heard during the interviews, I benefited greatly from O. van der Hart, E. R. S. Nijenhuis, and K. Steele, *The Haunted Self: Structural Dissociation and the Treatment of Chronic Traumatization* (New York: Norton, 2006).

31. P. Bourdieu et al., *The Weight of the World: Social Suffering in Contemporary Society* (Cambridge: Polity, 2002), 625ff.

32. A *dunam* was a unit of measurement in the Ottoman Empire; it is still in use in various countries that belonged to the empire. Originally, it designated a parcel of land 40 steps wide and 40 steps long, although currently the meaning varies somewhat from place to place. It amounts to roughly a quarter acre.

33. Pies with savory fillings (meat, potatoes, cheese, spinach) are a traditional Bosnian dish. They are served either hot or cold.

34. E. Stites, S. Lautze, D. Mazurana, and A. Anić, *Coping with War, Coping with Peace: Livelihood Adaptation in Bosnia Herzegovina, 1989–2004* (Tuzla: April 2004), http://nutrition.tufts.edu/docs/pdf/famine/bosnia_livelihoods_study.pdf. They describe how tasks that seemed temporary became permanent.

35. Interview with Hatidža Habibović.

36. Interview with Hatidža Mehmedović.

37. Bringa, *Being Muslim in the Bosnian Way,* ch. 4, 119–143.

38. Interview with Nezira Sulejmanović.

39. Interview with Sevda Hasanović.

40. Kravica is where a large number of Bosnian Serb men were murdered by Bosniaks in 1993. The place has symbolic significance; a memorial was built there in contrast to or as a counter to the cemetery in Potočari.

41. Debate, *Human Rights Watch* 10:9 (November 1998); a denial can be found in the NIOD Report.

42. S. Weine et al., "Individual Change after Genocide in Bosnian Survivors of 'Ethnic Cleansing': Assessing Personality Dysfunction," *Journal of Traumatic Stress* 11:1 (1998), 147–153; S. Weine et al., "Family Consequences of Refugee Trauma," *Family Process* 43:2 (2004), 147–158.

43. The *kolo,* or "circle," is a group folk dance performed in the round.

44. Interview with Behara Hasanović.

45. Interview with Zehta Ustić.

46. Over the years, I have repeatedly informed various ambassadors that the condition of the survivors is deplorable. Once, when I described it graphically, I was told by the Dutch ambassador in Bosnia that I was wrong; he severed relations with me. Things changed when Karel Vosskuehler took that post. There was another push for change after the publication of Alok van Loon's *Vrouwen van Srebrenica* (Amsterdam: Contact, 2005). The first section of that book is a personal report of her bewilderment at seeing all the squalor and distress. This led to a Dutch parliamentary inquiry, which resulted in a report: D. Karadzin and E. Polojac, *Inventory of the Psychosocial Assistance Provided to the Survivors of the Srebrenica Fall, 1995* (Sarajevo: Royal Netherlands Embassy, 2006).

3. War Is Coming

1. G. Duijzings, *Geschiedenis en herinnering in Oost-Bosnië: De achtergronden van de val van Srebrenica* (Amsterdam: Boom, 2002), part of the NIOD Report, 101ff.

2. Ibid., ch. 5, "De machtsovername door de nationalisten," 101–139. Duijzings describes in detail the party struggles at the local level.

3. *Zemlijšna karta sa Nacionalnom Strukturom Republike Bosne i Hercgovine* (Sarajevo: Bank of Sarajevo, 1992).

4. Interview with Šefika Begić, 2004.

5. The Podrinje is the region around Bratunac. There was a massive exodus of its residents in 1992 and 1993 to Srebrenica; most wound up in Potočari or fled through the woods. The Podrinje includes a part of the valley of the Drina River and extends to the other "safe area," Gorazde.

6. C. Rogel, *The Breakup of Yugoslavia and the War in Bosnia* (Westport, Conn.: Greenwood, 1998).

7. Duijzings, *Geschiedenis en herinnering in Oost-Bosnië,* 143.

8. Ibid., 167ff.

9. Information compiled by Selma Kapidzić, researcher, and Jagoda Gregulska, collaborator.

10. Skrbić, "Counting the Dead."

11. Interview with Šuhra Sinanović, 2004.

12. Institute for War and Peace Report, *Balkan Crisis Report* (October 8, 2004).

13. Interview with Binasa Sarajlić.

14. H. Nuhanović, *The Role of International Factors in Srebrenica* (unpublished manuscript, 2002), 25. This work contains a collection of survivors' statements on the role of the international community in the genocide against the population of "Srebrenica—Unsafe Area." There is a Bosnian version as well, but I refer to the English version.

15. In the Serb salute, the thumb and the index and middle fingers are held up. Traditionally, the gesture refers to the Christian Trinity. This old custom became a symbol of Serb nationalism and took on a broader and more nationalistic meaning in the region. Especially in Bosnia and Kosovo, it meant that one wished the other dead.

16. Interview by Ger Duijzings with Mirsada Bakalović, June 1998.

17. "'A Closed, Dark Place': Past and Present Human Rights Abuses in Foća," *Human Rights Watch* 10:6 (July 1998).

18. A. Delić, "Žrtvujemo li ih Povno?" [Are We Sacrificing Them Again?], *Sumejja bosanska* 19 (January–February 2006).

19. Interview with Edina Karić.

20. Interview by Ger Duijzings with Mitko Kadrić, November 1992.

21. C. Carmichael, "Violence and Ethnic Boundary Maintenance in Bosnia in the 1990s," *Journal of Genocide Research* 8:3 (2006), 283–293.

22. Interview with Abdulah Purković.

23. See n. 15 above.

24. This refers to the murders in the region around Srebrenica in 1942, which were begun by the Germans and the Croats. The Croats carried out a reign of terror that year in East Bosnia. The Muslim population sought and gained protection from the Croatian Ustaša. Duijzings describes (*Geschiedenis en herinnering in Oost-Bosnië,* 63f.) how the Muslims managed to deter the slaughter of Bosnians by Croats, but those unavenged mass murders became part of the local Serb nationalist mindset. Even though the 1942 murders had not been committed by Muslims, the Serbs regarded the occupation of Srebrenica as an act of revenge.

25. Interview with Vahida Ahmetović.

26. B. Lieberman, "Nationalist Narratives, Violence between Neighbors and Ethnic Cleansing in Bosnia-Herzegovina: A Case of Cognitive Dissonance?" *Journal of Genocide Research* 8:3 (2006), 295–309.

27. See also the testimony of Milorad Krnojelac (IT-97-25), www.un.org/icty/transe25/0103it.htm, which was brought to my attention by Lieberman's article.

28. Lieberman, "Nationalist Narratives," 299.

29. Ibid., 300.

30. Lieberman is referring to Norman Naimark's excellent book, *Fires of Hatred: Ethnic Cleansing in Twentieth Century Europe* (Cambridge, Mass.: Harvard University Press, 2001).

31. D. Adjuković and Dinka Corkalo, "Trust and Betrayal in War," in E. Stover and H. M. Weinstein (eds.), *My Neighbour, My Enemy: Justice and Community in the Aftermath of Mass Atrocity* (Cambridge: Cambridge University Press, 2004), 287–302.

32. Ibid., 290.

33. Waller, *Becoming Evil.* I am aware that this question is raised regarding every mass murder. The most systematic thoughts on this issue are in J. Sémelin, *Purifier et détruire: Usages politiques des massacres et genocides* (Paris: Seuil, 2005). See in particular ch. 5, "Les vertiges de l'impunité."

34. Waller, *Becoming Evil,* 272.

35. Interview by Anna Albers with Muská Omerović-Begović.

36. Interview by Arieke Duijzer with Zejna Jasarević-Fejić.

37. Interview with Sevda Hasanović.

38. Interview with Šefika Begić.

39. See Duijzings, *Geschiedenis en herinnering in Oost-Bosnië,* 102–156, in which the leadership role of her husband, Hamed Efendić, is apparent.

40. Interview with Fazila Efendić.

41. S. Leydesdorff, L. Passerini, and P. Thompson (eds.), *Gender and Memory* (Oxford: Oxford University Press, 1996; reprint, New Brunswick, N.J.: Transaction, 2005).

4. Living on the Run, Living in Danger

1. "The Tide of Misery," *Economist* (May 23, 1992).

2. See B. Hayden, "What Is in a Name? The Nature of the Individual in Refugee Studies," *Journal of Refugee Studies* 19:4 (2006), 471ff.

3. One of the most inspiring books about what it means to flee is Michael Marrus, *The Unwanted: European Refugees in the Twentieth Century* (Oxford: Oxford University Press, 1985).

4. Interview with Šuhra Alić.

5. Peter Read, *Returning to Nothing: The Meaning of Lost Places* (Cambridge: Cambridge University Press, 1996).

6. Benjamin Lieberman, *Terrible Fate: Ethnic Cleansing in the Making of Modern Europe* (Chicago: Dee, 2006), 327.

7. Y. Bauer, "The Death Marches, January–May, 1945," *Modern Judaism* 3:1 (1983), 1–23.

8. For example, Isnam Taljić, *The Story of Srebrenica* (Kuala Lumpur: Silverfish, 2004); Sadik Salimović, *The Road of Death* (Sarajevo: Mothers of the Enclaves of Žepa

and Srebrenica, 2008); Nihad Nino Ćatić and Ljudi Beznađa, *Mensen van de Wanhoop* (Eindhoven, Netherlands: Platform, 2007).

9. For example, P. McCarthy, *After the Fall: Srebrenica Survivors in St. Louis* (St. Louis: Missouri Historical Society Press, 2000).

10. S. Leydesdorff, "Nederland wil deportaties in Bosnië niet zien," *De Volkskrant* (April 8, 2005).

11. Interview with Jasmina Ljeljić.

12. P. Bell, I. Bergeret, and L. Oruč, "Women from the Safe Haven: The Psychological and Psychiatric Consequences of Extreme and Prolonged Trauma on Women from Srebrenica," in S. Powell and E. Duraković-Belko (eds.), *Sarajevo 2000: The Psychological Consequences of War: Results from the Empirical Research from the Territory of the Former Yugoslavia,* 32–37, at www.insanbilimleri.com/en/books/srajevo-2000.htm.

13. Interview with Ramiza Zukanović.

14. A. Stefansson, "Urban Exile: Locals, Newcomers, and the Cultural Transformation of Sarajevo," in X. Bougarel, E. Helms, and G. Duijzings (eds.), *The New Bosnian Mosaic: Identities, Memories and Moral Claims in Post-War Society* (Hampshire, Burlington, England: Ashgate, 2007), 59–79.

15. In research on the refugees in the Republika Srpska, Nadeža Savjak observed that problems in being able to provide the basic necessities of life can form a barrier to the processing of events. N. Savjak, "Displacement as a Factor Causing Posttraumatic Stress Disorder," in Powell and Duraković-Belko, *Sarajevo 2000,* 42–47.

16. Interview with Devleta Omerović.

17. Interview with Magbula Pašalić.

18. Interview with Mejra Hodžić.

19. For the fate of the children, see the lovely autobiography by Nadja Halilbegovich, *My Childhood under Fire* (Tonawanda, N.Y.: Kids Can Press, 2006).

20. Christopher S. Stewart, *Hunting the Tiger: The Fast Life and Violent Death of the Balkans' Most Dangerous Man* (New York: Dunne, 2008).

21. Interview with Šuhreta Mujić.

22. Foreword by Paule du Bouchet, in Bouchet, *Le Livre noir de l'ex-Yougoslavie: Purification ethnique et crimes de guerre* (Paris: Arlea, 1993).

23. T. Gjelten, *Sarajevo Daily: A City and Its Newspaper under Siege* (New York: Perennial, 1995).

24. Bouchet, *Le Livre noir,* 115, based on the report of the UNHCR, 1992.

25. L. de Barros-Duchêne, *Srebrenica: Histoire d'une crime international* (Paris: Harmattan, 1997).

26. For the shock, see I. Kaksić, "In Search of Safe Haven," in R. Benmayor and A. Skotness (eds.), *Migration and Identity* (New Brunswick, N.J.: Transaction, 2005), 19–35.

27. B. Franz, *Uprooted and Unwanted: Bosnian Refugees in Austria and the United States* (College Station: Texas A&M University Press, 2005).

28. Interview by Arieke Duijzer with Zejna Jasarević-Fejić.

29. Interview with Nura Duraković.

30. Ibid.

31. Interview with Kadira Rizanović.

32. E. Suljagić, *Postcards from the Grave* (London: Saqi, 2005), 61ff.

33. Hatidža Hren, *Srebrenica, het verhaal van de overlevenden* (Amsterdam: Van Gennep, 1999), 66, 67.

34. Interview with Vahida Ahmetović.
35. Interview with Sevda Hasanović.
36. Interview with Hanifa Muhinović.
37. Interview with Šuhreta Mujić.
38. Interview with Zehta Ustić.
39. Interview with Šida Omerović.

5. A Human Shooting Gallery

1. According to information from the RDC (December 2006), 378 Bosniak civilians, 99 Serb civilians, 454 Bosniak soldiers, and 192 Serb soldiers fell in 1992.

2. I. Maćek, "'Imitation of Life': Negotiating Normality in Sarajevo under Siege," in Bougarel, Helms, and Duijzings, *New Bosnian Mosaic*, 39–59.

3. Ibid., 55.

4. Ger Duijzings.

5. Gjelten, *Sarajevo Daily*, 136ff.

6. Convention on the Prevention and Punishment of the Crime of Genocide, adopted by Resolution 260(III)A of the United Nations General Assembly on December 9, 1948.

7. Interview with Alma Mustafić by Lara Broekman.

8. Interview with Ajša Begtić.

9. Kirsti S. Thorsen, *Médecins sans Frontières: Humanitarian Aid Program in Srebrenica*, 4.12.1992–21.7.1994, NIOD Report; Thorsen, *Swedish Rescue Services Agency: Swedish Shelter Project Srebrenica*, 1.3.1994–11.7.1995, NIOD Report; Thorsen, *Norsk Folkehjelp: Humanitarian Aid Programs in Srebrenica and Bratunac 1992–1995*, NIOD Report. Access to these materials was made possible by permission from NIOD; it is unclear whether the materials on which they are based are available for perusal.

10. Thorsen, *Norsk Folkehjelp*, paragraph 2.3.1. Access to this report was made possible by researcher Ger Duijzings.

11. NIOD Report, 1259.

12. Thorsen, *Médecins sans Frontières*.

13. Ibid.

14. *Report of the Secretary-General Pursuant to General Assembly Resolution 53/35* (1998), http://www.un.org/peace/srebrenica.pdf.

15. Interview with Hafiza Malagić.

16. See, for example, E. Ringelblum, *Notes from the Warsaw Ghetto: The Journal of Emmanuel Ringelblum* (New York: Schocken, 1974); Charles G. Roland, *Courage under Siege: Starvation, Disease, and Death in the Warsaw Ghetto* (New York: Oxford University Press, 1992); M. Weitzman, D. Landes, and A. Klein, *Dignity and Defiance: The Confrontation of Life and Death in the Warsaw Ghetto* (Los Angeles: Simon Wiesenthal Center, 1993); I. Trunk, *Lodz Ghetto: A History* (Bloomington: Indiana University Press, 2006).

17. Interview with Rukija Hasić.

18. NIOD Report, 1283.

19. Interview with Sabra Kulenović.

20. Ibid.

21. Interview with Razija Smajlović.

22. Interview with Magbula Pašalić.

23. T. Mazowiecki, *Question of the Violation of Human Rights and Fundamental Freedoms in Any Part of the World with Particular Reference to Colonial and Other Dependent Countries and Territories: Situation of Human Rights in the Territory of the Former Yugoslavia* (August 22, 1995), http://www.unhchr.ch/Huridocda/Huridoca.nsf/o/c0a6cfd5274508fd802567900036da9a?Opendocument.

24. P. von Recklinghausen, "Inside Srebrenica: City of the Damned," *Newsweek* (April 21, 1993).

25. Yugoslav Tribunal, IT 03-68, *ICTY Prosecutor versus Naser Orić*, 16304.

26. *Report of the Secretary-General Pursuant to General Assembly Resolution 53/35* (1998), 15.

27. Yugoslav Tribunal, IT 03-68, *ICTY Prosecutor versus Naser Orić*, 14350.

28. Ibid., 14351.

29. Ibid., 9671 (August 24, 2005).

30. Hunt, *This Was Not Our War*, 56.

31. Interview with Hatidža Mehmedović.

32. The story of Jezero, located close to Skelani, is comparable to the role of Kravica in Serb propaganda. It was used in the Orić trial to show how brutally the Muslims acted in Serb villages. No one can deny that the Muslims murdered in 1992, but what happened is used to demonstrate Muslim cruelty and to minimize the crimes committed in Srebrenica. See also UN Security Document A/46/171 S/25635, June 2, 1993, Memorandum on War Crimes and Crimes of Genocide in Eastern Bosnia (Communes of Bratunac, Skelani, and Srebrenica) Committed against the Serbian Population from April 1992 to April 1993, at www.srpska-mreza.com/Bosnia/Srebrenica/UN-victims.html.

33. Yugoslav Tribunal, IT 03-68, *ICTY Prosecutor versus Naser Orić*, judgment.

34. Ibid., 9680.

35. Ibid.

36. Ibid.

37. Sheri Fink interviewed people from MSF, although she was not in Srebrenica during the siege. Her *War Hospital: A True Story of Surgery and Survival* (New York: Public Affairs, 2003) gives a penetrating account of the primitive health-care situation and what it was like to be a doctor or nurse under those conditions.

38. T. Pontus, *J'étais médicin dans Srebrenica assiégée: Un prelude du grand massacre* (Paris: Harmattan, 2005).

39. He is referring to the events in the Vercors, a low mountain range close to Grenoble. Members of the resistance who controlled the plateaus were waiting for Allied drops. They had been betrayed. The Gestapo landed instead, and a mass murder followed.

40. Pontus, *J'étais médicin*, 85.

41. Ibid., 86.

42. H. Hren (ed.), *Srebrenica, het verhaal van de overlevenden* (Amsterdam: Van Gennep, 1999).

43. E. Suljagić, *Postcards from the Grave* (London: Saqi, 2005).

44. X. Bougarel, "Death and the Nationalist: Martyrdom, War Memory, and Veteran Identity among Bosnian Muslims," in Bougarel, Helms, and Duijzings, *New Bosnian Mosaic*, 167–193.

45. Ibid.

46. Suljagić, *Postcards from the Grave*, 62.

47. Ibid., 25.

48. Interview with Ćamila Omanović.

49. Paul Thompson and Hugh Slim wrote that no longer having sowing seed is the most important phase in a famine. H. Slim, P. Thompson, O. Bennett, and N. Cross, *Listening for a Change: Oral Testimony and Community Development* (London: Panos, 1993).

50. Interview with Ćamila Omanović.

51. Interview with Ramiza Zukanović.

52. P. Andreas, "The Clandestine Political Economy of War and Peace in Bosnia," *International Studies Quarterly* 48 (2004), 29–51.

53. H. Praamsma, J. Peekel, and T. Boumans (eds.), *Herinneringen aan Srebrenica: 171 soldatengesprekken* (Amsterdam: Bert Bakker, 2005).

54. NIOD Report, 1488.

55. Ibid., 1489.

56. Ibid., 1492.

57. Ibid., 1497.

58. Ibid., 1529.

59. Ibid., 1532.

60. Praamsma, Peekel, and Boumans, *Herinneringen aan Srebrenica*, 114.

61. Ibid., 149.

62. "Conduct of Dutch UN Military in the Former Yugoslavia," letter to Minister of Defense J. J. C. Voorhoeve from the commander of the army, Th. J. P. Karremans, May 12, 1995, no. TK9567. Available only in Dutch at http://ikregeer.nl/document/kst-22181-96.

63. NIOD Report, 1599–1647, ch. 9, "Het intern functioneren van DutchBat tot de VRS-aanval."

64. Ibid., 1642.

65. "Conduct of Dutch UN Military in the Former Yugoslavia."

66. Interview with Munira Subašić.

67. Praamsma, Peekel, and Boumans, *Herinneringen aan Srebrenica*, 126.

68. Ibid., 201.

69. Interview with Vahida Ahmetović.

70. Interview with Sabra Alemić.

71. L. de Barros-Duchêne, *Srebrenica: Histoire d'une crime international* (Paris: Harmattan, 1997), 90.

72. Interview with Šefika Begić.

73. For information on the small health centers, the *ambulantas,* see NIOD Report, 1271f.

74. Interview by Lara Broekman with Alma Mustafić.

75. Interview with Devleta Omerović.

76. Interview with Vahida Ahmetović.

77. Interview with Sabra Alemić.

6. Violence

1. See D. Diner, "Historical Experience and Cognition: Juxtaposing Perspectives on National Socialism," in Diner, *Beyond the Conceivable: Studies on Germany, Nazism,*

and the Holocaust (Berkeley: University of California Press, 2000), 160–173, which says the same thing about the victims of the Holocaust.

2. NIOD Report, 2685.

3. See his correspondence with German historian Martin Broszat in M. Broszat and S. Friedländer, "A Controversy about the Historicization of National Socialism," *New German Critique: Special Issue on the Historikerstreit* 44 (1988), 85–126, reprinted in P. Baldwin (ed.), *Reworking the Past* (Boston: Beacon, 1990), 102–133. See also M. Broszat and S. Friedländer, "A Controversy about the Historicization of National Socialism," *Yad Vashem Studies* 19 (1988), 1–47.

4. L. Langer, *Holocaust Testimonies: The Ruins of Memory* (New Haven, Conn.: Yale University Press, 1991).

5. K. Derderian, "Common Fate, Different Experiences: Gender-Specific Aspects of the Armenian Genocide, 1915–1917," *Journal of Holocaust and Genocide Studies* 10:1 (2005), 1–25.

6. Ibid.

7. For the debate over gendercide, see A. J. Jones, *Gendercide and Genocide* (Nashville, Tenn.: Vanderbilt University Press, 2004), 10. The debate began with Jones's article in 1996, "Does 'Gender' Make the World Go Round? Feminist Critiques of International Relations," *Review of International Studies* 22 (1996), 405–429.

8. J. D. Popkin, "Holocaust Memories, Historians' Memoirs: First-Person Narrative and the Memory of the Holocaust," *History and Memory* 15 (2003), 40–84.

9. O. van der Hart, E. Nijenhuis, and K. Steele, *The Haunted Self: Structural Dissociation and the Treatment of Chronic Traumatization* (New York: Norton, 2006).

10. M. Marshall Clark, "Holocaust Video Testimony, Oral History, and Narrative Medicine: The Struggle against Indifference," *Literature and Medicine* 24:2 (2005), 266–282.

11. M. Rothberg and J. Stark, "After the Witness: A Report from the Twentieth Anniversary Conference of the Fortunoff Video Archive for Holocaust Testimonies at Yale," *History and Memory* 15:1 (2003), 85–96.

12. Interview with Šuhra Sinanović.

13. Hren, *Srebrenica,* 155.

14. Gemeinschaft für Bedrohte Völker, Document 20/99, at www.gfbv.ba/index.

15. H. Nuhanović, *Under the UN Flag: The International Community and the Srebrenica Genocide* (Sarajevo: DES, 2007).

16. Ibid.

17. Yugoslav Tribunal, *ICTY Prosecutor versus Janković,* IT 98-23.2, 5752ff. The quotations here are translated from the Dutch.

18. Van der Hart, Nijenhuis, and Steele, *The Haunted Self.*

19. Interview with Nermina Smajlović.

20. Florence Hartmann, *Paix et châtiment: Les Guerres secretes de la politique et de la justice internationale* (Paris: Flammarion, 2007).

21. I am grateful to trauma specialist Onno van der Hart for his insights.

22. R. Leys, *From Guilt to Shame: Auschwitz and After* (Princeton, N.J.: Princeton University Press, 2007).

23. RDC, Witness no. 8561/95, woman born in 1971.

24. J. Zur, "Remembering and Forgetting: Guatemalan War Widows' Forbidden Memories," in K. Lacy Rogers, S. Leydesdorff, and G. Dawson (eds.), *Trauma: The Life Stories of Survivors* (New Brunswick, N.J.: Transaction, 2004), 45–60.

25. Ibid., 51.

26. Interview by Velma Sarić with Zumra Šehomerović.

27. Interview with Šida Omerović.

28. Interview with Ajša Begtić.

29. RDC, Witness no. 8545/95, woman born in 1947.

30. See also NIOD Report, 2605f.

31. Interview with Vahida Ahmetović.

32. Interview with Mejra Hodžić

33. Interview with Fazila Efendić.

34. Interview with Hatidža Habibović.

35. This was further compounded by the fact that some Dutch soldiers "temporarily" laid their weapons in a pile; NIOD Report, 2640. For more regarding giving up uniforms and weapons, see 2685.

36. Interview with Munira Subašić.

37. Interview with Šuhreta Mujić.

38. Interview with "Suada."

39. I am grateful to Velma Sarić for research she did for me under the supervision of Smail Čekić, a professor in Sarajevo.

40. Interview with Fazila Efendić.

41. Ibid.

42. Interview with Munira Subašić.

43. Interview with Nezira Sulejmanović.

44. A. Stiglmayer, *Mass Rape: The War against Women in Bosnia Herzegovina* (Lincoln: University of Nebraska Press, 1993). This book was published before the fall of Srebrenica, but noted the events that led to it. See also Irfan Ajanović (ed.), *I Begged Them to Kill Me: Crimes against the Women of Bosnia-Herzegovina* (Sarajevo: CID, 2000).

45. Amnesty International, *La justice pour qui? En Bosnie-Herzégovine, les femmes attendant toujours: Conclusions et recommandations* (EUR 63/00602009, September 30, 2009).

46. Yugoslav Tribunal, *ICTY Prosecutor versus Erdemović*, no. 15.7.2005, 56ff.

47. For a more theoretical approach to silence, see L. Passerini, "Memories between Silence and Oblivion," in K. Hodgkin and S. Radstone (eds.), *Contested Pasts: The Politics of Memory* (London: Routledge, 2003), 238–255.

48. Regarding the politics of memory, see A. Assmann, *Der lange Schatten der Vergagenheit: Erinnerungskultur und Geschichtspolitik* (Munich: Beck, 2006).

49. Interview with Ćamila Omanović.

50. Interview with Hadžira Ibrahimović.

7. Departure without Arrival

1. Ervin Staub's *The Roots of Evil: The Origins of Genocide and Other Group Violence* (Cambridge: Cambridge University Press, 1989) is very important.

2. Ervin Staub, "Preventing Genocide: Activating Bystanders, Helping Victims, and the Creation of Caring," *Other Voices* 2:1 (February 2000).

3. A. J. Veltlesen, "Genocide: A Case for the Responsibility of the Bystander," *Journal of Peace Research* 27:4 (2000), 519–532.

4. F. Grünfeld, "The Role of the Bystanders in Rwanda and Srebrenica: Lessons Learned," in R. Haveman and A. Smeulders (eds.), *Supranational Criminology: Towards a Criminology of International Crimes* (Antwerp: Intersentia, 2008).

5. Interview with Sevda Hasanović.

6. Interview by Anna Albers with Muška Omerović.

7. Interview with Šuhra Sinanović.

8. Interview with Sabra Alemić.

9. Interview with Mejra Hotić.

10. Interview with Hanifa Muhinović.

11. Interview with Šefika Begić.

12. Interview by Lara Broekman with Alma Mustafić.

13. Interview by Arieke Duijzer with Zejna Jasarević-Fejić.

14. Interview with Magbula Pašalić.

15. Interview by Mark de Vries with Muriz Bektić.

16. Interview by Esther van Zeijden with Ramo Ramić.

17. Interview with Hidajet Malagić.

18. Interview by Ragna Louman with Fadil Hotić.

19. J. Mertus, *War's Offensive on Women: The Humanitarian Challenge in Bosnia, Kosovo, and Afghanistan* (Sterling, Va.: Kumarian, 2000).

20. Interview with "Suada."

21. Interviews with Kada Hotić and Zumra Šehomerović.

22. UNHCR, *Survey of Displaced Persons in Tuzla Canto from the Podrinje Area, Eastern Republika Srpska* (Tuzla: 2003).

23. Interview with Fadila Memišević.

24. Interview with Kada Hotić.

25. A. Stefansson, "Urban Exile: Locals, Newcomers, and the Cultural Transformation of Sarajevo," in Bougarel, Helms, and Duijzings, *New Bosnian Mosaic,* 59–79.

26. *Southeastern Europe* (July 14, 2000).

27. "Activities," *Journal of the Association "Mothers of the Enclaves Srebrenica and Žepa"* (2000).

28. Various interviews. See also U.S. Department of State, *Human Rights Report for 2000: Bosnia Herzegovina,* http://www.state.gov/g/drl/rls/hrrpt/2001/eur/8236.htm.

29. See the coverage in *Večerne novine* (Sarajevo) (May 12, 13, 14, 2000).

30. See B. S. Nelson, "Post-War Trauma and Reconciliation in Bosnia-Herzegovina: Observations, Experiences and Implications for Marriage and Family Therapy," *American Journal of Family Therapy* 31:4 (July 2003), 305–316.

31. Interview with Šuhra Sinanović.

32. E. Helms, "'Politics Is a Whore': Women, Morality, and Victimhood in Post-War Bosnia Herzegovina," in Bougarel, Helms, and Duijzings, *New Bosnian Mosaic,* 235–255.

33. E. Mujawayo and S. Belhaddad, *Survivantes* (Paris: Aube, 2004), especially ch. 20.

34. A. Portelli, *The Order Has Been Carried Out: History, Memory, and Meaning of a Nazi Massacre in Rome* (New York: Palgrave, 2003), especially ch. 8, "A Strange Grief."

35. Ibid., 215.

36. The Serbs tried to camouflage their crimes by moving bodies from mass graves to areas where they were less likely to be found. Some bodies had been moved several times and mixed with earth from different places.

37. For this kind of information and for so much more, I am grateful to Asta Zinbo, ICMP.

38. L. Vollen, "All That Remains: Identifying the Victims of the Srebrenica Massacre," *Cambridge Quarterly of Health Care Ethics* 10 (2001), 336–340; Sarah Wagner, *To Know Where He Lies: DNA Technology and the Search for Srebrenica's Missing* (Berkeley: University of California Press, 2008).

39. C. A. Brkić, *The Stone Fields: Love and Death in the Balkans* (New York: Picador, 2005).

40. Interview with Haša Selimović.

41. Vervaeke learned this statistic at an NGO meeting.

42. Interview with Rukija Hasić.

43. Interview with Hatidža Habibović.

44. Interview with Hatidža Mehmedović.

45. M. F. Kett, "Internally Displaced Peoples in Bosnia-Herzegovina: Impacts of Long-Term Displacement on Health and Well-Being," *Medicine, Conflict, and Survival* 21:3 (July 2005), 199–215.

46. Yugoslavia Tribunal, *ICTY Prosecutor versus Krstić*, July 27, 2000, 5815ff., testimony of psychologist Teufika Ibrahimefendić.

47. Interview by Arieke Duizer with Zejna Jasarević-Fejić.

48. Yugoslav Tribunal, ICTY witness Nicolic, 02/60/1, October 23, 2003.

49. Nancy Fraser, "Rethinking Recognition," *New Left Review* 3 (2000), 107–120; Nancy Fraser and Axel Honneth, *Redistribution or Recognition?* (London: Verso, 2003).

50. Shoshana Felman, *The Juridical Unconscious: Trials and Traumas in the Twentieth Century* (Cambridge, Mass.: Harvard University Press, 2009), 124, 125.

51. Cathy Caruth, *Unclaimed Experience: Trauma, Narrative, and History* (Baltimore, Md.: Johns Hopkins University Press, 1996).

52. See also Michael G. Levine, *The Belated Witness: Literature, Testimony, and the Question of Holocaust Survival* (Stanford, Calif.: Stanford University Press, 2006).

53. Besides the Shoah Visual Foundation, this is the largest audiovisual archive on genocide in the United States. Compared to the former, the Fortunoff Collection is more academic in its approach.

54. Shoshana Felman and Dori Laub, *Testimony: Crises of Witnessing in Literature, Psychoanalysis, and History* (London: Routledge, 1992), 71n18.

55. A description can be found in Tone Bringa, *Being Muslim in the Bosnian Way: Identity and Community in a Central Bosnian Village* (Princeton, N.J.: Princeton University Press, 1995).

56. For example, see Lisa DiCaprio's article on the 10th memorial: "The Betrayal of Srebrenica: The Ten-Year Commemoration," *Public Historian* 31:3 (August 2009), 73–106. The photography of Tarik Samariah is also of interest. See also Olivera Simic, "Gender, Conflict, and Reconciliation: Where Are the *Men?* What about *Women?*" (August 2009), at www.globalizacija.com, and Simic, "A Tour to a Site of Genocide: Mothers, Bones, and Borders," *Journal of International Women's Studies* 9:3 (May 2008), 320–330.

INDEX

DutchBat and, 171–172
fall of Srebrenica, xi
fugitive status, xiv, 147
Karremans and, Th. J. P., 131
as model for anti-Muslim behavior,
68
photos of, 12
on Potočari, 152, 171–172
Morillon, Philippe, 112, 121, 136,
192–193
Mothers of the Enclaves of Srebrenica
and Žepa (and variants thereof)
Hotić and, Kada, 120
members, 193
office space, 1
president, 1
Sabra and, 114
Srebrenica
A Cry from the Grave (film), 19
Subašić and, Munira, 131, 157
Mothers of the Plaza de Mayo, 197
Movement for Peace Disarmament and
Freedom, 110
Mujawayo, Esther, 198
Mujić, Šuhreta (survivor). See Šuhreta
(survivor)
Munira (survivor). See Subašić, Munira
murder
robbery as a motive for, 58
Serb murders of spouses and
children from mixed marriages,
62, 80
in Serb strategy, 15
Muriz (survivor), 188
Muška (survivor), 68–70, 181–183
Mustafić, Alma (survivor), 109, 137, 186

narod status, 31
nationalism
among Serbs (Bosnian Serbs),
30–31, 64
hatred, 67
nationalistic behavior, 67–68
Nermina (survivor), 16–18, 147,
199–200
Netherlands Institute for War
Documentation (NIOD), xiii
New York Review of Books (journal), 22

Nezira (survivor), 164–166
NGOs
"collective lodgings" built by, 91
rape victims, 22
reports about wartime Srebrenica,
110–111
reports of betrayal, 210
women's organizations becoming,
198
Zene Srebrenice, 115
Nietzsche, Friedrich, 10
Nijenhuis, Ellert, 147
NIOD report (Netherlands Institute
for War Documentation)
conclusions, xiii
DutchBat in Srebrenica genocide,
xiii, 130, 141
follow-up investigation, xiv
Karremans' leadership, questioning
of Th. J. P., 131
killings in May 1992, 53
publication of, xiii
refugees in Srebrenica, 111
size, xiii
sources, 110
"nonviolent communications," 37
NorBat (Nordic Battalion), 179
Norwegian People's Aid (Norsk
Folkehjelp), 110–111
Nourija (survivor), 132
Nova (television program), 131
Novi Sveskigrad (New Swedish Town),
111
Nuhanović, Hasan, 57, 145
Nura (survivor), 96–97, 132
Nuruddin, Derviš, Ahmed, 22

Office of the High Representative
(OHR), 195, 197
Omanović, Ćamila (survivor). See Ćamila
Omarska, West Bosnia, 112
Order Has Been Carried Out, The
(Portellia), 199
Orić, Naser (survivor)
International Criminal Tribunal for
the Former Yugoslavia (ICTY)
proceedings against, 107, 118,
119–120, 123

SELMA LEYDESDORFF is Professor of Oral History and Culture at the University of Amsterdam. She is author of *We Lived with Dignity: The Jewish Proletariat of Amsterdam, 1900–1940* and editor (with Nanci Adler, Mary Chamberlain, and Leyla Neyzi) of *Memories of Mass Repression: Narrating Life Stories in the Aftermath of Atrocity.*

KAY RICHARDSON is a retired editor with thirty years of experience in international scholarly publishing. During her thirteen years of residence in the Netherlands, she gained fluency in Dutch and developed an abiding interest in Dutch history and culture.